JPS GUIDE

AMERICAN
JEWISH
HISTORY

JPS GUIDE

AMERICAN
JEWISH
HISTORY

Norman H. Finkelstein

2007 • 5767
The Jewish Publication Society
Philadelphia

The Jewish Publication Society
2100 Arch Street
Philadelphia, PA 19103

www.jewishpub.org

Composition and design by Masters Group Design, Philadelphia

Manufactured in the United States of America

07 08 09 10 11 12 13   10 9 8 7 6 5 4 3 2 1

ISBN 13: 978-0-8276-0810-8
ISBN 10: 0-8276-0810-1

Library of Congress Cataloging-in-Publication Data
        Finkelstein, Norman H.
  JPS guide : American Jewish history / Norman H. Finkelstein. — 1st ed.
      p. cm.
  Includes bibliographical references and index.
  ISBN-13: 978-0-8276-0810-8 (alk. paper)
1. Jews—United States—History. 2. United States—Ethnic relations. I. Title.
  E184.35.F565 2006
  973'.04924—dc22
                            2006028015

JPS is a nonprofit educational association and the oldest and foremost publisher of Judaica in English in North America. The mission of JPS is to enhance Jewish culture by promoting the dissemination of religious and secular works, in the United States and abroad, to all individuals and institutions interested in past and contemporary Jewish life.

For Rosalind:

She is clothed with strength and splendor;
She looks to the future cheerfully.
Her mouth is full of wisdom,
Her tongue with kindly teaching.

PROVERBS 31:25–26

Acknowledgments

"Remember the days of old,
consider the years of ages past;
ask your father, he will inform you,
your elders, they will tell you."
(Deuteronomy 32:7)

American Jewry has a long and distinguished past that provides the foundation to its present and future. With this book I have attempted to provide an overview of American Jewish history for contemporary readers that puts the past in perspective.

I am grateful to the scholars, curators, librarians, and archivists who assisted me in researching this book: Dr. Jonathan Sarna of Brandeis University; Dr. Solomon Schimmel of Hebrew College; Julie Koven of the American Jewish Historical Society; Nicholas Graham of the Massachusetts Historical Society, Ellen Healy of the Gomez Mill House; Rev. Salomon L. Vaz Dias of Congregation Shearith Israel in the City of New York; Ruth Hoffman, Collections Director, Congregation Mikveh Israel, Philadelphia; and the staff of the Hebrew College Library.

I particularly appreciate the dedicated support of the entire staff at The Jewish Publication Society, especially Dr. Ellen Frankel and Carol Hupping for their vision, Janet Liss and Emily Law for their meticulous editing and questioning, and Robin Norman for her production assistance.

I continue to be blessed with the support of my family: my wife, Rosalind—the book's first critical editor—my children, Jenn, Jeff, Rob, and Risa, and my grandchildren, Tova and Joseph. Without their understanding and good humor, this book could not have been written.

Contents

When you think of the early history of the Jews in America, what image comes to your mind? Do you picture New York City's Lower East Side around 1900, its tenements, streets, and sweatshops crowded with Yiddish-speaking immigrants?

If you do, you are not alone. The great Eastern European wave of immigration at the end of the 19th century has become the touchstone for contemporary Jewish life in America, and to many people, it represents the experience of this country's "first" Jewish residents. But that wave of immigrants—primarily Russians, Poles, and Lithuanians—was only one in a long succession of Jewish groups who traveled to the New World. Those who arrived between 1880 and 1920 were preceded by German-speaking Jews in the early- to mid-19th century. In turn, they followed in the footsteps of a hardy band of 23 Jewish settlers from Brazil who first set foot in New Amsterdam in 1654. Although we date the beginnings of Jewish life in America to the arrival of those 23 Jews, Jewish presence in the New World began with another group of intrepid Hispanic Jews, largely forgotten today, who came ashore even earlier.

Working in a Sweatshop
For most people, the earliest Jewish immigration to America is exclusively represented by photographs from the late 19th and early 20th century, depicting teeming ghetto streets or, as in this case, harsh working conditions. In fact, by the time this photograph was taken, Jews had already been finding their way to the New World for several centuries. Library of Congress

Persecution of Iberian Jewry

After Muslims invaded the Iberian Peninsula in 711 C.E., Jewish inhabitants enjoyed centuries of relative tolerance and freedom under their new rulers—a sort of Golden Age. But by the middle of the 14th century, *la Reconquista* (the Reconquest, or the movement by Christian leaders to regain control over the Iberian Peninsula) had succeeded in reestablishing most of Spain under Christian rule. Spaniards, suspicious of their non-Christian neighbors, spread wild rumors about Jews, and local governments enacted laws curbing the rights of Jews. Violence against Jews increased, as did entreaties for their conversion. Most attacks were incited by religious fanatics and carried out by street mobs bent only on rape and plunder. In 1355, nearly 1200 Jews were killed in Toledo during one particularly savage attack. In 1371, King Henry II, following a practice instituted by Pope Innocent III in 1216, decreed that Jews had to wear distinctive badges on their clothing and could no longer have Christian names.

The Golden Age

We who are the remnant of the captive Israelites, are dwelling peacefully in the land of [Spain] ... called in the sacred tongue *Sefarad* ... The land is rich, abounding in rivers, springs, and aqueducts; a land of corn, oil and wine, of fruits and all manner of delicacies; it has pleasure-gardens and orchards, fruitful trees of every kind, including the leaves of the tree upon which the silkworm feeds ... There are also found among us mountains covered by crocus and with veins of silver, gold, copper, iron, tin, lead, sulphur, porphyry, marble and crystal.
(From a letter by Hasdai ibn Shaprut)

Hasdai ibn Shaprut (925–975) was the first Jew to attain prominence in Moorish Spain. He was a physician to the caliph and because of his language skills became a trusted and influential adviser. He is credited with establishing a major Talmudic academy in Cordova where Spanish Jews developed their own religious traditions independent of the existing centers of learning in Babylonia. His bridging of the worlds of secular learning and religion became a model for Jewish life in other countries.

Church initiatives to convert Jews met with surprising success. Historian Cecil Roth writes, "In some places, the Jews did not wait for the application of compulsion, but anticipated the popular attack by coming forward spontaneously, clamoring for admission to the Church ... It was a phenomenon unique in the whole of Jewish history."[1] Conditions worsened for Jews. In some areas they were not allowed to associate with Christians and were restricted to *Juderias*—ghettos.

Moses ben Maimon—Maimonides (1135–1204)

Born in Cordova, Spain, Maimonides was a physician, scholar, and philosopher. He remains the best-known Jewish intellectual of all time, a prime example of the Golden Age of Spanish Jewry. His *Guide of the Perplexed* provided the Jews of his time with an understanding of how to accept religious faith in the "modern world."
www.legadoandalusia.com

13

Interior of Toledo's Santa Maria la Blanca Church. Library of Congress

They were not permitted to build new synagogues and were prohibited from appearing in public on Christian holy days. Slowly, the Jewish community weakened materially and morally.

In June 1391, mobs in Seville went on a terrible rampage. Continual preaching by Fernan Martinez, the archdeacon of Ecija, incited the anti-Jewish violence. "Spain for Christians," the mobs shouted. Homes in the Jewish quarter were robbed, burned, or destroyed. Four thousand Jewish men, women, and children were savagely killed. Thousands more quickly converted to Christianity in order to save their lives. Even as the king, anxious to keep the peace, ordered a halt to the atrocities, mob violence intensified and spread. Magnificent synagogues were ransacked or transformed into churches. Today, visitors to Cordova's Church of St. Crispin or Toledo's Santa Maria la Blanca Church stand in what were once Jewish houses of worship.

Many Jews were offered a cruel choice: convert or die. Jews not so easily swayed from their religion either fled their homes or were killed. Others, scared for their lives, accepted baptism and suddenly found themselves Christians. One conservative estimate of the number thus converted is 35,000.[2] Once converted, whether voluntarily or by force, there was no turning back: the Church considered anyone baptized to be a Christian forever. Even New Christians who managed to flee the country after conversion were, when found, still subject to Church law.

New Christians, Old Problems

The New Christians could be divided into three groups. The first was composed of a very small number of Jews who enthusiastically discarded their Jewish culture and began leading totally Christian lives. A second group was made up of wealthy and powerful Jews who, although converted, quietly honored their Jewish roots. Within a generation their children had lost whatever attachment their parents once had to their old faith. Those in the third and largest group converted only to save their lives and livelihoods but retained a strong sense of Jewish identity. They were far from sincere in their new faith and tried to keep Jewish tradition alive for themselves and their children. Those who had not been very observant as Jews now continued as unobservant Christians.

New Christians were at first sincerely welcomed into Spanish society. Christians rejoiced that the conversion of the Jews would hasten the Second Coming of

14

Christ. Legally, at least, these converted Jews, as New Christians, were entitled to all the benefits due a Christian. "From the standpoint of the Church the anti-Jewish campaign had one aim—conversion … The moment a Jew embraced Christianity, all discrimination against him was to end."[3] It did not take long for the original welcome to turn cold as Old Christians began to realize that the newcomers were now able not only to continue with their successful business lives, but also to enter all aspects of Spanish life previously closed to them, even within the Church. "They were Jews in all but name and Christians in nothing but form."[4] The Church grew increasingly concerned about their new converts, suspicious of their true religious commitment. Some unconverted Jews likewise viewed their former coreligionists as opportunists and traitors, but overall, the Jewish attitude toward their baptized brothers was one of empathy and understanding.

Laws were passed prohibiting New Christians—increasingly referred to by the derogatory term *Marranos* (Spanish, meaning *pigs*)—from holding certain appointed positions in the government or the Church. Jews who had not converted called them, more sympathetically, *anusim*—the forced ones. Old Christians politely called them *Conversos*. Yet, no matter how Christian these Marranos had become, their Jewish bloodline still made them impure in the eyes of their neighbors.

Welcoming the Descendants of *Anusim*

Descendants of *anusim* have found difficulty in obtaining religious acceptance from many religious authorities who question their authenticity. One who went out of his way to make them welcome was Rabbi Chaim David Halevy, the chief rabbi of Tel-Aviv. Writing in an Israeli newspaper, he stated:

There should be no concern regarding their return to Judaism. No doubt, if they desire to return to Judaism … the return of anusim to the Jewish world will signify the final victory of Judaism over those who tried to destroy it. It is the ultimate act of publicly praising God's name, and a tribute to the large numbers who died on the altar.
(Translated from *Hatzofeh*, April 1, 1991, 4)

The foundation for the modern acceptance by Jews of *anusim* can be traced back to Maimonides in his *Epistle on Forced Conversion*, written in 1165:

How can God not reward a Jew who has been coerced by force of persecution yet secretly performs some commandments … one who transgresses under duress is not called a sinner, nor wicked, nor is he disqualified … It is improper to reject those who desanctify the Sabbath or to despise them, rather one should welcome them and encourage them.

A Prayer for *Anusim*

May He who blessed our fathers, Abraham, Isaac, and Jacob, Moses and Aaron, David and Solomon, bless, preserve, guard and assist all our brethren imprisoned by the Inquisition. May the King of kings bless them and make them worthy of His grace, and hearken to the voice of their supplication, and bring them forth from darkness to light. May such be thy divine will! And let us say Amen.

Sephardic Prayer Book (Quoted in Halevy, *Anusim in North America*, http://www.cs.tau.ac.il/~ nachumd/sch/sch/Anusim.html)

Although life for Jews who had not converted grew increasingly difficult, New Christians maintained ties with them, to the consternation of Church authorities. The earliest Conversos still retained Jewish memories and the ability to read Hebrew. These ties weakened with each succeeding generation, resulting in the diminishment of their Jewish practices and knowledge. Meanwhile, hatred among the masses toward their New Christian brethren increased, as did the scale of violence. "Charges were built up, by a clergy which [sic] sentiment was at one with the populace, about the religious hypocrisy of the *Marranos*, about their secret practices of Judaism—about the danger they represented to the purity of the Christian faith."[5] Major attacks against New Christians in 1467 and 1473 occurred in Toledo and Cordova.

Horrors of the Inquisition

In 1478 the pope issued approval for the establishment of an official Inquisition tribunal in Spain. Two years later, the first inquisitors began their work of ferreting out disloyal Christians. The concept of the Inquisition was not new. The Church had used courts of this sort previously to search out those who were not "good" Catholics and suspected of "Judaizing." Contrary to popular opinion, the Inquisition was permitted to deal only with Catholics who had strayed from the Church, not uncon-

Horrible Cruelties Inflicted by Order of the Inquisition
The officers of the Inquisition followed the settlers to the New World and arrived in Mexico in 1571, decades after the first Conversos. Some Conversos who secretly practiced Judaism were tortured and tried by the Inquisition, while others escaped detection. There were also Conversos who did not practice Judaism, but were falsely accused of doing so. Library of Congress

verted Jews. Spies were everywhere. Although punishment given out by the Inquisition varied, two common practices were confiscation of property and torture, often leading the condemned to be burned at the stake. Some believe that New Christians were convicted more often to claim their property than for their souls.

The Inquisition soon became a second government in the country, with its own network of spies, prisons, and tribunals. Those condemned to death who accepted Christianity at the end were mercifully strangled to death before their corpses were burned. Those who went to death maintaining innocence were burned alive. The inquisitors refined torture to such an extent that even innocent prisoners, after weeks and months of painful torture, often confessed to deeds they had not committed. As converted Jews attempted to "toe the line" and live exemplary Christian

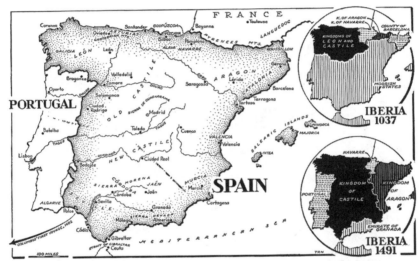

1519 Spain

The Moslem invasion of Spain in 711 opened a new era of tolerance for Jews that was still largely in place in 1037, although the peninsula's former Christian rulers had begun their *Reconquista.* By 1491, however, only Granada still remained free of Christian control. By 1519, all Iberian Jews had either fled the peninsula, been killed, or converted to Christianity—or so it appeared.
www.libro.uca.alfonso6

lives, unconverted Jews were often removed to separate quarters of Spanish cities to prevent any contact between Jews and Marranos. Jews were subject to nearly constant humiliation and the threat of violence. Blood libel rumors— that Jews required the blood of young Christian children for their rituals—were widespread. Yet, in spite of these dire warning signs and the cruelty and uncertainty that befell their Converso brethren, unconverted Jews did not recognize the impending danger to themselves.

Expulsion

By the autumn of 1492, it was all over. With the capitulation of Granada on January 2, 1492, all of Spain was finally unified under Christian rule. On March 31, King Ferdinand signed a decree ordering all Jews to convert within four months or leave the country. An estimated 100,000 Spanish Jews sought safety in adjoining Portugal. When Portugal banned Judaism in 1497, most of those Spanish refugees were forcibly converted, sometimes in mass baptismal ceremonies. By the end of that year, it could be legally claimed that no Jews remained on the Iberian Peninsula.

The New World

The expulsion of Iberian Jews set in motion a series of events that ultimately led to the arrival of the first Jews to the New World. The first European to set foot in the New World was a Converso: Luis de Torres, who sailed with Columbus in 1492. Within a few years, Spain took possession of lands in the New World and began to settle them in two main areas. "New Spain" consisted of what is today a good part of southwestern United States, Mexico, Central America, and the Caribbean

Hernando Cortés and Hernando de Soto in the camp of the Inca at Caxamalca. When Cortés triumphantly seized the capital of the Aztec Empire—today's Mexico City—on August 13, 1521, Conversos were among the conquistadors who accompanied him. Library of Congress

islands. "Peru" was the name given to the rest of South America, with the exception of Brazil, which was claimed by Portugal in 1500. Jews and Conversos used deception, forged documents, and bribery to make their way across the Atlantic to establish new homes and find refuge from the Inquisition. Over the years, Spanish rulers periodically issued orders forbidding Jews to live anywhere in the New World. Yet as early as 1495, Converso settlers could be found in Hispaniola. As New Christians they were not affected by bans on Jewish travel, yet records from 1515 show Conversos being sent back to Seville, Spain, to face trial by the Inquisition.

Keeping the Faith in the New World

The Conversos of New Spain, isolated from the Jewish mainstream, adapted their secret practices of Judaism from Christian custom, past memories, and distorted interpretations of Jewish laws and customs. Few, if any, were learned in Jewish studies. Of course there were no synagogues, but they gathered in private homes or rooms in commercial buildings to conduct their own impro-vised services. New Christians would be married publicly in a church ser-vice and then privately in a vaguely Jewish ceremony. Sabbath observance for those who cared included the secret lighting of candles, or changing into finer clothes than were usually worn during the week. Some women were known to light a candle in Church while whispering a Jewish prayer. Women were largely responsible for maintaining their family's tenuous Jewish identity from generation to generation. Transmitting religious knowledge was perilous. Relying on Christian Bibles and prayers, Conversos tried to retain Jewish concepts and specific words or phrases. Because nothing was written and all knowledge was passed down orally from one generation to the next, prayers often became garbled versions of the original. Most prayers were transformed into Spanish with only hints of their original structure. Hebrew was generally limited to a few words such as *Adonai* or *Shema*.[6]

Poetic Testimony

The careful note-taking by Inquisition courts provides a wealth of firsthand information about the religious lives of *anusim*. One of Luis de Carvajal's sisters, who went to her death in the *auto da fé* of 1596, was a writer whose poetry masked Jewish content. In this fragment from one of her poems, she warned of the consequences of revealing a hidden Jewish life.

> In all of your homes
> Do not light a flame
> On the Sabbath day of rest
> Because your soul will
> Be condemned for this act.

(Hamilton 2000, 82)

Holidays presented particularly difficult challenges, as the Inquisition spies were well aware of the Jewish calendar. To bypass that threat, holidays—particularly Hanukkah, Passover, and Purim—were sometimes not observed directly on their assigned dates on the Jewish calendar. Purim evolved into a Festival of Saint Esther, with Christian blessings inserted to avoid suspicion. The Purim story of the Jewish queen who hid her religious background and ultimately saved her peo-ple from death was particularly meaningful. They read in the book of Esther, "Esther did not reveal her people or her kindred." For the first generations after the Expulsion, rabbis continually ruled that Conversos had a legitimate place within the Jewish community according to Jewish law. Their rulings reflected the close kinship Jews had with those of their people who, in spite of their legal Catholic status, secretly maintained connections with Judaism.

To throw off suspicion while fasting on Yom Kippur, servants were sent on long errands during mealtimes. On Passover, some substituted tortillas for matzos, while others sought out excuses to explain why they were avoiding leavened food. With no *haggadot*, some just opened their Christian Bibles and read aloud the story of the Exodus. Prayers and hymns were rephrased from Catholic ritual but

Signs of Judaizing

The network of spies reporting to the Inquisition was extremely vigilant in rooting out those whose behavior indicated even a remote tie to Judaism. Many accused were totally innocent, inadvertently doing or saying something that a spy interpreted as having a Jewish connection. Inquisition officials provided a laundry list of suspicious activities that could "reveal" someone as a lapsed New Christian:

*Wearing clean blouses and
    other clothing on holidays
Putting clean tablecloths on tables and
    clean sheets on beds to honor the
    Sabbath
Cleaning and draining blood from meat
Fasting on the Grand Fast Day
    [Yom Kippur]
Laying of hands by father on a
    son's head to sanctify him
Breaking off a piece of dough
    when baking bread.*

(Liebman, *The Jews in New Spain*, 96)

sometimes included references to Jesus and Mary to discourage detection.[7] They adapted other signs and rituals from the Catholic Church, including offering prayer on one's knees.

Adhering to the laws of kashrut—keeping kosher—also presented obstacles. Secret Jews tended to substitute beef for pork whenever possible, although the koshering of meat was symbolic at best. Pork products were often kept on hand to serve to guests so as not to raise suspicions of friends and neighbors.

Often, Conversos didn't feel safe enough to tell even close family members of their true heritage. Parents waited until children were old enough to handle the information with maturity and discretion before telling them about their Jewish roots. Sometimes parents would allow a son to join a Catholic order, to provide the perfect cover as he ministered to his family's true spiritual needs. And as a terrible irony, as Conversos struggled to remember the traditions of their Jewish faith, the Inquisition was there with its official lists of suspicious activities to remind them of what Judaism was—how it sounded, how it looked, what rituals it included.[8] In time, many Conversos simply melded into the greater Christian society, but a sizeable number over the generations continued to secretly practice their limited Judaism.

The Inquisition's Long Arm

In 1571, Philip II of Spain established an Inquisition tribunal in Mexico. Over the next decades, Conversos spread northward into what is today New Mexico, Texas, California, Colorado, and Arizona to escape detection. This large land area, stretching through Eastern Mexico to today's American Southwest, was known as Nuevo León, a section of New Spain. It was heavily settled by Conversos, thanks in large measure to Luis de Carvajal de la Cueva, a New Christian known as "el Conquistador" because he had accompanied Cortés.

Born in 1539 in Portugal to Jewish parents who had been forced to convert to Christianity, Carvajal led his own life as a committed Catholic and eventually was made governor of the New Kingdom of León in Northern Mexico. While visiting Spain to be rewarded for his conquistador exploits, he was given permission to bring 100 people back to Mexico without having to prove that they belonged to Old Christian families. Many who returned with him were New Christian relatives.

LISTA DAS PESSOAS,

Que fahiraõ, & fentenças que fe leraõ no Auto Publico da Fé que fe celebrou na Igre-
ja do Convento de Saõ Domingos def-
ta Cidade de Lisboa em Domingo
26. de Novembro de 1684. &
condenaçoés que tiveraõ.

SENDO INQUISIDOR GERAL O ILLUSTRISSIMO
Senhor Arcebifpo.

DOM VERISSIMO DE LANCASTRO

do Confelho de Eftado de Sua Mageftade , & feu
Sumiller da Cortina.

DEFUNTO NOS CARCERES ABSOLUTO DA INSTANCIA.

Num. Idades.   Penas.

1.   48.   [R] Odrigo Nunes Delcanho M. X. N. mercador
              natural da Villa de C,elorico Bifpado da Guar-
              da & morador nefta Cidade Originario do Rey-
              no de Caftella.

ABJURAÇAM DE LEVE.

2.   64.   FRancifco Rodrigues o auzente de alcunha trabalhador na-   3. annos para
              tural & morador do lugar de Caparica termo da Villa de   Caftro Marim.
              Almada do Arcebifpado de Lisboa por culpas de blafphemia.

3.   39.   Luis Leyte expulfo de certa Religião Subdiacono natural   Sufpenfo das Or-
              defta Cidade de Lisboa,& morador na da Bahia de todos os San-   dens que tem, &
              tos do eftado do Brafil , por dizer Miffa & adminiftrar nella a   inhabilitado pa-
              Comunhaõ a muytas peffoas não fendo Sacerdote.   ra as mais , &
                                                              6. annos de Gal-
                                                              lès.

4.   46.   João Cardozo Alferes de Infantaria natural da Villa das La-   Açoutes & 5.
              gens na Ilha das Flores & morador nefta Cidade por cazar fe-   annos de Gallès
              gunda vez fendo viva fua primeyra mulher.

5.   35.   Francifco Pimentel Barbeyro natural & morador do lugar de   O mefmo.
              Santo Antonio na Ilha de Saõ Miguel pela mefma culpa.
                                                              PRI-

The first page of a list of people tried at the November 26, 1684 "Auto Publico da Fé" in Lisbon, and the penalties they received.
Jewish Theological Seminary Library

21

Back in Mexico, Carvajal busied himself with establishing silver mines, expanding settlements, building churches, and converting natives to Christianity.

In spite of his constructive work as a devout Catholic, the Inquisition arrested him in 1589. His devoted relatives, although outwardly Catholic, had been found practicing Judaism. Under severe torture, he and his relatives identified others who were secret Jews. Carvajal's failure to denounce them before his arrest led to his death. Found guilty, he appeared as a penitent on February 24, 1590, and

A Final Reckoning

In 1649, Thomas Trebino de Sobremonte went his death proclaiming to his priest confessor, "Do not exert yourself to convince me, for I must die as a Jew. It would be best to convert yourself to Judaism." Then, as the flames began consuming his body, he said, "Throw in the wood. I pay for it anyway." (Wiznitzer 1962, 237)

The Fate of the Governor's Nephew

Born in 1566, Luis de Carvajal el Mozo (the Younger) was the governor's namesake and heir—and one of those named by his uncle under torture. Upon the shocking discovery of his Jewish descent, Luis immersed himself in Jewish studies and ritual and began to preach the "law of Moses." Arrested by the Inquisition, he confessed to past Jewish observances but claimed he had returned to the Christian faith. He was reconciled to the Church in 1590 and sentenced to life as a church hospital servant. Eventually reassigned to a religious school where religious materials in the library refueled his passion for Judaism, he began writing clandestine memoirs, Jewish liturgy, and poetry.

Freed in October 1594, he was rearrested three months later and tortured, along with his mother and sister, until they revealed names of other secret Jews. He changed his name to Joseph and converted his cell mate, a priest, to Judaism. He was burned at the stake in 1596, as were his mother and sisters, after revealing more names under torture.

Padre Contreras, a priest who witnessed his execution, recorded the following:

He was always such a good Jew and he reconciled his understanding, which was very profound and sensitive, with his highly inspired Divine determination to defend the Law of God—the Mosaic—and to fight for it. I have no doubt that if he had lived before the incarnation of our Redeemer, he would have been a heroic Hebrew and his name would have been as famous in the Bible as are the names of those who died in the defense of their law when it was necessary. (Liebman 1970, 182)

was sentenced to forfeiture of his wealth and expulsion. His secret Jewish relatives were condemned at the same time. While awaiting transport into exile, he died in his jail cell at age 51, a man broken in spirit and body, still maintaining his allegiance to the Church.

Carvajal's niece, Dona Isabel Rodriguez de Andrade, was stripped to the waist before the Inquisition tribunal, her arms tied and twisted in torture behind her. Admitting her guilt, she succumbed to the pain and implicated her entire family except for her uncle, the governor, whom she described as "a good Christian." When her mother appeared before the tribunal and was about to be stripped to the waist she screamed:

Strangle me now, but do not strip me; do not insult me.
I prefer a thousand deaths. Remember that I am a woman
And an honest widow! I have already told you that I
Believe in the Law of Moses and not in that of Jesus
Christ, and I have nothing more to say!
(Wiznitzer 1962, 186–87)[9]

The Inquisition continued its work, as the arrival of more Conversos continued into the 1600s. New arrivals connected with settled families and relied on one another for support. They even established ad hoc "synagogues" where they gathered on Shabbat and holidays. They had no knowledge of Hebrew but rather used their memory of occasional words or phrases. Some even used the forms of Catholic ritual, within which they inserted their forms of Jewish prayer.

No one knows exactly how many Conversos made their way to New Spain. Most of our information about their lives comes from the detailed records kept by Inquisition authorities, whose *auto da fés* continued well into the early 18th century. In spite of their secrecy needs, Conversos tried to maintain contact with Jewish communities elsewhere, even raising funds for poor Jews in Palestine. Records exist through the 16th century of responsa between far-flung Converso communities and European rabbinical authorities on religious questions. These letters dwindled in number over time, signifying a decline in adherence by Conversos to the secret Judaism of their ancestors. Intramarriage among Converso families was strongly encouraged. Some secret Jews found refuge in rural Indian villages, where they intermarried. Their descendants, known as *mestizos*, managed to pass down distorted bits and pieces of their receding Jewish memory to succeeding generations.

Increasingly, the legal and societal barriers to practicing Judaism, along with the lack of authentic Jewish scholarship among Conversos, took their toll. Jewish adherence in New Spain was transformed into a crypto-Judaism of superstition and simplistic rote observance of limited practices, such as adapting Sabbath customs, fasting, and denying Christ. A Portuguese archbishop chided Jewish penitents at an *auto da fé* in 1705 with these words:

Miserable relics of Judaism! Unhappy fragments of the synagogue; last remnants of Judea! Scandal of the Catholics and detestable objects of scorn to the Jews, for you are so ignorant that you cannot observe the very law under which you live.[10]

By the mid-17th century, nearly all traces of crypto-Judaism had been eradicated.[11] Today, in widespread areas of Mexico and the Southwestern United States, people who steadfastly practice their Roman Catholic faith continue to observe—some consciously, most unwittingly—certain religious and cultural practices, passed down to them from previous generations, that strongly identify them as likely descendants of Jews expelled from Spain in 1492.

To many, the story of crypto-Jews is nothing more than an interesting sidebar in the story of American Judaism. Yet, the vestiges of Jewish memory that continue indicate a legacy of persistence that honors ancestors who tried, in their own brave but futile way, to keep the flame of Judaism alive. In the end, though, in spite of their pain and

Crypto-Jews Today

During the past century, signs pointing to Jewish ancestry began to surface among totally committed Catholics in Mexico and the American Southwest. Some families play a Christmas game with a four-sided top. At Easter, some celebrate the Feast of Saint Esther, although no such saint exists in Catholicism. Still others fast in her name. Around Passover, some eat a special bread made without lard—*pan de Semita*—which substitutes for matzah. Some slaughter chickens with a specially sharpened knife, allowing all blood to drain before cooking. Perhaps most pervasive is the secret lighting of candles on Shabbat.

When asked about these practices, people simply respond that they are following family customs, passed down from generation to generation. Most have no idea that these practices might indicate Jewish antecedents. These rituals are all that remain of a Jewish tradition diluted by time and persecution. Although genetic and DNA testing can authenticate a Jewish connection, today's crypto-Jews are themselves conflicted about their heritage. Some have formally converted to Judaism even as other Jews question their authenticity. By the early 20th century, those *anusim* who remained conscious of their authentic Jewish roots had lost touch with the main currents of Judaism.

suffering, they did not succeed in creating a lasting Jewish foothold in the New World. That credit belongs to other Hispanic Jews who followed them and laid the foundation for a vibrant American Jewish community, proud in faith and unafraid of publicly proclaiming their heritage. The historian Meyer Kayserling wrote, "Where the history of the Jews in Spain ends, that of the Jew in America begins: The Inquisition is the last chapter of the confessors of Judaism on the Pyrenean peninsula, and the first chapter on the continent of the Western hemisphere."[12]

MID-1300s–1654
A TIMELINE

Mid-1100s
End of a centuries-long "Golden Age" for Iberian Jews under Muslim rule

1391
Anti-Jewish riots throughout Spain kill thousands of Jews

1413
Thousands of Spanish Jews convert; some continue to lead Jewish secret lives

1449
Violence between Old and New Christians in Toledo

1478
Inquisition begins to seek out disloyal New Christians

1492
Jews expelled from Spain. Many flee to Portugal; New Christians remain

1497
Most Spanish refugees forcibly converted en masse

1519
New Christians among conquistadores accompanying Hernando Cortés to capture Mexico

1531
Inquisition established in Portugal. Many New Christians flee abroad

1569
Philip II of Spain orders establishment of Inquisition in New Spain

1571
Inquisition instituted in Mexico

1587
First record of Conversos in Hispaniola

1590
Luis de Carvajal de la Cueva, governor of Nuevo León, burned at the stake

1654–1812

The Earliest Settlers

The very names recorded here are strange,
Of foreign accent, and of different climes;
Alvares and Rivera interchange
With Abraham and Jacob of old times.

—Henry Wadsworth Longfellow,
"The Jewish Cemetery at Newport," stanza 4

In this poem, Longfellow lyrically reminds us of something we tend to forget, if we ever knew it: the first Jewish settlers in America were Hispanic. More accurately, they were Sephardic (from a Hebrew word for *Spain*), because although they came from Brazil, their family roots were in Spain and Portugal. Unlike the "secret Jews" of New Spain who preceded them, whose memory exists mainly in Inquisition records, this later group of arrivals stepped ashore openly as Jews and went on to establish the first successful Jewish settlement in North America. Although Ashkenazic Jews from Central Europe would soon outnumber them, these pioneer Sephardic settlers laid religious and cultural foundations for future generations of American Jews.

From Brazil to the Battery

In early September 1654, a French ship, the *Sainte Catherine,* entered the harbor of New Amsterdam. Among her passengers were 23 Jewish men, women, and children who became, quite by accident, the vanguard of a vibrant Jewish presence in the United States. Their original destination was Holland. After a storm-tossed voyage from Recife, they were forced to land on Spanish territory in Jamaica. Most of their belongings were confiscated, and some passengers who had been born Christian were detained by the authorities while 23 of the Jewish refugees were allowed to leave. This group quickly left Jamaica for the busy port of Cape Saint Anthony in Cuba where, one step ahead of the Inquisition, they boarded the *Sainte Catherine* for New Amsterdam.

Sephardim and Ashkenazim

Sephardim trace their lineage back to Spain and Portugal. After 1492, Jews who were expelled from those countries migrated especially to the Middle East and North Africa—but also to the New World. Ashkenazim are Jews whose ancestors migrated from France and Germany to Eastern Europe. Sephardim and Ashkenazim shared basic religious tenets, but the Ashkenazim, forced to lead insular lives, became stricter in observance, while the Sephardim, although also orthodox in practice, were more liberal in their interpretations and worldlier. For example, European Sephardic communities provided secular education for their children and did business with Christians. Being first to create Jewish institutions in the New World, their cultural, social, and religious practices became models for the Ashkenazim.

Sixteenth-century Brazilian sugar mill shown with African slave laborers. www.antislavery.org

The Jewish presence in Brazil dated back 150 years with the arrival from Portugal of Conversos, Jews who were outwardly "New Christians" but secretly Jewish in their hearts and memories. Their ancestors had been forced from Spain in 1492 and required to convert to Christianity in Portugal. With the discovery of Brazil by Portuguese explorers in 1500, Conversos flocked to the new haven, which they hoped would take them as far as possible from the Inquisition's "corporate headquarters" in Lisbon. They came to establish permanent homes and are credited with creating the profitable sugar trade. The first sugar mill in Brazil began operation in 1516, and by the end of the 16th century, there were 200 sugar mills in the country, most owned and operated by Conversos. Yet, despite the Conversos' success in their new home, they kept their Jewish roots hidden lest they be discovered and shipped back to Portugal for punishment.

In 1580, Philip II of Spain gained control over Portugal and broadened the scope of the Inquisition to include Portuguese colonies across the Atlantic. Although an official Inquisition office never existed in Brazil, local Church officials had the authority to send suspects back to Lisbon for trial. The tightening of Inquisition activities in Portugal led more Marranos, whose families had now been living in Portugal for generations, to flee—some to Brazil. In 1587, with Portugal's intellectual and financial base diminishing because of the steady outflow of people, the king issued an order halting the departure of additional New Christians from Portugal. The ban was lifted in 1601 to encourage further population of overseas colonies.[1]

Under Dutch Rule

The Dutch invasion of Brazilian territory, which began in 1624 with the capture of Bahia, brought relief to the secret Jews, who quickly shed their New Christian disguises to support the overthrow of Portuguese rule. When the Portuguese regained control a year later, though, the Jews were forced to flee Bahia for other Brazilian settlements. In 1630 the Dutch capture of Pernambuco, which they renamed Recife, provided a new haven for Jews. The tolerance of the Dutch was well known, so Conversos felt safe to publicly proclaim their Judaism. As Jewish immigration to Recife increased, a vital Jewish community emerged, complete with synagogue and religious schools. In 1642, a large group of Jewish immigrants arrived from Holland, including Isaac Aboab da Fonseca, the first rabbi in the New World.

In 1645, the Dutch issued a message that became, in effect, the first charter for Jews in the New World. Jews were "to be protected from any damage to person or property in the same manner as … all the citizens of the United Netherlands." In the 17th century, this was an astonishing statement for a Christian nation to make.[2] That year witnessed the arrival of the first Jewish professionals with full permission to actively practice their skills: the first Jewish attorney, first physician, and first engineer. While Jews rejoiced, Old Christians in the Portuguese community were upset to see their formerly New Christian neighbors now openly returned to Judaism.

30

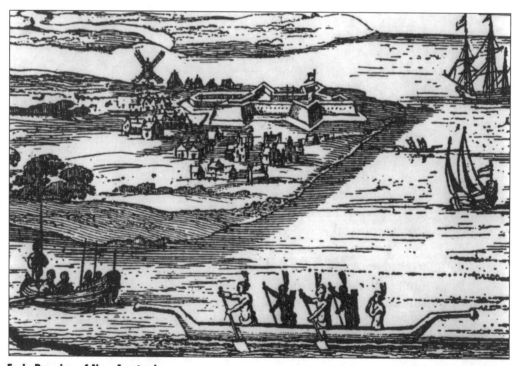

Early Drawing of New Amsterdam
The first Jewish settlers arriving in 1654 aboard the *Sainte Catherine* beheld a similar view of New Amsterdam. New York Public Library Picture Collection.

The End of the Beginning

This unprecedented religious freedom ended when the Portuguese ultimately retook Recife in 1654, ending their long military campaign to recover lost colonies in Brazil. The die was cast for the Jews of Brazil. Once out of the closet, it was impossible to go back in. With the imminent return of the Inquisition, Jews had no choice but to leave their homes and businesses as quickly as possible. Most went to Amsterdam or one of the Dutch-controlled Caribbean Islands. But one small group inadvertently reached the Dutch colony of New Amsterdam, forever altering the course of Jewish history.

An Uncertain Refuge

Nearly penniless, weary from the hazardous journey, and uncertain of their welcome, the 23 Jewish refugees aboard the *Sainte Catherine* disembarked onto Dutch soil at New Amsterdam. The history of the Jews in the United States begins with their arrival and their early quest for religious and civil rights. They were not the first Jews to arrive in North America. Earlier Converso arrivals had settled in New Spain but had never established viable Jewish communities. Individual Jews had followed the Conversos to other emerging colonies, not as settlers but as itinerant traders. Records indicate that in 1649, a Jewish traveler named Solomon Franco arrived in Puritan Boston where, after a brief stay, he was unceremoniously encouraged to leave. In New Amsterdam, two Jewish traders—Jacob Barsimson and Solomon Pieterson—had arrived only weeks earlier.

Peter Stuyvesant
Stuyvesant governed New Amsterdam from 1647 to 1664 on behalf of the Dutch West India Company. His numerous roadblocks to the Jewish settlers were challenged by the newcomers, who quickly found a permanent home in North America. New York Public Library Picture Collection

The welcome received by the first Jewish settlers in North America was less than auspicious. The ship's captain instituted a court case against them, since funds for their passage had not arrived from coreligionists in Holland. The court ordered two of the new arrivals imprisoned and the belongings of all 23 passengers sold at auction. In addition, the flinty governor of New Amsterdam, Peter Stuyvesant, "deemed it useful to require them in a friendly way to depart." He did not want the "repugnant" Jews, members of a "deceitful race," to remain, and he wrote to the directors of the Dutch West India Company in Amsterdam with his views.[3]

31

The Jewish refugees also wrote a letter—to their friends and relatives in Holland—asking for help. They had come this far to safety and had no desire to leave. In turn, well-to-do Jewish residents of Amsterdam sent a petition to the directors of the Dutch West India Company in January 1655 on behalf of their coreligionists in the New World. The petition referred to the sacrifices made by the Jews of Recife as well as to the loyalty shown the Dutch by Jewish inhabitants wherever they lived. The petition also reminded the directors that the Company had invited people to come and settle in the Dutch colonies of the New World.

> It is well known to your Honors that the Jewish nation in Brazil have at all times been faithful and have striven to guard and maintain that place, risking for that purpose their possessions and their blood.

> Yonder land is extensive and spacious. The more of loyal people that go to live there, the better it is in regard to the population of the country.[4]

Then, in a sublime and unsubtle example of understatement, the Holland Jews wrote:

> Your Honors should also please consider that many of the Jewish nation are principal shareholders in the Company.

The directors thought things over and sent their reply to Stuyvesant.

> These people may travel and trade to and in New Netherland and live and remain there, provided the poor among them shall not become a burden to the Company or to the community, but be supported by their own nation.[5]

Asser Levy

Asser Levy was the apparent leader of the first band of Jewish settlers to set foot in New Amsterdam. From the moment they arrived, Levy's name appears and reappears in the traces of legal proceedings we have from that time, challenging Governor Stuyvesant in demanding equal rights for himself and his fellow Jews. He probably came from Amsterdam originally, ending up in Recife, Brazil, to engage in business. He may have been the only Ashkenazic Jew who disembarked from the *Sainte Catherine*. His name appears in the wills of Christian neighbors as a trustee and administrator. In 1671, he even contributed money to the building of the first Lutheran Church in New York. He died in New York in 1682.

Soon, other Jews began arriving directly from Holland and other European countries. Unlike the Catholics of Spain and Portugal, the Protestant Dutch did not normally obsess over matters of religion. They were a merchant nation whose concern for trade and profit overrode religious zeal.

The Fight for Equal Rights

Although forced to tolerate a Jewish presence, Governor Stuyvesant did everything possible to restrict the rights of the newcomers. In response, some Jews insisted on and fought for the same rights and benefits accorded to other residents. When a question arose about Jews serving in the militia, Stuyvesant and the governing council responded "that owing to the disgust and unwillingness of the trainbands to be fellow soldiers … Jews cannot be permitted to serve as soldiers, but should be exempt."[6] But the council also ruled that those exempt from military service should pay a monthly tax. While most Jews nodded and grumbled, Asser Levy chose to speak out. Stuyvesant had finally met his match in a Jew who was proud and unafraid. On November 5, 1655, Levy presented a petition that he and Jacob Barsimson be allowed to stand guard duty like other male residents of New Amsterdam or be excused from paying the unfair tax. The issue at hand was not money but the belief that equal treatment requires equal responsibility. True to form, the council denied the request and ended its message with a pointed admonition to the men that if they didn't like living there, they were free to leave.[7] Levy probably appealed directly to Amsterdam, for records indicate that he later did guard duty with other men of New Amsterdam.

Stuyvesant was an equal-opportunity denier of rights. His prejudices extended as well to anyone who was not a member of the Dutch Reformed Church. In a letter to Amsterdam he wrote: "To give liberty to the Jews will be very detrimental there, because the Christians there will not be able at the same time to do business. Giving them liberty, we cannot refuse the Lutherans and Papists."[8] The directors, however, were more interested in profit than prayer. They reiterated the right of Jews to "enjoy the same liberty that is granted them in this country" but without extending to them the right to worship publicly "in synagogues or gatherings." Stuyvesant rhetorically responded, "What they [the Jews] may be able to obtain from your Honors time will tell."[9]

While Jews and Christians of denominations other than the Dutch Reformed Church were not at first allowed to build their own houses of worship, they were not prohibited from practicing their religions in private. The first Jewish congregation in North America, Shearith Israel (Remnant of Israel), dates its beginnings to April 26, 1655. Earlier that year, Abraham de Lucena had arrived in the colony bearing a Torah scroll sent by the Amsterdam synagogue. On February 16, 1656, Dutch officials gave permission for the purchase of "a little hook of land" outside the city for use as a Jewish burial ground.[10]

The Beginnings of American Judaism

Even after New Amsterdam fell to the British in 1664 and became known as New York, permission for the building of a synagogue was still not forthcoming. Services continued to be held quietly in individual homes until 1695, when the Duke of York finally granted permission. The community rented a house on Mill Street for "the Jews synagogue." Not until 1728 was the Jewish community able to begin construction of a proper synagogue for Congregation Shearith Israel in the City of New York.

The congregation quickly evolved into a uniquely American institution. Interestingly, while Portuguese was the first official language of record, it wasn't long before English become standard. To growing numbers of Ashkenazic immigrants who followed, the orderly worship service and "Americanized" customs of Shearith Israel represented a refreshing change from the rigid religious practices

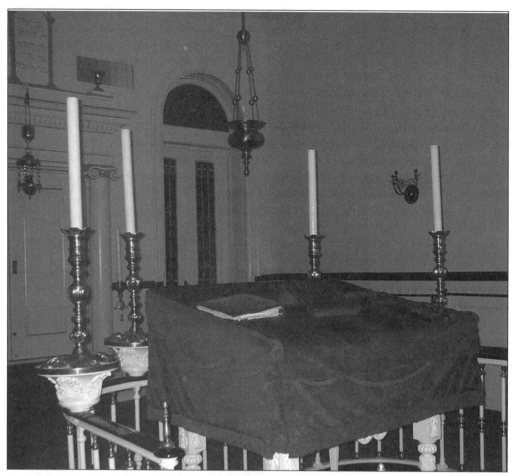

The "Little Synagogue"of Congregation Shearith Israel
The "Little Synagogue," located in the current home of Congregation Shearith Israel in New York City, is a representation of the congregation's first house of worship, built in 1730 in Mill Street. This restoration retains the "costly and elegant" look of the original interior. The reader's desk and the candlesticks have been in use by the congregation since 1730. Norman H. Finkelstein

of European ghettos. To arrivals from Poland and Germany, the sophisticated and worldly-wise Sephardic community represented an ideal to emulate. Until the early 1820s, the authority of Jewish religious observance in North America rested generally on Sephardic tradition and specifically on the reputation of Shearith Israel, the "mother synagogue" of America.

Other congregations soon followed the example of Shearith Israel: Savannah, Georgia (1733); Charleston, South Carolina (1740); Philadelphia, Pennsylvania (1740); and Newport, Rhode Island (1750). The first group of Jews arriving in Savannah brought with them enough men to constitute a minyan—a prayer quorum of 10. They also brought with them "a Safer Tora [sic] with two cloaks, and a Circumcision Box, which was given to them by Mr. Lindo, a merchant in London, for the use of the congregation they intended to establish."[11] In each of these communities, one synagogue served all Jews. Although Ashkenazic Jews soon outnumbered the original settlers, Sephardic ritual prevailed in practice. By 1700, the Jewish population in the colonies numbered between 200 and 300 people. By the outbreak of the American Revolution in 1776 the number had risen to 1,000 to 2500 out of a total population of 2.5 million.[12]

Making a Living

The business of these early Jewish settlers was business. While some were petty traders or craftsmen, the most visible were wealthy merchants and shipowners who used their Sephardic connections around the world to amass great fortunes. They experienced a degree of religious and social freedom unknown to most European Jews. In 1672, the Jewish-owned merchant ship *The Trial* was seized off Jamaica. The courts affirmed the seizure by ruling that under the Navigation Acts only British-owned and crewed ships could trade between England and the colonies and therefore Jewish ships were not allowed. On appeal, The Council for Plantations in London affirmed that anyone who had legal standing in New York also had trading rights covered by the Navigation Acts. By the overturn of the original ruling, colonial Jews for the first time were officially recognized as British citizens. (Jews living in England had to wait nearly another 100 years for such legal recognition.)

In 1705, Luis Moses Gomez, the patriarch of what would become one of the most influential Jewish families in America, received a Letter of Denization (naturalization) from Queen Anne granting him and his heirs the right to "peaceably, freely & fully have, possess, use & enjoy each and all franchises & privileges as any of our loyal and faithful subjects born within this kingdom, without any disturbance, molestation, hindrance or vexation, and without annoyance or complaint by our heirs and successors."[13] This seminal document, while not in itself a grantor of full equality, was an early marker of Jewish rights in America.

For Jews in the 17th and 18th centuries, America was geographically and spiritually far removed from the ghettos and restrictions of Europe. Here, in spite of lingering and annoying restrictions that would gradually disappear, they lived, worked, and socialized freely among their neighbors. "For the first time, Jews lived essentially as equals among Christians"[14] and were subject to the same civil laws.

Luis Moses Gomez

Born of a Converso family around 1660 in Spain, he made his way to France and England, eventually reaching New York in 1703. A member of a well-connected international merchant family, he requested and received a Letter of Denization directly from Queen Anne. He was a philanthropist, heavily invested in Congregation Shearith Israel where he and a succession of sons served as *parnas* (president). In 1714 he purchased 6,000 acres just north of Newburgh, New York, along the Hudson River where he built a trading post. That fort, sold by his sons eight years after his death in 1740, was modified by subsequent owners. Today, the Gomez Mill House is a historical site, recognized as the oldest Jewish homestead in the United States.

Beyond New York

In spite of the important concessions won by Levy and his fellow travelers upon their arrival, some Jewish settlers did not feel fully comfortable and left New

Amsterdam for other colonies. A small number went to Rhode Island, where Roger Williams had established a colony welcoming people of all religious backgrounds. The colony's 1647 Code of Laws stated: "These are the lawes [sic] that concern all men ... and otherwise than ... what is herein forbidden, all men may walk as their consciences persuade them, everyone in the name of his God." In 1658, 15 Jewish Converso families arrived in Newport from Holland, joining the few Jews already there. In that year, they established a congregation called Yeshuat Israel (Salvation of Israel), meeting in private homes for the next 100 years. They led quiet lives, engaging in trade, shipping, and manufacturing as Newport steadily grew into a significant port. When another group of wealthy Converso merchant families arrived directly from Portugal in the mid-1700s, the sleepy backwater began to rival New York in its importance as a Jewish community.

The new arrivals, particularly the Lopez and Rivera families, promptly resumed public practice of their long-hidden Jewish faith. Ashkenzic Jewish merchant families, the Polocks, Harts, and Hays, soon joined them. Together they turned Newport into the center of the country's whale oil, candle, and soap industries. Jews and non-Jews in Newport "met on equality on the street, in the home, in the club or society, at the library, in the factory, on the vessel and in the store."[15] By the start of the American Revolution, Newport was the most important center of Jewish life in the country.

With the number of Jewish residents growing, the community leaders set out to build a synagogue. In 1759, the congregation sent letters to New York's Shearith Israel and other established Sephardic congregations in Europe and the Caribbean seeking financial assistance. Aaron Lopez was one of the signers and was given the honor of laying the cornerstone of the building. A noted architect, Peter Harrison, designed the building, which was completed four years after the cornerstone was laid.

Not all colonies were as welcoming. The Puritans who dominated Massachusetts biblical names. Reverence for the original Abraham, Isaac, and Jacob did not, however, extend to their 17th-century descendants. Jews were welcome in the abstract but not in the flesh, unless they converted to Christianity.

Nearby, the founding of Rhode Island College, later Brown University, set a more inviting atmosphere for Jews. At their annual meeting in 1770, the trustees voted "that the children of JEWS may be admitted into this Institution, and intirely [sic] enjoy the freedom of their own Religion, without any Constraint or Imposition whatever."[16]

Adapting Jewish Practices to Colonial Life

In the main, the lives of colonial Jews mirrored those of their neighbors and class. The main difference lay in their practice of Jewish rituals and law. Much like Jews of today, their interpretations of what it meant to be Jewish depended on individual beliefs, style, and commitment. In America, even as the early congregations tried to impose standards on their communities, early settlers quickly realized that adherence to these standards was voluntary. Particularly for Jews who lived beyond the major cities, keeping a Jewish home—including keeping kashrut (following Jewish dietary regulations), observing holidays, and educating the young—presented significant challenges. One young woman, Rebecca Samuels, who with her watchmaker husband settled in rural Virginia, wrote her parents in Germany, "The way we live here is no life at all. Jewishness is pushed aside here. We do not know what the Sabbath and holidays are."[17]

Some rural Jews, struggling in isolation to adhere to Jewish laws and customs, moved to New York or Philadelphia just to be close to an active Jewish community. Others interpreted their Jewish practices to fit their business and personal needs. As one correspondent of the time wrote of the Jewish community, "In this country each acts according to his own desires."[18]

Jewish settlers quickly learned to adapt to the availability of specific foods and adjust their recipes accordingly. Native fish, corn, and beans were abundant and accompanied the familiar dishes

Aaron Lopez

Lopez was one of the wealthiest merchants and shipowners, and the most successful Jewish merchant of his time. Born in Lisbon in 1731, he was baptized, given the name of Duarte, and raised as a good Catholic. He married his wife, Anna—also from a Converso family—in a church ceremony. Upon his arrival in Newport around 1754, he immediately underwent ritual circumcision, changed his name to Aaron and his wife's to Abigail, and remarried her in a Jewish religious ceremony. For the rest of his life, Lopez adhered strictly to Jewish law and observance, even prohibiting his ships from leaving Newport harbor on a Saturday (Gutstein 1939, 42). He was "distinguished for hospitality and benevolence, and his fine gentlemanly manners, united with a character of irreproachable integrity, secured him the respect and esteem of all who know him" (Kohut 1902, 141).

As a Patriot, he and his extended family left Newport in 1775 for Leicester, Massachusetts. Sadly, as he returned to Newport after the Revolutionary War in 1782, he drowned in a freak accident. His good friend, the Reverend Ezra Stiles, wrote that Lopez was "without a single Enemy and the most universally beloved by an extensive Acquaintance of any man I ever knew." Parenthetically, the good Reverend also bemoaned the fact that Lopez never "perceived the Truth as it is in Jesus Christ ..." (Kohut 1902, 139). The Lopez house in Massachusetts became the home of Leicester Academy.

brought with them from Spain and Portugal such as almond puddings, egg custards, stew, and fish fried in olive oil.[19] In rural areas men learned to ritually slaughter their own meat. In the large communities, that responsibility was delegated to an individual who acted as *shochet*. A brisk trade developed in the shipping of kosher meat to the Caribbean. Aaron Lopez, the Newport shipowner, recorded shipments of "Jew beef" bearing a kosher stamp certifying the legitimacy of the cargo.

Dedication of the Newport Synagogue

On December 2, 1763, Reverend Isaac Touro led the new synagogue's dedication service. The synagogue attracted much attention in its day not only for the simplicity of its exterior design and stunning interior, but also for its angled placement, which allowed the ark to face east toward Jerusalem. The *Newport Mercury* glowingly described the dedication ceremony:

The Order and Decorum, the Harmony and Solemnity of the Musick, together with a handsome Assembly of People, in an Edifice the most perfect of the Temple kind perhaps in America, & splendidly illuminated, could not but raise in the Mind a faint Idea of the Majesty & Grandeur of the Ancient Jewish Worship mentioned in Scripture.

Today, this synagogue—now Touro Synagogue—is the oldest in the country.

Colonial Jewish Women

The role of women during those early years is not largely documented. While the influence of Dutch liberality allowed New Amsterdam women to engage in business pursuits, most busied themselves with family life and responsibilities. Yet, we know of women who operated businesses, particularly after being widowed. Abigail Minis of Savannah, with eight children to support following the death of her husband in 1756, successfully took over his farm and tavern. Others found work as seamstresses or boardinghouse proprietors. Most colonial women who worked were small shop owners. Even women from upper-middle-class families worked. A few were engaged in the import-export shipping trade, in roles normally reserved for men.

In the Community

By the mid 1700s, Jews in the colonies who had first called themselves members of the Jewish (or Portuguese) nation began to identify themselves as part of the greater American fabric—as in "The Jewish Society of Philadelphia." Although Jews experienced moments of discrimination, they were better integrated in community life than their counterparts in Europe. First under the Dutch and then under the British, laws and regulations hindering Jewish equality with other residents gradually diminished. In 1727 the General Assembly of New York voted that Jews could omit the words "upon the true faith of a Christian" when taking an oath. Some upper-class Jews found easy entry into the social world of their contemporaries. In Newport, two Jewish merchants, Moses Lopez and Abraham Hart, were founding members of the prestigious Redwood Library in 1747. The Plantation Act of 1740 passed by the British Parliament permitted the naturalization of immigrants to the American colonies who had resided there for seven years. Because Jews were not specifically excluded, they were, of course, automatically included.

Education of the young was a concern for colonial-era parents. Knowledge was imparted to children primarily through family and religious institutions. Jews, a minority wherever they lived, recognized the importance of transmitting religious traditions to their children. Private tutors filled some of the void, but the level of Jewish knowledge in the colonies was not very high.[20] The leaders of Congregation Shearith Israel in New York established a school and in 1746 published a list of regulations which stated that "school hours were fixed at 9-12 and 2-5 ... English language, reading and writing were taught …"[21] Of course, Jewish subjects were an integral part of the curriculum, similar to today's Jewish day schools.

Jews mingled freely in the higher strata of colonial society through business relationships, wealth, common interests—and Freemasonry. No other institution in the 18th century had as much impact on bringing Jews and Christians together. The legacy of the fraternal order in Western Europe included the admission of Jewish men as fully equal members. This open-mindedness extended to the New World and provided one of the few opportunities for Jewish and Christian professionals to "meet on the level" in the lodge meeting room. "The relationship of the Jews to the Order brought them naturally more directly in contact with their Christian brethren than would otherwise have probably been the case…"[22]

Jewish society in any community required a consecrated burial ground for Jewish dead. In New Amsterdam, a Jewish cemetery was established in 1655 under the control of Shearith Israel. In Philadelphia, the first cemetery dates to 1740 and marks the beginning of Congregation Mikveh Israel (Hope of Israel). Since synagogues in early America were not allowed to incorporate, these plots of land were purchased by members of the congregations and later deeded over to the synagogue. In 1701, Luis Moses Gomez and three of his sons, David, Daniel, and Mordecai, purchased a parcel of land near Chatham Square in New York as a Jewish burial ground. They in turn transferred legal ownership to three other leaders of Congregation Shearith Israel—Jacob Franks, Abraham Isaacs, and Nathan Levy—who "bound themselves in penalty of a thousand pounds never to sell or encumber said property."[23] Jewish patriots and soldiers of the American Revolution are buried in the Jewish cemeteries of Mikveh Israel in Philadelphia, Shearith Israel in New York, Yeshuat Israel in Newport, and in other cities such as Savannah and Charleston.

Letters from Abigail

The letters of one woman, Abigail Levy Franks, provide a glimpse into family life. By the 1730s she had given birth to nine children, two of whom died in childhood.

Her letters detail the uncertainties of life for an early-18th-century Jewish merchant family. She describes politics, disease, tragic death, tight family connections and disappointments, shipwrecks, and lost fortunes. When her eldest child, Naphtali (whom she called Hertsey, a Yiddish endearment for "Dear Heart"), moved to London, her only connection with him was through a decades-long series of letters.

The greatest disappointment in Abigail's life was the intermarriage of two of her children. Indicative of the comfortable relations between Christians and Jews of the time, Phila secretly married Oliver DeLancey, a member of one of New York's most important families. For Abigail, this was a catastrophe of the first order, and she severed all contact with her daughter for the rest of their lives. A year later, son David married a Christian woman from Philadelphia. Their first child was named Abigail in honor of her grandmother but was baptized. Abigail wrote to Naphtali that she was "in the Midst of my many griefes [sic] …"

She was an active supporter of Congregation Shearith Israel, raising funds for the new building consecrated in 1730. For her good works, a separate prayer for the dead continues to be offered in her memory in the synagogue on Yom Kippur, on the anniversary of the building's consecration and on the anniversary of her death.

39

At Worship

From the very beginning, American Jews insisted on creating their own American forms of Jewish observance—a legacy that continues today. Being Jewish in early America was too often an exercise in compromise and creativity. The earliest settlers from Brazil came with a memory of forced conversions and minimal religious knowledge. They brought with them the Sephardic rituals of their ancestors, which were also adopted by the Ashkenazic Jews who followed. When a Christian minister visited the Mill Street synagogue of Shearith Israel in New York in 1712, he observed that many of the congregants came from Poland, Hungary, and Germany.[24] By 1720, Ashkenazic Jews outnumbered the Sephardim, but Sephardic ritual prevailed.[25]

Although Ashkenazic Jews from Germany and Poland sometimes looked askance at the liberal ritual flexibility of the Sephardim, they accepted the Sephardic religious practice they found already in place. That is not to say there were not internal squabbles. A minister wrote in 1739 to a friend in Germany about the Savannah Jews. "They have no synagogue, which is their own fault; the one element hindering the other in this regard. The German Jews believe themselves entitled to build a Synagogue and are willing to allow the Spanish Jews to use it with them in common, the latter, however, reject any such arrangement and demand the preference for themselves."[26]

Intermarriage between Sephardic and Ashkenazic families brought both groups together, but not always amicably. When Isaac Mendes Seixas married Rachel Levy (Moses Levy's daughter and Nathan Levy's sister) in 1740, Abigail Franks wrote, "The Portugueze [sic] here are in a great ferment about it and think very ill of him."[27] Yet, intermarriage between both groups was inevitable because of the

---

Freemasonry

The institution of Masonry was brought to America from England early in the 18th century—possibly initially by Jews (Oppenheim 1910, 92). As a society of secret rites, Masonry had been formed to promote morality and fraternal accord among its members. Open to any male who vouched a belief in God, Freemasonry from the beginning eschewed any sectarian requirements. In Europe, where Jews had no legal rights of emancipation, Masonry offered a rare avenue to assimilation in the larger society. Acceptance of new members was by secret ballot, and Jewish candidates continued to receive the various degrees of the Order.

In America, Masonry continued to provide a common ground for Jews and Christians. Among its members were the most influential business and political figures of the time, including George Washington, who was the Grand Master of Masons in Virginia. Jews served as Masters of individual lodges as well as Grand Masters of a number of states. In some communities, Masonry and Judaism were inseparably intertwined. When the Jewish community of Savannah, Georgia, dedicated its new synagogue in 1820, the ceremony was conducted with Masonic rituals and trappings (Faber 1992, 115–16).

Many Jews who fought as Patriots were Masons. Benjamin Seixas, Haym Salomon, Michael Gratz, Jonas Phillips, Mordecai Manuel Noah, and Solomon Bush are but a few historically recognizable Jewish Masons. The gravestone of Moses Seixas, a leader of Newport's Yeshuat Israel, said: "He was Grand Master of the Grand Lodge of the Masonic Order of this State."

Shearith Israel Cemetery, New York
Buried in this cemetery, close by Chatham Square in New York, are members of the earliest Jewish families in North America as well as Jewish fighters in the American Revolution.
Norman H. Finkelstein

small numbers of Jews in the colonies—and one of Isaac and Rachel's six children, Gershom Mendes Seixas, went on to lead two of America's most significant congregations. Of greater danger to the cohesion of the small Jewish population was growing intermarriage outside of the faith. Freedom in the New World also meant choice, and the casual relationships between practitioners of different religions sometimes led to conversions and intermarriages. Jews, long constrained by civil and religious authorities in Europe, were quick to throw off the ancient restrictions and create lives of their own making.

Jews from Europe found themselves largely without the support base that had previously governed their lives in the Old Country. They were isolated from religious authority, and sending a question of ritual or prayer via letter to Europe meant waiting months for a reply. In America, Jewish affiliation was voluntary and individuals chose their own levels of religious observance. Synagogues were not immune from the spirits of freedom of choice and democracy that energized the new nation as a whole. The opening words of Shearith Israel's new constitution in 1790 were "We the members… ," mirroring the opening of the Declaration of Independence.

Except for an occasional visiting clergyman from across the ocean, there were no permanent fully trained rabbis in America until the 1840s. Laymen, with varying

The Rabbi from Hebron

Although no American synagogue prior to 1825 had an ordained rabbi at its helm, a number of itinerant rabbis appeared from time to time, usually to collect alms for Jews in Palestine. The best known was Rabbi Haym Isaac Karigal. Born in Hebron, the rabbi set out after his ordination at age 17 to visit far-flung Jewish communities from Constantinople to Curaçao and then to the British colonies.

During a three-month stay in Newport in 1773, he often led services in the synagogue. He also became fast friends with Reverend Ezra Stiles, the minister of Newport's Second Congregational Church. Stiles wrote in his diary: "We conversed much and freely" about Jewish learning; and the rabbi helped the minister improve his knowledge of Hebrew. Stiles later observed that his friend was "learned and truly modest, far more so than I ever saw a Jew" (Lebeson 1950, 91). When Stiles was called to the presidency of Yale University a few years later, he instituted a Hebrew language requirement for undergraduates.

knowledge and background, led the scattered congregations. At first, following the European model, Congregation Shearith Israel in New York viewed itself as having the universal mission of governing all Jews within its reach.[28] Until 1825, it was the only Jewish house of worship in the city and provided religious and educational services to the small Jewish population. It did not take long, however, for the spirit of America to derail the traditional powers of the synagogue over its congregants. "Jews in post-revolutionary America made their own rules concerning how to live Jewishly, and there was little that the synagogue-community could do about it."[29] Religious leadership fell upon a paid knowledgeable employee of the congregation. Responsibility for the religious care of the community was vested in a *shamash*—a ritual functionary, or a *hazzan*—a cantor. His job was to arrange and usually lead the services, make kosher candles, and bake the matzot for Passover. He also saw to the charitable needs of the congregation for poor, widowed, and distressed members.[30]

The religious education level of congregants was quite low, prompting Isaac Pinto in 1765 to translate the Hebrew prayer book into English because, he said, "many congregants did not fully understand the prayers and some understood none at all."[31] Although Sephardic ritual was the norm for the established synagogues of the time, friction between Ashkenazim and Sephardim began to grow. In 1802, a group of Ashkenazim withdrew from Philadelphia's Congregation Mikveh Israel to establish their own congregation, which they called Rodeph Shalom. This turning point marked the transition from a single-entity Jewish community to the multicentered world that has characterized Jewish religious life in America ever since.

In the Arts

The earliest Jews in America left no lasting legacy in the fine arts, literature, or music. They were merchants, busily engaged in forging a new life for themselves and their families in a new land of opportunity and challenges. The major exception was Myer Myers of New York. Like many of his contemporaries, he was a merchant, but he was also an artisan in silver and gold. A contemporary of Paul Revere, Myers was one of the few silversmiths of his time who produced intricate items with artistic flair—ultimately earning him election as president of New

York's Gold and Silversmith Society. His candlesticks, jugs, baskets, and teapots were much in demand by the wealthy, and he also produced items such as flatware for middle-class clients. His workmanship was unparalleled in one area: that of synagogue ritual silver. His Torah adornments, particularly *rimonim*—crowns for the tops of wooden scroll holders—were important and lasting. Today, they are among the prized possessions of Congregations Mikveh Israel in Philadelphia, Shearith Israel in New York, and Yeshuat Israel in Newport, and many of his creations can be seen in important American museums and in traveling exhibitions.

Lasting images of the most prominent Jewish families of the colonial and Revolutionary periods exist today in the form of portraits done by important contemporary painters such as Gilbert Stuart, Charles Willson Peale, and Thomas Sully. These beautiful paintings not only provide a window into the lives of these individuals and their families, but also indicate their financial support of the artists they commissioned.

A Prayer for the King

Isaac Pinto's 1765 translation of the prayer book "according to the Order of the Spanish and Portuguese Jews" contained the following prayer for the king:

May he that dispenseth Salvation unto Kings, and Dominion unto Princes: whose Kingdom is an everlasting Kingdom: that delivered his Servant David from the destructive Sword: that maketh a Way in the Sea, and Path through the mighty Waters: Bless, preserve, guard, and assist, our most Gracious Sovereign Lord, King George, our gracious Queen Charlotte, their Royal Highnesses George Prince of Wales, the Princess Dowager of Wales, and all the Royal Family. May the supreme King of Kings, through His infinite Mercies preserve them, and grant them Life and deliver them from all Manner of Trouble and Danger. May the supreme King of Kings aggrandize and highly exalt our Sovereign Lord the King, and grant him long and prosperously to reign. May the supreme King of Kings inspire Him and, and his Council, and the States of his Kingdoms, with Benevolence towards us, and all Israel, our Brethren. In his, and our Days, may Jehudah be saved, and Israel dwell in Safety: And may the Redeemer come unto Tzion: Which God of his infinite Mercies grant; and let us say. Amen

In the colonies, after the king and royal family, the governor and magistrates were also mentioned in the prayer.

Jewish Presence in the Revolution

The role of Jews in the events leading up to the American Revolution is largely unrecognized, given that they represented only a tiny percent of the overall

Myer Myers

Known best for his artistry in silversmithing, Myer Myers was also a Patriot, a loyal congregant, and a twice-married father of 12. His family came from Holland, but he was born (1723), raised, and educated in New York, probably in the school then maintained by Congregation Shearith Israel. He served twice as *parnas* of Shearith Israel (1759 and 1770) and also in the militia. As the British advanced on New York in 1776, he removed his business to Norwalk, Connecticut, and when the British fired that town, fled to nearby Stratford. He then joined family and friends in Philadelphia. After his return to New York in 1783, he and two other synagogue leaders delivered greetings on behalf of the Jewish community to Governor Clinton.

Tale of a Converted Jew

Harvard University had a problem. Hebrew language was a course requirement for all students, but no one was qualified to teach. Enter Judah Monis. Little is known about his early years. In 1722, he was hired as an instructor in Hebrew by Harvard under the condition that he convert to Christianity, since none but professing Christians could teach there. This he did, in a public baptism attended by the leading local clergy. To honor the occasion, Monis published a book of essays "dedicated to the Jewish Nation" and containing "nine principal Arguments the modern Jewish Rabbins [sic] do make to prove, the Messiah is yet to come: with answers to each." The Reverend Increase Mather wrote in the preface, "The conversion of Mr. Monis to Christianity, is an effect of divine grace," and expressed his hope that "God grant that he (who is the first Jew that ever I knew converted in New England) may prove a blessing unto many and especially to some of his own nation ..." (Kohut 1902, 40–41).

Although Monis affirmed a sincere and lasting loyalty to his new religion, even marrying a Christian woman, he also continued to observe the Jewish Sabbath. He remained at Harvard until 1759 and in 1735 published the first Hebrew grammar book in America. When he was laid to rest in a church cemetery in Northborough, Massachusetts in 1761, his tombstone was inscribed as follows:

A native branch of Jacob see,
Which once from off its olive broke,
Regrafted from the living tree
Of the reviving sap partook . . .

population. Like other colonial Americans, their loyalties were divided, with a sizeable majority favoring the Patriot vision of an independent America. When revolutionary fervor grew after Britain's imposition of the onerous Stamp Act in 1765, Jewish merchants' signatures appeared on the various non-importation resolutions adopted by individual colonies. Like other Americans, they opposed the power of the British Parliament to tax the colonies. But some Jews probably had mixed feelings, given the freedoms they enjoyed under British rule.

A number of Jews fought in the Revolution, probably about 100. The first Jew to die fighting for American independence was, ironically, also the first Jew elected to public office in the colonies: Francis Salvador.

Mordecai Sheftall of Savannah, Georgia, was the head of the local revolutionary committee and was responsible for provisioning soldiers. In 1778, he was appointed Deputy Commissary General for Federal troops, but before Congress could approve, the British captured and imprisoned him and his son in December 1778. Both were taken to a notorious British prison ship, the *Nancy*, where they were treated poorly. Eventually paroled to a town under British supervision where local Tories beat and killed Patriots as British troops evacuated under fire from American forces, both Sheftalls escaped by sea, only to be recaptured and sent to Antigua. They were freed in 1780 and made their way to Philadelphia to rejoin their family.

Reuben Etting of Baltimore enlisted the moment he heard about the Battle of Lexington and headed north to Massachusetts. He was taken prisoner by the British who, when they discovered he was Jewish, gave him only pork, which he refused to eat. He was able to survive on scraps of permitted food from fellow prisoners. Weakened by such treatment, he died shortly after his release.[32] A cousin bearing the same name, born in 1762, also fought in the war and was appointed as a United States marshal in 1801 by President Thomas Jefferson.

Abigail Minis supplied provisions to American troops in 1779, angering British authorities. She received permission from them, however, to move with her daughters to safety in Charleston, South Carolina. She died in 1794 at the age of 94.

The war inflicted great hardships on individuals and communities alike. Many Jewish merchants suffered dislocations and reverses, and many a personal fortune disappeared as merchants found their trade interrupted. Haym Salomon, later to gain fame as the mythic Jewish financier of the Revolution, began the war as a wealthy merchant whose unstinting financial sacrifices helped to keep the Revolution going. He died penniless.

Francis Salvador

Francis Salvador was born into a wealthy Jewish family in London in 1747. In 1773, a reversal of financial fortune led him to family-owned land in South Carolina, where he joined the Patriot cause. In 1775, he was the first Jew elected to public office, as a member of the Provincial Congress of South Carolina. On July 1, 1776, when Cherokee Indians attacked settlers, Salvador rode 30 miles to warn outlying residents. On July 24, not knowing that the Declaration of Independence had been issued, he set out with other militia members on a campaign against Loyalist residents and Cherokees (Hühner 1903, 109–113). On August 1, Salvador was shot and scalped—the first Jew to give his life for his new country.

British attacks forced residents, including Jews, from the cities of Newport, Philadelphia, Boston, and Charleston. Of the approximately 1,500 Jews scattered among the 13 colonies on the eve of the American Revolution, about 200 lived in Newport—the largest concentration of Jews in the colonies. Aaron Lopez was one of the Newport Jews who opposed British rule and abandoned the city where they had developed roots and prospered. Lopez led his extended family and members of the Rivera and Mendes families, numbering nearly 70 people, to temporary settlement in Leicester, Massachusetts.[33] The renowned synagogue was closed, and its spiritual leader, Isaac Touro, who professed Loyalist tendencies, sailed with his family to Jamaica where he lived out his life under British rule. According to the diary of the Reverend Ezra Stiles, the few Jews remaining in Newport were "very officious as Informing against the Inhabitant—who are one + another frequently taken up + put in Gaol."[34] [sic]

Haym Salomon

The name of Haym Salomon has become inextricably linked with the story of the American Revolution. He was indeed an ardent Patriot and came to be known as the "financier of the Revolution"—perhaps a bit of an exaggeration. Born in Poland in 1740, he married into the wealthy Franks family and lived in New York until 1778, when he moved to Philadelphia. There, he became a successful financier and used his knowledge and connections to sell bonds for the patriotic cause. He worked closely with Robert Morris to strengthen the weak American financial system, and died in Philadelphia in 1785.

The First American "Rabbi"

Gershom Mendes Seixas was a self-taught cantor committed to fostering Jewish religious life in the new land. He was elected *hazzan* of Shearith Israel in 1768, and although he was neither an ordained rabbi nor a biblical or talmudic scholar, he was considered the spiritual leader, religious authority, and public representative of the fledgling New York Jewish community. A Christian visitor to a Shabbat service in 1776 described him as "a handsome young man of about 25, dressed in a black Gown, such as is worn by Bachelors of Arts" (DeSola Pool 1950–1951, 187). Seixas officiated at Jewish marriage ceremonies, since Jewish tradition did not require the presence of an ordained rabbi to conduct a valid Jewish wedding. He also performed the services of a mohel—religious circumciser—often traveling distances to perform this mitzvah, which sometimes took place days after the traditional eighth day after birth.

He left New York during the Revolution, taking with him books, Torah scrolls, and ceremonial objects for fear they would be damaged or taken by invading British troops. In 1780, with a war-related influx of Jews swelling its community, Philadelphia's congregation asked Seixas to assume the religious leadership of Congregation Mikveh Israel. On September 13, 1782, he officiated at the dedication of the synagogue building, delivering a powerful sermon invoking God's protection for the Revolution. In 1784, after a series of negotiations with synagogue representatives, he returned to New York and Shearith Israel along with the items he had removed for safekeeping.

He was named a trustee of Columbia University in 1787 and held that position until 1815, a year before his death.

In New York, as the British fleet appeared in the harbor, Reverend Gershom Mendes Seixas called his congregants to the Mill Street Synagogue. There he delivered a powerful patriotic address and shortly thereafter left the city for safety in Stratford, Connecticut. While most other patriotic Jews also left the city, a small number remained behind and, together with the few Loyalist Jews, kept the synagogue open. During the war, the congregation was led first by a Tory sympathizer and later by a Jewish Hessian officer who fought with the British and remained after the hostilities ended.

Like some other American families, some Jewish families were divided within themselves in their loyalties. David Franks was the King's sole agent in the northern colonies providing food and supplies to British troops; but other members of the Franks family, David Salisbury Franks and Isaac Franks, served as officers in the Continental Army.

For Jews, participation in the war marked the first time since their exile from Jerusalem that they could take their place alongside their Christian neighbors as equals in a fight for freedom. Jews were present at Bunker Hill, Valley Forge, and other battle sites throughout the colonies. Behind the scenes, they provided logistic support by equipping soldiers, shipping supplies, and raising funds. Shipowners such as Isaac Moses of Philadelphia outfitted privateers to harass British shipping, and their ships engaged in running the British blockade to provide necessary provisions to the needy Revolutionary forces.

What Happened Afterward

After the war, some Jews returned to Newport, but by then the fortunes of the venerable port had declined. The Jews who had increased Philadelphia's population during the war returned to New York, leaving Mikveh Israel financially troubled. Indeed, the remaining members made a communitywide appeal in 1788 for funds to keep the congregation alive. Among the subscribers was Benjamin Franklin, who is recorded as having donated five pounds to the cause.

The cordial relations between Jews and Christians of that period were illustrated by the Grand Federal Procession held in Philadelphia on July 4, 1788 to commemorate the ratification of the Constitution. The Constitution and the 1791 First Amendment made the United States the first country in nearly 2000 years to guarantee its Jewish residents full and equal citizenship. The "Jewish rabbi [*sic*] [Jacob Raphael Cohen] of that city walked between two Christian ministers to show that the new republic was founded on religious toleration."[35] Following the parade, kosher food was served at a separate table at the reception, permitting Jews to enjoy the festivities with their Christian neighbors. A year later, when George Washington was inaugurated as the first president of the United States, Reverend Gershom Mendes Seixas was one of 14 invited clergymen who participated in the festivities.

Ever Nervous

Despite much evidence of personal and official acceptance of them, Jews of the early Republic were wary. For 2000 years, their ancestors had lived precarious lives at the whims of unfriendly governments. Even in America, where unlike most Catholics, African Americans, and Native Americans, they had found a generally open climate of acceptance and legal rights, undercurrents of anti-Jewish feelings were never far from the surface. Remembering their rather lenient treatment by the departing British, Jews had reasonable concern about their position in an independent America. In New York, the leaders of Shearith Israel, who returned to the city after the British withdrawal,

The Franks Family Divided

Born in 1720, David Franks lived primarily in Philadelphia. Despite strongly supporting Congregation Mikveh Israel, he married a Christian woman, and their children were raised as Christians. Like his father before him, he provided food and supplies to the British Army, and he ran a successful shipping, export, and import business with Nathan Levy. Although Franks signed the Non-Importation Agreement of 1765, he remained a Loyalist, serving as a British officer during the war (Phillips 1896, 198–99). In 1778, he was arrested by order of Congress. With his fortune gone, he went to England but returned in 1783 to resume his business. He died in 1793.

A nephew, David Salisbury Franks, came from England to Montreal as a merchant in 1774. He supported the American Revolution actively as well as financially, joining a Massachusetts militia regiment and ultimately attaining the rank of major under General Benedict Arnold. During the general's trial for treason, he came under scrutiny but was quickly exonerated. He died in 1794.

At age 17, Patriot Isaac Franks saw heavy fighting during the Battle of Long Island, retreating afterward with the American forces to New York. He later recalled the day in July 1776 when his unit "attended the first communication of the Declaration of Independence ... when we all, as with one voice, declared that we would support and defend the same with our lives and fortunes" (Jastrow 1897, 9). In 1794, he was named Lieutenant Colonel of the Second Regiment of Philadelphia County Brigade of the Militia of the Commonwealth of Pennsylvania. Franks died in 1822.

47

> ## Letter to Governor Clinton
>
> From the members of Shearith Israel:
>
> We the Members of the Ancient Congregation of Israelites, lately returned From Exile beg leave to Welcome Your Arrival in this City, with our Most Cordial Congratulations.
>
> Though the Society we Belong to is but small when compared with other Religious Societies, yet we flatter ourselves that none have Manifested a more zealous Attachment to the Sacred Cause of American in the War with Great Britain. We derive therefore the Highest Satisfaction from reflecting, that it pleased the Almighty Arbiter of Events, to dispose us to take part with the Country we lived in, and we now look forward with Pleasure to the happy days we expect to enjoy under a Constitution Wisely framed to preserve the inestimable Blessing of Civil, and Religious Liberty.
>
> Taught by our Divine Legislator to Obey our Rulers and prompted thereto by the Dictates of our own Reason, it will be the Anxious endeavor of the Members of our Congregation to render themselves Worthy of these Blessings by Discharging the Duties of Good Citizens . . .

addressed a letter to Governor George Clinton pledging loyalty on "Behalf of the Antient [*sic*] Congregation of Israelites."

A Presidential Response

The leaders of all the Jewish congregations in the United States decided to create a single letter of congratulations to the new president, George Washington, rather "than troubling him to reply to every individual address." But the best of intentions sometimes go awry, particularly when they involve the dynamics of divided, independent, geographically dispersed communities, linked only by the vagaries of a fledgling postal service. Long delays in deciding on the wording led the frustrated congregations in Newport and Savannah to submit their own letters, followed months later by the joint letter finally edited and sent on behalf of the remaining congregations in Philadelphia, New York, Charleston, and Richmond. It was President Washington's response, in 1790, to the Jewish Congregation of Newport that became the iconic affirmation of acceptance by successive generations of American Jews. "To bigotry no sanction" was actually a phrase used by Moses Seixas in his letter to Washington on behalf of the congregation. In his response, the president incorporated those words. "For happily the Government of the United States, which gives to bigotry no sanction, to persecution no assistance, requires only that they who live under its protection, should demean themselves as good citizens."

By the end of the 18th century, no more than 3,000 Jews lived in the new country, with over half living in the South. For the most part they continued to immerse themselves in all aspects of American life. One reason for the low population rate was the small number of Jewish immigrants. Another was the alarming rate of intermarriage and conversion. In an ironically positive way, intermarriage could be interpreted as a sign of ultimate acceptance of Jews by the larger Christian population. But for the Jewish community, it was a problem of the greatest order. Pioneer Jewish families had arrived in America a century earlier as Conversos, proudly abandoning that identity to become loyal Jews. Within two or three generations of their arrival, many of their descendants were no longer Jewish.

To the Hebrew Congregation in Newport Rhode Island

Gentlemen.

While I receive, with much satisfaction, your Address replete with expressions of affection and esteem, I rejoice in the opportunity of assuring you, that I shall always retain a grateful remembrance of the cordial welcome I experienced in my visit to Newport, from all classes of Citizens.

The reflection on the days of difficulty and danger which are past is rendered the more sweet, from a consciousness that they are succeeded by days of uncommon prosperity and security. If we have wisdom to make the best use of the advantages with which we are now favored, we cannot fail, under the just administration of a good Government, to become a great and a happy people.

The Citizens of the United States of America have a right to applaud themselves for having given to mankind examples of an enlarged and liberal policy: a policy worthy of imitation. All possess alike liberty of conscience and immunities of citizenship. It is now no more that toleration is spoken of, as if it was by the indulgence of one class of people, that another enjoyed the exercise of their inherent natural rights. For happily the Government of the United States, which gives to bigotry no sanction, to persecution no assistance, requires only that they who live under its protection should demean themselves as good citizens, in giving it on all occasions their effectual support.

It would be inconsistent with the frankness of my character not to avow that I am pleased with your favorable opinion of my administration, and fervent wishes for my felicity. May the Children of the Stock of Abraham, who dwell in this land, continue to merit and enjoy the good will of the other Inhabitants; while every one shall sit in safety under his own vine and figtree, and there shall be none to make him afraid. May the father of all mercies scatter light and not darkness in our paths, and make us all in our several vocations useful here, and in his own due time and way everlastingly happy.

George Washington

Despite the risks to their population inherent in intermarriage and conversion, Jews in America continued to gain solid footholds. Georgia elected the country's first Jewish governor, Daniel Emanuel. With the purchase of the Louisiana Territory in 1803, the boundaries of the new country expanded and drew a number of Jewish immigrants, mainly Ashkenazic, westward. The ubiquitous "Jew peddlers" forged links between far-flung wilderness communities. They helped found towns like St. Louis, Nashville, Detroit, and Cincinnati. Few Jews in the first years of the 19th century became lawyers, doctors, or teachers, but a small number did serve as officers in the fledgling armed forces of the United States. Simon Magruder Levy was one of the two members of West Point's first graduating class in 1802. Others fought valiantly in the War of 1812, most notably Uriah Phillips Levy, a controversial officer, later to become a commodore in the United States Navy.

Honoring Those Who Fought

Today, members of Congregation Shearith Israel in New York gather each year on Memorial Day at their Chatham Square cemetery to honor the memories of those buried there who laid the foundation for a Jewish presence in America. In particular, they honor the members of the Jewish community who fought in the Revolutionary War. Although small in number, these early settlers made it possible for a uniquely American version of Jewish life, culture, and religious practice to develop on these shores. In so doing, they left their greatest legacy to future generations of American Jews.

1654–1812

A TIMELINE

1654
Arrival of 23 Sephardic Jewish settlers to New Amsterdam

1657
Jews in New Amsterdam accorded full Dutch citizenship rights

1664
British capture New Amsterdam and rename it New York; Jews granted right of British citizenship

1677
Newport Jews purchase land for cemetery

1695
First synagogue in rented house in New York

1761
First English-language prayer book published in New York

1775
Francis Salvador is first Jew elected to public office

1776
Revolutionary War begins

1788
Ratification of the United States Constitution

1790
President Washington's letters to American Jewish communities

1791
Bill of Rights codifies rights for all Americans, including Jews

Founding of New York Stock Exchange includes three Jewish founders: Benjamin Mendes Seixas, Ephraim Hart, and Alexander Zuntz

1797
Maryland Jews petition for equal status

1801
Reuben Etting appointed United States Marshal for Maryland

1802
Philadelphia's Rodeph Shalom is first organized Ashkenazic congregation

1812
War between the United States and Great Britain

1813–1880

Settling In

In the early 19th century, European Jews were still experiencing the effects of racially fueled hatred and nationally sponsored discrimination. But in America, by and large, Jews had found a safe haven. Article VI of the United States Constitution guaranteed that, at least on the national level, "no religious test [would] ever be required as a qualification to any office or public trust under the United States"—meaning that Jewish citizens could hold any federal office, including the presidency. Their small numbers in the population meant that Jews did not present a religious or social threat. Of course, they were still targeted by Christian missionaries: Many in colonial times thought of their Jewish neighbors in the abstract as living incarnations of their biblical ancestors and viewed them as prime candidates for conversion. Yet, in spite of religious differences and missionary zeal, Jews were openly accepted in most communities.[1] Their integration into community life allowed them to live quietly and nearly invisibly. Indeed, they assimilated so well, and intermarried in such large numbers, that Jewish life in America was in jeopardy of disappearing. Jews were doing to themselves what fervent Christian missionaries could not. Joseph Lyons of Savannah wrote pessimistically in 1833, "Certainly, a synagogue, as it exists under the present organization, will not be found in the United States fifty years hence."[2]

The Jew Bill

Beginning in 1797, Jewish citizens of Maryland had regularly, but unsuccessfully, petitioned their legislature for equal status "on the same footing with other good citizens." In 1818, when Maryland's Jews numbered about 150, a Presbyterian member of the state legislature named Thomas Kennedy filed a bill to "extend to those persons professing the Jewish religion, the same privileges that are enjoyed by Christians." The Scottish-born Kennedy told his colleagues, "There are not Jews in the country from whence I came nor have I the slightest acquaintance with any Jew in the world." Kennedy simply believed that religion was "a question which rests, or ought to rest, between man and his Creator alone."

Opposition to the bill was rampant. Year after year the bill was defeated. In 1823, a "Christian Ticket" organized and defeated Kennedy at election time by a margin of 2 to 1. Kennedy was reelected in 1824, the same year he finally succeeded in getting the "Jew Bill" passed. It went into effect in 1826, and later that year two Jews were elected to the Baltimore City Council.

Local Obstacles to Equality

The United States Constitution and the Bill of Rights notwithstanding, barriers to full equality in local and state governments still existed. Individual states operated under their own constitutions, and some maintained discriminatory legal practices well into the 19th century. Maryland's 1649 Act Concerning Religion granted freedom of religion only to those who did not "deny our Saviour Jesus Christ to bee the sonne of God ... ," effectively rendering Jews ineligible to serve in the state militia, practice law, or hold any state government appointment until passage of the "Jew Bill" nearly two centuries later, in 1826. Until 1868, Jews and Catholics in North Carolina were prohibited from holding political office. Not until 1877 were similar rules in New Hampshire finally eliminated.

In spite of these obstacles, Jews participated in the electoral process, joined the military, and got themselves elected to political offices. In 1813, Mordecai Manuel Noah was named as consul in Tunis—the first Jew to be appointed to a diplomatic position. But within two years he was unceremoniously recalled by Secretary of State James Monroe, who used Noah's Jewishness as a pretext for firing him instead of citing the real reasons.

Others embarked on military careers. Uriah Phillips Levy's passion for the sea carried him from the lowly position of cabin boy at age 10 to commodore, the highest rank in the United States Navy—but his passage there was fraught with obstacles. By the time he was 20, he was part owner of a schooner, the *George Washington*. He joined the fledgling United States Navy and fought in the War of 1812, along with 40 other Jews, and was captured by the British. He was commissioned as a naval officer in 1817 and received much praise for his command of the Mediterranean fleet. During his rocky ascent through naval ranks, he constantly battled institutional anti-Jewish discrimination, which resulted in one duel and six court martials in which he was exonerated of blame. The duel was fought with Lt. William Potter, who called Levy "a damned Jew." Potter was killed. Levy was adamantly opposed to the practice of flogging as a form of punishment for sailors in the U.S. Navy and is largely credited with its abolishment by Congress in 1850. Besides his naval activities, he served as the first president of Washington Hebrew Congregation. In 2005, a newly constructed Jewish chapel at the United States Naval Academy in Annapolis, Maryland, was named after him.

Mordecai Manuel Noah

Mordecai Manuel Noah, of Portuguese descent, was born in Philadelphia in 1785. In 1813, President James Madison appointed him consul to Tunis, where he negotiated the ransom of American sailors kidnapped by pirates. He was criticized for paying too much, allowing his political enemies to lobby for his removal. Less than two years after his appointment, he was relieved of duty by Secretary of State James Monroe, who said: "At the time of your appointment it was not known that the Religion which you profess would form any obstacle to the exercise of your Consular function."

Noah returned home to resume his career as a journalist, playwright, and author. In 1822 he was appointed high sheriff of New York, but bigotry still dogged his career. In a widely repeated story, a citizen remarked, "It would be a pity to have a Jew hang a Christian," to which Noah responded, "Fine Christian that had to be hanged" (Marcus 1989, 481).

Noah is best remembered today for his attempt to create a Jewish homeland called "Ararat" on Grand Island, New York, as a refuge from anti-Jewish hatred. Many influential Christians supported the concept of a Jewish homeland to fulfill their own religious agendas. Despite its grand opening in 1825, however, Ararat never caught on with American Jews, who were more interested in assimilating than in distancing themselves from other Americans. Still, Noah's utopian vision marked him as the first modern political Zionist. Eventually, Noah came to believe that Palestine was the true homeland for Jews. He died in 1851.

55

Translating Ashkenazic into American

The Ashkenazic newcomers who arrived in the 1820s were heirs to the relatively brief tradition of liberal ideas born in the French Revolution. Prior to the

Revolution, European Jews were considered out-siders, subject to virulent discrimination, violence, and expulsions. In many countries, Jews were geographically restricted. In the liberal atmosphere created by the Revolution, a debate opened concerning the treatment of Western European Jews. "The Jew should be denied every-thing as a nation," the Count of Clermont-Tonnerre argued in 1789, "but granted everything as individu-als." Jews were no longer relegated to second-class status legally, but the old hatreds still lingered. Real emancipation took decades to implement, but oppor-tunities in business, education, and the arts began to flourish.

Uriah Phillips Levy

Born in Philadelphia in 1792 to a Sephardic family , Levy was a longtime admirer of Thomas Jefferson. In 1836, 10 years after Jefferson's death, Commodore Levy purchased the former president's run-down home at Monticello and devoted the rest of his life to restoring and maintaining the home as a national treasure. His own mother was buried on the property. Levy died in 1862, leaving behind a contested will in which he left the home and property "to the people of the United States." His nephew, Congressman Jefferson Monroe Levy, bought Monticello in 1879, and the property remained in the Levy family until it was turned over to the Thomas Jefferson Foundation in 1923.

Library of Congress

Debates over reforming Jewish religious practice were also beginning to develop in Germany. Yet most new arrivals to America wanted to re-create the kind of traditional worship they had left behind in Europe. They looked askance at the adapted "home-grown" religious practices that had developed in America and chose to form new congregations. These synagogues began as traditional Ashkenazic houses of worship reflecting the familiar rituals of the Old Country. Yet, far removed from the learned rabbis of Europe and their scholarship, American Jews "instinctively chose positions compatible with an American ethos, making many European *halakhic*

religious rulings at best irrelevant, and at worst, divisive."[3] On the other hand, their cohesiveness and communal unity dampened the growing tendency of Jewish intermarriage with Christians among descendants of the original Sephardic settlers and provided stability to Jewish continuity.

Signs of Reform in the 1820s

Contrary to popular belief, the reformation of Jewish religious practice in the United States did not begin with the mass mid-19th-century migration from central Europe. It began much earlier, in 1824, as a local rebellion in Charleston's only synagogue. Some members of Congregation Beth Elohim, where traditional Sephardic-Orthodox liturgy prevailed, petitioned their leadership for modifications

Beth Elohim in Charleston
This 1812 drawing of Congregation Beth Elohim's synagogue indicates the openness with which Jews of the period expressed pride in their religion and a feeling of security in the new country.
Library of Congress

in the religious service. They requested a shorter service that included the use of the English language. Their petition was denied, and the group—led by noted journalist, educator, and dramatist Isaac Harby—withdrew from the congregation to establish the Reformed Society of Israelites. On November 21, 1825, Harby, the Society's first president, delivered an address in which he stated the group's goal: "to promote true principles of Judaism according to its purity and spirit." The "reforms" Harby and his group instituted were "the abolition of rabbinical interpolations and of useless repetitions and to read or chant with solemnity."[4] Like subsequent American reformers, the Reformed Society of Israelites was concerned with the decorum of religious services and looked to their neighboring Protestant churches as models of propriety.

Synagogues of the time were in constant flux, so it was not unusual when the Charleston reformers rejoined Beth Elohim several years later. But this did not mean the end of debate on reforming the congregation. The spirit of reform led to ritual changes that included the introduction of confirmation classes for boys and girls, family seating, and elimination of the observance of a second day for festivals. In 1843 another rift occurred when the congregation introduced organ music into the services—the first American synagogue to do so—leading some traditional members to leave and form a separate congregation, Shearith Israel (not to be confused with the New York congregation by the same name). These early flirtations with reform did not signify the formal establishment of Reform Judaism in America; rather they were indications that American Jews were exploring new paths to religious practices that fit American sensibilities. In 1841, at the dedication ceremony of the new synagogue building of Beth Elohim, Rabbi Gustavus Poznanski declared: "This country is our Palestine, this city our Jerusalem, this house of God our Temple."[5]

Isaac Leeser

Arriving in the United States in 1824 at the age of 18, Isaac Leeser set out at once to learn English and become acculturated to American life. He received a basic Jewish education in Germany and assimilated Sephardic ritual in Richmond, Virginia, where he settled. Leeser became the best-known religious figure of his time. He wrote, preached, and published, putting particular emphasis on combating the ubiquitous Christian missionaries who relentlessly pursued their Jewish neighbors. His antidote to the missionaries was to unite the scattered Jews of America and provide them with a knowledge base to vitalize religious practice. Library of Congress

Break with Centrality

Until 1825, Congregation Shearith Israel was the only synagogue in New York City. Although the congregants adhered to the long-established religious traditions, a majority of congregants was no longer of Sephardic lineage. That year a group of congregants sent a letter to the synagogue trustees requesting the use of a room in which to conduct their own services. "We have a large portion of our brethren who have been educated in the German and Polish *minhag*— custom, who find it difficult to accustom themselves to what is familiarly called the Portuguese *minhag* ..."[6] The trustees refused, leading the petitioners to establish a second congregation in the city, B'nai Jeshurun. Although the 171-year monopoly of Shearith Israel was now broken, relations between the two congregations were cordial. These early congregations operated without rabbinic authority. Questions of Jewish law were put before learned members of the congregation or sent to European rabbis for resolution.

A Strong Call for Unity and Decorum

The most widely known and respected spokesman of the American Jewish community prior to the 1850s was Isaac Leeser, despite the fact that he never claimed to be a talmudic scholar and indeed was not an ordained rabbi. In 1829 he was hired as the *hazzan* of Congregation Mikveh Israel in Philadelphia. Despite ongoing disagreements with the trustees and congregants, he had the "determination to educate and organize American Jewry and to assert his own role as teacher and leader."[7]

Zealous to maintain Orthodox tradition and practice, he understood that education and adaptation were necessary for Judaism to flourish on American soil. At a time when Jews carefully observed the behavior of their Christian neighbors, he was concerned about the lack of decorum in American synagogues. In his periodical, the *Occident and American Jewish Advocate*, he suggested four rules for congregations: punctuality, silence, controlling young children, and remaining until the end of services. "There is no reason," he wrote, "why a Jew cannot observe the Sabbath and the dietary laws meticulously and yet be a cultured educated person."[8]

Always seeking ways to unite American Jews, Leeser proposed the creation of a union of congregations. He was also a realist. Writing in the *Occident* in February 1844, Leeser recognized that "there are difficulties in the way of such a union; there are … many inveterate prejudices among our people, owing to no religious differences, but to the fact that some are native, others new-comers; some wealthy, others poor; some professing love for the German *Minhag*, others again for the Polish or Portuguese; some have reform ideas, whilst others at last refuse even the smallest concession …" The time was not yet ripe, and the only two congregations who even bothered to respond both opposed his suggestion.

Finding Work in America

Many of the Ashkenazic Jews who arrived in the early 19th century settled in the large port cities of the East where they landed, although some made their way inland to smaller but growing cities such as Rochester, Pittsburgh, Chicago, and Cincinnati. They entered the business world, but in a manner different from their Sephardic predecessors, who were mainly merchants, and different from other immigrants of the time, who quickly spread out into the interior and the farming life. Because the new Ashkenazic arrivals were mostly poor and uneducated, with little English-speaking ability, they tended to live together in clearly defined areas of cities where they entered into occupations that did not require knowledge of English or the possession of capital funds. For many of them, this meant garment-making or peddling.

Helping the Poor

When the original 23 settlers landed in New Amsterdam in 1654, they were allowed to stay under the condition that the fledgling Jewish community would be responsible for the care and feeding of the poor among them. Beginning in the 1820s, the establishment of new congregations diluted the monopolistic

Not Just a Dead-End Job

Peddling was more than just a way to make a living; it was also a route to Americanization. It allowed impoverished Jewish immigrants to accumulate money to start their own businesses and accustom themselves to American ways. Rabbi Isaac Mayer Wise later described the journey many newcomers made from peddler to storekeeper: "At first one is the slave to the basket or the pack; then the lacking of the horse, in order to become, finally the servant of the store."

Rebecca Gratz

Born in 1781 to a prominent Jewish family in Philadelphia, Rebecca Gratz was a well-educated woman who devoted her life to the betterment of others. Her sister Richea, 11 years older, was the first Jewish woman to attend college in America, entering Franklin College in Lancaster, Pennsylvania, in 1787.

Rebecca strongly believed in the Jewish education of the young and founded America's first Hebrew Sunday School in Philadelphia. Some claim that she was the model for Rebecca in Sir Walter Scott's *Ivanhoe*. She died in Philadelphia in 1869. Library of Congress.

community controls of the earlier Sephardic congregations. Jews also began to create separate social and philanthropic organizations outside the direct control of the synagogues. Free matzot at Passover, coal for the winter, burial of the dead, and education of poor children were seen as communal responsibilities. In 1815, Rebecca Gratz founded the Philadephia Orphan Asylum, and in 1819 she helped found the Female Hebrew Benevolent Society in Philadelphia to aid the city's impoverished Jews. Hovering over Jewish community needs was the threat posed by Christian missionaries who used aid as a key to conversion, ready to pounce on vulnerable Jews. The greatest accomplishment of these missionaries was to encourage Jewish philanthropy, which by the end of the 19th century had become the dominant connective factor in American Jewry.

The Next Big European Influx

America in 1820 still had fewer than 3,000 Jewish residents. Between 1840 and 1860, according to rough estimates, America's Jewish population jumped from fewer than 15,000 Jews[9] to 200,000.[10] This dramatic increase stemmed mainly from a new flood of Central European Jews who were seeking refuge from ongoing revolutionary strife, worsening economic conditions, and repressive anti-Jewish legislation in the German-speaking countries. This second, larger wave of Ashkenazic Jews, generally more educated and often more financially secure than earlier German Jewish immigrants, created a new era in Jewish communal life. "The bewildered newcomers of one decade became the solid and settled gentry of the next."[11] Mid-19th-century Jewish immigrants brought with them a tradition of culture, charity, and reform Jewish practice, and quickly found ways to incorporate these traditions into their new American life while maintaining their Jewish connections.

In the professions, there were few lawyers or physicians in America prior to 1800, with only a handful of Jews among them. With the mid-19th-century wave of immigrants came a number of professionally trained physicians. The opening of Jews Hospital (later known as Mount Sinai) in New York City in 1852 marked the beginning of Jewish-sponsored hospitals in American cities. Originally founded

280 JAN. 20, 1866.

NO ADMITTANCE

ARRIVAL AT CASTLE GARDEN

Arriving at Castle Garden
Before Ellis Island, New York's Castle Garden was the major arrival center for immigrants between 1855 and 1890. This scene, from *Frank Leslie's Illustrated Newspaper*, shows a group of new arrivals in 1866. Library of Congress.

partly to assure a high quality of care to Jews and partly to provide working venues for Jewish physicians, these hospitals evolved into community institutions serving all residents.

Finding Success in the Hinterlands

A fascinating aspect of Jewish settlement was the move westward and southward. There, far from the established Jewish communities they had left behind in Europe, daring young men formed the first Jewish outposts in the most remote and "untamed" sections of America and dreamed of making their fortune. Most succeeded. Many Jewish merchants were elected to political offices and traded with the numerous Native American tribes. Just like their counterparts in the

Walter J. Judah, Physician

Dr. Judah died in 1798 while tending to victims of a yellow fever epidemic in New York. He was buried in the cemetery of Congregation Shearith Israel. The following is inscribed on his tombstone:

Zealous he was in his labor, the labor of healing. Strengthening himself as a lion and running swiftly as a hart to bring healing To the inhabitants of this City, treating them with loving kindness When they were visited with the Yellow Fever. He gave money from his own purse to buy for them beneficent medicines. But the good that he did was the cause of his death.
(Hühner 1914, 163)

larger cities, many began their business lives as peddlers. Eventually they settled in small towns to open small stores. In time, these Jews and their children became respected members of their communities, and the stores they opened often grew larger. Some of their stores—Macy's, Filene's, Kaufmann's, and Meier and Frank, to name a few—became enormous mercantile successes.

Often, Jews founded towns where they ultimately opened their stores. Sometimes, like Henry Castro who settled in Castroville, California, in 1842, they were respected enough to have their town named after them. Jews were fully accepted members of their communities in spite of an undercurrent of anti-Semitism. There were Jewish mayors, sheriffs, and other elected officials. Between 1820 and 1880, 20 Jews were elected to the United States Congress,[12] with most representing districts containing small Jewish populations. David Levy Yulee of Florida was the first Jew to be elected to the United States Senate, in 1845.

Solomon Nunes Carvalho
Born in Charleston, Carvalho became a well-known painter and photographer who accompanied John Fremont on his 1853–1854 expedition through the territories of Kansas, Colorado, and Utah, in search of a railway route to the Pacific. Carvalho took daguerreotypes on this expedition, most of which were destroyed in a fire. Library of Congress

Jews fought at the Alamo, and some made forays into the wilderness. The Gold Rush enticed young Jews to the Pacific, where they opened small shops servicing the miner hordes. An ambitious and innovative young man could become successful without fear of discrimination. One was Levi Strauss, whose sturdy canvas pants became a staple of American life. But it was a lonely existence for the early Jewish pioneers in their scattered towns, and many eventually moved to larger cities to be among other Jews.

From Peddlers to Philanthropists

Other German Jews became icons of industry and finance. The names Guggenheim, Rosenwald, Straus, Schiff, and Kahn became synonymous with modern philanthropy supporting both Jewish and secular charities. Meyer Guggenheim, a Swiss immigrant, began life in America peddling in Pennsylvania. Identifying a need, he invented and bottled a better stove polish that became an instant success. In the 1870s he and his sons bought silver mines in Colorado and in the 1880s opened smelting plants, making the family one of the wealthiest in America. They joined a handful of other wealthy German Jewish families who became the self-anointed elite of the American Jewish community. Most belonged to Reform temples, associated with others within their select group, and highlighted their place in the upper stratosphere of American social circles, taking the strong view that "American Jews are differentiated from American Christians in religion only not in nationality ..."[13]

New Communal Opportunities

In Europe, central Jewish communal structures still controlled the lives of Jews. But in America, Jews supported both secular and religious institutions, seeing attachment to either as a way of considering themselves part of the American Jewish community. They understood that unlike European models, belonging to these American associations was voluntary but also a positive way of actively participating in their local communities.

As in colonial times, Freemasonry continued to offer an opportunity for Jewish men to interact with others in their community in a supportive setting. Rabbi Isaac Mayer Wise justified Jewish participation in fraternal orders: "Masonry is a Jewish institution whose history, degrees, charges, passwords and explanations are Jewish from the beginning to the end."[14] Still, not all Masonic lodges were equally receptive to Jewish members, leading Jews to establish their own fraternal self-help organizations such as B'nai B'rith, founded in 1843, which historian Hasia Diner called the "secular synagogue." The non-synagogue-based fraternal, social, and philanthropic groups allowed rabbis and their congregants to focus on religious practice, leaving much of the social and philanthropic responsibilities to other groups. Over time, this array of organizational choice and commitment to communal services became a hallmark of American Jewish identity.

Judah Touro

Sometimes called America's first philanthropist, Judah Touro was born in Newport in 1775. His father was Isaac Touro, the *hazzan* of Congregation Yeshuat Israel who moved his family to Jamaica as the Revolutionary War was ending and died shortly thereafter. Orphaned by the age of 12, Judah Touro was raised and educated by his uncle, Moses Michael Hays, in Boston. In 1802, he moved to New Orleans, where he became wealthy in real estate and mercantile businesses and was severely wounded during the defense of New Orleans in 1815. He joined with Amos Lawrence of Boston, each giving $10,000, to build the Bunker Hill Monument. Touro never married, and when he died in New Orleans in 1854, he left more than $500,000 to charities, Jewish and non-Jewish.

Further Decentralization Leads to Further Reform

"In Germany, reform was viewed as a precursor to acculturation and integration. In America, acculturation and integration proved to be the precursors of reform."[15] With increasing numbers of Jews arriving from Central Europe, cracks continued to widen in the once monopolistic synagogue structure in American cities. Although earlier Ashkenazim had allied themselves with existing Sephardic congregations, cultural differences kept them from full social acceptance. "Acculturated native American [Jews] found the newcomers alien, abrasive and uncouth, while immigrants found their Americanized fellow Jews lax in religious

The Founding of the B'nai B'rith

The 12 men who gathered in the Sinsheimer Café in New York City on the October 13, 1843, were Jewish immigrants from Germany. Tired of the heavy-handed dogma that surrounded synagogue life, they founded an organization based on Jewish ideals that could unite all Jews in a fraternal setting.

The Independent Order of B'nai Brith, in the preamble to its constitution, stated its dedication to "uniting Israelites in the work of promoting their highest interests and those of humanity; of developing and elevating the mental and moral character of the people of our faith; of inculcating the purest principles of philanthropy, honor, and patriotism; of supporting science and art, of alleviating the wants of the victims of persecution; providing for, protecting and assisting the widow and orphan on the broadest principles of humanity." They formed themselves as a secret organization with regalia, degrees, and passwords, adopting rituals commonly used by other fraternal organizations such as Masons and Odd Fellows. By 1880 there were over 300 B'nai B'rith lodges throughout the country with thousands of members.

observance."[16] In America, each congregation independently developed its own interpretations of religious practice. Unlike the European communal model of *kehillah,* whose leaders represented the entire community, affiliation with local American congregations was thoroughly voluntary.

During the years 1840 through 1850, as many Jews left the established Jewish communities behind to spread out into America, new congregations emerged one after the other in Cleveland, Boston, Rochester, Chicago, Buffalo, Pittsburgh, and Memphis.[17] This demographic shift quickly diluted what remained of the original Sephardic dominance in religious and communal life. As congregations proliferated far beyond the original East Coast settlements, debates evolved about the importance of maintaining traditions while recognizing the need to adapt to the cultural and societal mores that surrounded them. Conflicts and secessions were common and usually resulted in small changes that laid the basis for further reforms. The innovations grew slowly. An example is today's familiar ceremony of confirmation, which was established on Shavuot 1869, in New York's Congregation B'nai Jeshurun.

In smaller cities with fewer Jews, religious observance tended to be more flexible, with individuals willing to compromise their personal practices for the sake of the larger community. In San Francisco, with a growing Jewish population, two congre-

Confirmation

The first confirmation ceremony took place in Germany in 1810 as a Reform alternative to bar mitzvah. It was introduced in the United States in 1846 at New York's Temple Emanu-El and was quickly adopted by other Reform congregations. While the centuries-old bar mitzvah ceremony focused on boys at the age of 13 and their ability to read from the Torah, confirmation included both boys and girls at age 16 or 17 when they were mature enough to fully grasp the tenets of Judaism. The confirmation ceremony is held on the holiday of Shavuot, which celebrates the giving of the Torah. "Today it has been widely adopted by the various branches of Judaism as an addition to the Bar or Bat Mitzvah" (Eisenberg and Scolnic 2001, 28).

Temple Emanu-El, New York

Congregation Emanu-El was established in 1845 by German Jewish immigrants as a Reform congregation. Dedicated with much celebration on September 11, 1868, at the corner of Fifth Avenue and 43rd Street, the building was called by one observer "the finest example of Moorish architecture in the Western world."

As members of Emanu-El grew more assimilated and wealthier, so did the congregation's religious reform. Beginning with the institution of organ music and the translation of the hymn-book into German, by 1855 the congregation had introduced family pews and had done away with prayer shawls and second-day observance of holidays.
Library of Congress.

65

gations were fully functioning by 1860: one Orthodox and the other Reform, both led by ordained rabbis. By 1880 there were about 20 congregations scattered throughout the Far West.[18]

The Growth of Reform

As the century unfolded, an increasing number of newly acculturated children of German immigrants left the traditional religious practices of their parents behind to become the bulwark of the emerging Reform movement in America. Before 1840, Beth Elohim in Charleston stood alone as a reforming congregation. Within a few years, other Reform-minded congregations arose (Har Sinai in Baltimore, 1842; Emanu-El in New York City, 1845; Beth-El in Albany, 1846). Just prior to the Civil War, other congregations, previously Orthodox in orientation, gradually acceded to the wishes of their congregants and adopted religious reforms. Historian Leon Jick wrote, "By the 1870s there were few congregations in America in which substantial reforms had not been introduced."[19] Many congregations were engaged in lively debate about the appropriate ritual road to follow. The Reform movement became increasingly popular.

Arrival of the Rabbis

The first ordained rabbis to serve American congregations arrived in the 1840s. What they found differed markedly from their previous European religious experiences. American Jews "expected that these men would serve not so much as interpreters of Jewish Law but as guides through the confusing rules and expectations governing the successful creation of an Americanized expression of Judaism."[20] Some rabbis failed to fully understand the implications of life in America, but those who did ultimately played a significant role in defining today's uniquely American forms of Judaism.

Bavaria Collides with Baltimore

Abraham Rice was the first ordained rabbi to lead an American congregation. He arrived from Bavaria in 1840 and became the religious leader of the Baltimore Hebrew Congregation. Rabbi Rice found out soon enough that Baltimore was not Bavaria, at least as far as rabbinic authority was concerned. Almost from the beginning, differences of opinion between the new rabbi and his congregants led to a divisive relationship. The learned rabbi was out of touch with the American conventions that had developed in Jewish religious life. For example, when lodge brethren of a deceased congregant conducted a Masonic funeral service as part of the religious burial service, Rice raised objections and found himself rebuffed by his congregants. Although Rice tried to raise the level of Jewish education by organizing an afternoon Hebrew school for children, other cultural differences and congregational attempts to introduce modest reforms widened the divide between rabbi and worshipers. While the congregation still observed the laws of kashrut and maintained separate seating during services, the decision to institute the use of an organ during services led a number of congregants to leave and form a new congregation, Har Sinai, America's first strictly Reform house of worship. In 1849, Rabbi Rice recognized the futility of his efforts. He withdrew from his pulpit and opened a store.

Fortunately, not all newly arrived religious leaders met the same fate as Rabbi Rice. Three rabbis who, like Isaac Leeser, understood the American perspectives of their congregants well enough to eventually influence them significantly were Isaac Mayer Wise, Dr. Max Lilienthal, and David Einhorn, all of whom grew to prominence before the Civil War began. They came to their congregations with differing outlooks on religious practice, but each saw the need to educate and organize the American Jewish community. But first, each had to overcome the reluctance of their congregations to fully accept their rabbinic leadership. American Jews were too accustomed to fashioning their own instinctive rules. In Europe, rabbis were the respected spiritual leaders and the undisputed arbiters of religious and cultural practices. In America, where congregational power rested in the hands of lay leaders, rabbis were considered paid employees subject to the whims of a less-educated laity. Rabbis like Wise, Lilienthal, and Einhorn undertook to redesign the synagogue following the model of Protestant churches, with the pulpit as the central feature.

Isaac Mayer Wise

Although there was no one single founder of American Reform Judaism, Isaac Mayer Wise is credited with organizing the movement. He arrived in the United States in 1846 to become rabbi of Congregation Beth-El in Albany, New York, an appointment that was not without controversy. From the beginning, Wise was a force to be reckoned with, asserting his pulpit rights as a rabbi at a time when laymen ran American congregations in a manner largely ignorant of the niceties of Jewish law. He instituted the use of family pews, abolishing separate seating for women; counted women in the *minyan* (prayer quorum); gave sermons in English; and presided over confirmation ceremonies. After enduring a series of conflicts with the congregation—including a punch on the nose delivered on the *bimah* on Rosh Hashanah by the congregation president—Wise assumed a new pulpit at Congregation Anshe Emeth.

After nearly eight years in Albany, Wise was named rabbi of Congregation Bene Yeshurun in Cincinnati, Ohio, and there he spent the last 46 years of his life. In 1857 he published a new prayer book, *Minhag America*, in both English and German editions, which was widely used. He hoped that all American congregations would adopt it, leading to a single ritual throughout the country that would unite all American Jews under a single religious umbrella. In this he was not totally successful, as more-traditional congregations rejected the idea. Certainly, though, Rabbi Wise "attracted a large following among the upwardly mobile, rapidly Americanizing Jewish burghers who were 'his people.'"[21]

Isaac Mayer Wise
Born in Steingrub, Bohemia, in 1819, Wise was educated and ordained in Germany. From his perspective as a German immigrant, he saw the need for training American native men as rabbis. In 1855 he opened Zion College with 14 students, an enterprise that soon failed, as did Isaac Leeser's Maimonides College, opened in 1867.

Nonetheless, Wise pursued the idea of unity. In 1873 he created the Union of American Hebrew Congregations, uniting 34 Reform congregations. Two years later, his dream for an American rabbinical school became a reality with the establishment of Hebrew Union College in Cincinnati, with 13 students. A major stumbling block to the creation of an authentic American form of Judaism had been the lack of home-grown Enlish-speaking rabbis. Hebrew Union College would produce rabbis committed to Judaism and "sensitive to the changing conditions of the American environment in which Judaism had to struggle for survival" (Martin 1980, 43). In 1889 Wise founded the Central Conference of American Rabbis to provide collegial support to succeeding generations of well-trained rabbis. He died in Cincinnati in 1900. Library of Congress

Rabbi Max Lilienthal

Dr. Lilienthal's reputation in Europe had preceded him to America. A graduate of the University of Munich, he was named principal of a Jewish school in Riga, Latvia, in 1839. Induced by the Russian government to help establish schools throughout the country that would teach Jewish students secular and religious subjects, he soon discovered that the ulterior motive of the Russian government was not benevolence but conversion. In disgust, he left for America. In an unusual arrangement upon his arrival, due to financial considerations, three "German" congregations in New York hired him as their joint rabbi. In the sermon on the occasion of his installation, he noted that Judaism was "split, at present into two parties ... The one exclaims: 'Hold fast to the ancient institutions' while the other says, 'Onward, onward, is our motto; "onward" is the watchword of the times.'" He called for the support of schools to provide religious education to children and told his congregants it was his duty to "introduce order and decorum into our houses of worship." He quickly devised a rotating system that allowed members of all the synagogues to assemble on the Sabbath to hear his sermons. Like Rabbi Wise, Dr. Lilienthal underwent an American baptism by fire before his leadership became accepted, but ultimately both these rabbis "legitimated new modes of Jewish practice that enabled congregants to feel that Jewish observance did not have to undermine their American respectability."[22]

Rabbi David Einhorn
In 1855, Rabbi David Einhorn arrived from Germany and took the helm of Baltimore's Har Sinai congregation. Only then, under Einhorn's outspoken liberal leadership, did the nation's first strictly Reform congregation begin to make major changes in its practice. He composed a creative prayer book, *Olath Tamid*, which removed all references to a return to Zion, the Yom Kippur *Kol Nidrei* prayer, and the *Musaf* (additional) service for the Sabbath and weekdays. In 1894, his prayer book became the model for the Reform movement's classic *Union Prayer Book*. Jewish Historical Society of Maryland

The views of the new religious leaders spanned the religious spectrum. While Leeser considered himself a traditionalist, Einhorn and Lilienthal gravitated to the left, with Wise taking a centrist position. By dint of personality and the courage of young lions, they taught, preached, and cajoled their fellow Jews. Their importance stretched beyond their individual congregations where, in many instances, their growing national reputations did not insulate them from the ever-present petty disagreements of daily congregation life. Yet they forged on in a community largely insulated from the tradition of Jewish scholarship.

To improve intellectual life, some influential Jewish leaders created books, journals, and newspapers. Isaac Leeser formed the short-lived American Jewish Publication Society in 1845 to publish serious books on Jewish religion. (The Society was not a forerunner of The Jewish Publication Society, founded in 1888.) A bit more successful was his periodical, the *Occident and American Jewish Advocate.* America's first Jewish newspaper was *The Jew,* established in 1823 primarily to refute the work of missionaries. In Baltimore, David Einhorn published *Sinai* in German. Together with weekly newspapers such as Robert Lyon's *Asmonean* (1849); Isaac Mayer Wise's *American Israelite* (1854) and his *Die Deborah,* geared to female readership (1855); and Samuel Isaacs's *Jewish Messenger* (1857), these publications served to connect a Jewish population increasingly fragmented by geography and religious practice.

Rabbi Wise is sometimes credited with creating Reform Judaism in the United States. Yet he and his contemporary religious leaders were only building on the reformist trends already in process in many American congregations. Their success lay in the fact that they were educated rabbis with charisma and vision who just happened to be endowed with strong organizational skills. While fearlessly leading, they simultaneously validated the adaptive, reformist tendencies of their congregations. They also encouraged the feeling among their congregants that America offered a new opportunity for changing the direction of Jewish thought. Isaac Mayer Wise summarized that attitude when he dedicated the Cincinnati's Plum Street Temple "in gladness not in perpetual mourning."

The Shul Shootout

As Reform Judaism gained in numbers, internal debates in some congregations led to walkouts, dissension, and withdrawals to form competing synagogues. Events in Portland, Oregon's Congregation Beth Israel took a publicly embarrassing and near tragic turn in 1880. Traditionally oriented congregants had engaged in furious debate with their Reform-leaning rabbi, Moses May, who accused his congregants of ignorance.

After years of vituperative charges, a faction favoring more traditional ritual took over the synagogue leadership. Relations with the rabbi disintegrated into mutual name-calling. On September 30, the rabbi passed the store of one of his most vocal detractors and shouted "You're a liar!" through the open door. Later, as the rabbi passed by the man on the street, the storekeeper knocked him to the ground and ripped his coat. The enraged rabbi pulled out a gun and shot twice, luckily missing his intended target. The fracas was reported widely in the local press, to the chagrin and embarrassment of the Jewish community. The storekeeper was arrested and paid a fine. The rabbi, sporting two black eyes, quickly left town.

69

Establishing Principles

The rise of Reform Judaism in Germany led to a series of rabbinical conferences in 1844, 1845, and 1846 to standardize religious practices. The tradition of these conferences carried over to America. The Philadelphia Conference in 1869 created the "Classical Reform Period" of a universal and scientific approach to Judaism. The Pittsburgh Conference in 1885 "distilled ideas that had been circulating in

Reform Jewish circles for two generations."[23] "We consider ourselves no longer a nation, but a religious community and therefore expect neither a return to Palestine, nor a sacrificial worship … We hold that all such Mosaic and rabbinical laws as regulate diet, priestly purity, and dress originated in ages and under the influence of ideas entirely foreign to our present mental and spiritual state … We accept as binding only it's [*sic*] [the Torah's] moral laws and maintain only such ceremonies as elevate and sanctify our lives." The creation of the Union of American Hebrew Congregations was "originally intended to include congregations of all shades of religious opinion."[24] It was part of Isaac Mayer Wise's dream of establishing the organizational foundation of his *Minhag America*, a single Jewish religious practice informed by American ideals and conventions. Despite wide differences in theology and ritual, by 1880 over 90 percent of American congregations were Reform. Their religious practices and beliefs varied greatly from one another, and it would be safe to say that the umbrella of Reform Judaism in America covered almost any congregation that was not Orthodox.

Ironically, it had been the lack of a central religious authority that allowed the spread of reformist innovations in all types of synagogues. Wise and other Reform-minded rabbis succeeded because they were able to validate the accommodations begun by their congregants, a reversal of the European experience that allowed Judaism to not only survive, but truly flourish in America.

Hannah Solomon

Born in Germany in 1858, Hannah Solomon came with her parents to Chicago, where her father became a successful businessman. The family was active in a Reform temple, and Hannah involved herself in social and cultural organizations. She and her sister were the first Jewish members of the Chicago Women's Club. She served as president of the organization she founded, the National Council of Jewish Women, until 1905. Solomon died in 1942.

Emerging Role of Women

Women were gradually becoming more visible in Jewish religious life. While it would take most of the century to see full equality of women in the Reform synagogue, women became actively involved in their synagogues through sisterhood organizations that originated in 1887 in New York's Temple Emanu-El and by the end of the century had taken root in nearly every Reform congregation in the United States. Sisterhoods and Ladies Auxiliaries took root in Orthodox and Conservative congregations throughout the country as well. In 1893, Hannah Solomon founded the National Council of Jewish Women, which provided leadership opportunities for women while attending to the charitable needs of Eastern European immigrants. In addition to women whose names are well known—Rebecca Gratz, creator of the first Jewish Sunday school; Henrietta Szold, founder of Hadassah; and Lillian Wald, founder of New York's Henry Street Settlement—were thousands of unsung women whose selfless contributions bettered the lives of American Jews. They were founders of labor unions and hospitals. Women were also at the forefront of educational activities in their communities, serving as teachers and fund-raisers.

While Jews were adjusting to their new lives in America, the hardship and discrimination they had escaped continued to affect Jews around the world. It did not take long for American Jews to use their new rights and privileges to politically organize in defense of fellow Jews overseas.

The Damascus Blood Libel

The early-19th-century Jews of the United States were less than cohesive in presenting a uniform national image. Divided by geographic, linguistic, and cultural origins, their lives revolved around family and local community. It took events thousands of miles away to bring the nascent national Jewish community to life. The mysterious disappearance of a Catholic monk in Syria in 1840 reawakened the medieval anti-Jewish blood libel. A number of Jews were arrested and tortured. People around the world were shocked. In America, Jewish communities organized public meetings and sent petitions of protest to President Van Buren, who issued an official denunciation of the affair. This marked the "first time that the Jews of the United States interested themselves and enlisted the interest of the government in the cause of suffering Jews in another part of the world . . ."[25]

When an American Jewish merchant was expelled from Switzerland in 1857, Isaac Leeser and Isaac M. Wise joined forces. Using their respective newspapers, they organized Jewish delegations from around the country to go to Washington and lobby government officials. American Jews discovered that their voices did matter and that a united front gained them access to the national centers of political power.

The Mortara Affair

The next year, another anti-Jewish act, this time in Italy, galvanized the world Jewish community. A young child, Edgar Mortara, secretly baptized by his devout Catholic nurse as an infant, was kidnapped by Vatican agents. His involuntary baptism was enough to make the little boy a Catholic in the eyes of the Church. Vatican officials removed the boy from his home to be raised as a Catholic. The feelings of Edgar's Jewish parents can scarcely be imagined. Jews and non-Jews everywhere were outraged, but pleas from around the world fell on deaf ears in the Vatican. Edgar was raised as a Catholic and grew up to become a priest.

A positive effect of the Mortara Affair was that it institutionalized American Jewish political action for the first time by leading to the creation of the Board

Edgar Mortara

Edgar Mortara was educated in a convent and was sometimes taken by Church authorities to Jewish ghettos, apparently to provoke the residents. He entered the Augustine order and served as a missionary, preaching in German churches and once even in an Italian Catholic church in New York. After he had taken orders, he was allowed to see his family members and attended his mother's funeral in Switzerland in 1895. He published a request in a Catholic newspaper for his friends to pray for his dead mother and for his family.
(Deutsch, www.jewishencyclopedia.com)

of Delegates of American Israelites in 1859, "for securing and maintaining civil and religious rights at home and abroad." The board, an early attempt to organize the disparate American Jewish community, did not have universal support from all leaders of the time. Rabbis Wise and Einhorn were opposed to its establishment, as were the venerable congregations of Shearith Israel and Emanu-El in New York and Mikveh Israel in Philadelphia. They objected to the creation of a not religiously affiliated organization to represent the entire Jewish community.

Although the board merged in 1878 with the Union of American Hebrew Congregations, at the time of its creation it was the first centralized organization to speak for American Jews. Together with such fraternal organizations as B'nai B'rith, it marked the emergence of a secular leadership in the Jewish community, which had formerly been dominated by the synagogue. Soon other organizations, social and philanthropic, would arise to represent the diverse needs of a growing Jewish population. Like their Christian neighbors, most Jews continued to identify with their religion. But with traditional dietary and dress customs falling by the wayside, they adapted their lives to fit an American lifestyle.

Education

Before the advent of quality public schools in the mid-19th century, Jewish parents relied on tutors or congregational schools to educate their children. They avoided the public schools, which were in many instances unofficial extensions of evangelical Protestantism. In 1854, day schools were associated with seven New York City congregations. "We are not illiberal," wrote Isaac Leeser in the December 1843 issue of the *Occident*, "but cannot shut our eyes to the dangerous tendency of placing Jewish children under the inclusive care of gentile teachers." The typical congregational school taught basic secular subjects as well as Hebrew and religion. Included in the curriculum of the B'nai Jeshurun Educational Institute in New York were classes in Hebrew, reading, writing, Bible, history, geography, penmanship, French, German, Spanish, algebra, drawing, and Latin. School hours were 9 to 4 daily, a precursor to the modern Jewish day school.

The success of congregational schools was short-lived due to improvements in public schools and the dearth of qualified Jewish teachers and textbooks. Although Leeser championed the establishment of day schools for children, he also supported Rebecca Gratz's Sunday school program, which she began in 1838, using the model followed by Protestant churches. He was concerned about ongoing efforts to convert Jews and welcomed efforts within the Jewish community to inoculate children against the entreaties of missionaries. Writing in the April 1843 issue of the *Occident*, Leeser reported on the fifth annual examination of students of the Sunday School. "In the absence of regular day-schools [this school] contributes, in an eminent degree, to disseminate much valuable and healthful instruction among a large number of children." The Sunday school model, which evolved into supplementary school programs, enhanced Jewish support of the American public school system.

Jews and the Arts

While education was prized, Jews by mid-19th century had contributed little to American or Jewish arts and literature. Isaac Harby and Mordecai Manuel Noah, involved as they were in Jewish affairs, were also early playwrights and journalists whose fame extended to the larger American community. The newspapers and journals of Leeser, Lyon, and Wise contributed, each in its own way, to the dissemination of literary works with Jewish themes, although to a small audience. Penina Moise not only composed hymns for her Charleston congregation, Beth Elohim, but also became the first person, male or female, to publish a book of poetry in America. It was not until 1867 that the first Jewish novel of any literary merit was published: *Differences,* by Dr. Nathan Mayer. But it was Emma Lazarus, best known for her sonnet engraved on the Statue of Liberty, who became the first truly acclaimed Jewish writer of the 19th century.

Penina Moise

Penina Moise was born in Charleston in 1797 to parents who had arrived from the Caribbean five years earlier. Her formal education ended when she was 12 years old, upon the death of her father, but she continued her love of reading. She became a protégé of the dramatist Isaac Harby, a fellow member of Congregation Beth Elohim, and began writing hymns and poems, mainly with Jewish themes. Her hymns were published as the nation's first Jewish hymnal in English. Moise was a strong advocate of Jewish rights who viewed her country as a haven for downtrodden immigrants, and her poems reflected her concerns. In the *Southern Patriot* in 1820, she wrote:

If thou out of that oppressed race
    Whose name's a proverb and
    whose lot's disgrace
Brave the Atlantic—
    Hope's broad anchor weigh;
A Western Sun will
    Gild your future day.

Penina Moise died in 1880.

The Civil War

The Civil War divided Jews as it did all Americans. Southern Jews supported the Confederacy; Northern Jews favored the Union. Prior to the war, Jews as a group never took a public stand on slavery. Although many shared antislavery opinions, they viewed the Christian-oriented abolitionist movement with suspicion.[26] A report to the 1853 meeting of a leading antislavery society accurately described Jewish attitudes:

The Jews of the United States have never taken any steps whatever with regard to the Slavery question. As citizens, they deem it their policy "to have every one choose whichever side he may deem best to promote his own interests and the welfare his country …"

The objects of so much mean prejudice and unrighteous oppression as the Jews have been for ages, surely they, it would seem, more than any other denomination, ought to be enemies of caste, and friends of universal freedom.

Two vocal Jewish abolitionists were Ernestine Rose and Rabbi David Einhorn. Rose, a Polish immigrant, was a popular speaker and an outspoken advocate of

Emma Lazarus

The daughter of a well-to-do family, Emma Lazarus was born in New York in 1849. She received a classical secular education and developed an avocation for poetry. She met and corresponded with Ralph Waldo Emerson and considered the renowned poet to be her mentor. Her poem "In the Jewish Synagogue at Newport" was a direct response to Henry Wadsworth Longfellow's downcast look at Judaism in "The Jewish Cemetery at Newport." The increase in Russian pogroms in the early 1880s profoundly affected her writing and led to poems on the Jewish experience, including "The Banner of the Jew" in 1870 (shown here is the fifth stanza):

Oh deem not dead that martial fire,
Say not the mystic flame is spent!
With Moses' law and David's lyre,
Your ancient strength remains unbent.
Let but an Ezra rise anew
To lift the Banner of the Jew!

Her most famous poem, "The New Colossus," written in 1883, includes the Statue of Liberty's welcome to the world's immigrants:

Give me your tired, your poor,
Your huddled masses
yearning to breathe free,
The wretched refuse
of your teeming shore.
Send these, the homeless,
tempest-tossed, to me:
I lift my lamp beside the golden door.

Emma Lazarus was only 38 years old when she died of cancer in New York.

women's rights. "Emancipation from every kind of bondage is my principle," she exclaimed. Einhorn, who had brought about American Judaism's first major reforms at Baltimore's Congregation Har Sinai, used his pulpit and his journal, *Sinai,* to preach, "It is the duty of Jews to fight bigotry since, for thousands of years, Jews have consciously or unconsciously fought for freedom of conscience."

Yet some Jews held other views of the slavery issue. Rabbi Morris Raphall of New York's Congregation B'nai Jeshurun was a dramatic orator and writer who had the distinction of being the first Jewish clergyman to deliver an opening prayer for a session of the United States Congress (February 1, 1860). On National Fast Day he delivered a widely reprinted sermon, "A Bible View of Slavery." In the North, many were disappointed with his words; Southerners viewed it with satisfaction. "Slavery has existed since the earliest time," the rabbi wrote. "Slave holding is no sin," he declared, since "slave property is expressly placed under the protection of the Ten Commandments ..." Rabbi Einhorn was aghast and forcefully rebutted Raphall's words in *Sinai.* Dismissing Raphall's literal interpretation of the Bible as representative of all Jewish thought in America, Einhorn insisted that just because a particular practice was condoned in the Bible did not make it right for modern times. The real question, according to Einhorn, was: "Is slavery a moral evil or not?" He argued that the spirit of Judaism, as opposed to its letter, demanded the abolition of slavery. "The Bible," he wrote, "merely tolerates this institution as an evil not to be disregarded and therefore infuses in its legislation a mild spirit gradually to lead to its dissolution."[27]

Thousands of Jews volunteered and many died on both sides of the conflict. An estimate by Congressman Simon Wolf "placed the number in the Union forces at about eighty-four hundred and in the Confederate forces at about ten thousand."[28]

Ernestine Rose

Ernestine Rose, daughter of an Orthodox rabbi, became one of America's best-known advocates for human rights. Born in Poland in 1810, she was a self-proclaimed "rebel at the age of five" and left home at 17 to travel through Europe. Arriving in America in 1836, she quickly became a prominent fighter for social justice. In response to a Boston editor's charge that Jews were "a troublesome people to live in proximity with," she wrote, "in spite of the barbarous treatment and deadly persecution they [European Jews] have suffered … Europe has been none the worse on their account." She died in England in 1892.

Library of Congress

Rabbi Raphall Petitions the President

Rabbi Morris Raphall, who inflamed passions with his 1860 sermon "A Bible View of Slavery," had a son serving in the Union Army. Seeking to obtain a promotion for him, Rabbi Raphall visited President Lincoln on what happened to be a national day of prayer on behalf of the army. Adolphus Solomons, a Washington publisher and friend of the president who was present that day, later recounted the meeting of the rabbi and President Lincoln.

After hearing the rabbi's request, Lincoln responded, "As God's minister is it not your first duty to be at home today to pray with your people for the success of our army as is being done in every loyal church throughout the North, East and West?" The Rabbi, evidently ashamed at his faux pas, blushing made answer: "My assistant is doing that duty." "Ah," said Lincoln, "that is different." The President then drew forth a small card and wrote the following upon it: "The secretary of war will promote Second Lieutenant Raphall to a First Lieutenantcy. A. Lincoln." Handing the card to the Rabbi he said, with a smile all his own: "Now, doctor, you can go home and do your own praying."

(Markens 1909, 135)

Other estimates differ, but it is clear that Jews fought on both sides in numbers greater than their percentage in the general population. There were nine Jewish generals in the North and several in the South. Jews fought not only for their respective causes, but also for equal treatment for themselves. Six Jewish soldiers in the Union army received the coveted Congressional Medal of Honor for their bravery. When the war ended, Jewish soldiers returned to their homes to rebuild their country and their lives.

In the North, two events galvanized the Jewish community at large during the war: the appointment of a Jewish chaplain to the military and General Grant's Order No. 11.

The First Jewish Chaplain

With the large number of Jews in the Union Army, the Board of Delegates of American Israelites began to press for the appointment of Jewish chaplains. They delegated Rabbi Arnold Fischel of New York's Shearith Israel to investigate conditions. Writing to the Board, Fischel noted:

Present at an Execution

Desertion from the Union Army was dealt with harshly by military commanders. In one case, a Jewish soldier of the 118th Pennsylvania Volunteers, George Kuhn, recently arrived from Germany, was found guilty of desertion by a court-martial and sentenced "to be shot to death by musketry in the presence of the Division" (George Kuhn archives, Maryland Jewish Historical Society). Rabbi Benjamin Szold of Baltimore was summoned to minister to the prisoner. After hearing his story, the rabbi approached President Lincoln to request a pardon. The President denied the request. At the execution, Rabbi Szold stood by Kuhn, a minister attended two Protestant prisoners, and a priest comforted a Catholic deserter. This was possibly the first case in American history of an all-denominational funeral.

Now that I have visited all the camps and hospitals in Virginia, I have a distinct idea of what has to be done, and what can be done. The number of Jews in the army is very large ... As a general rule, they are not known as Jews, but hundreds with whom I have conversed express their anxiety and hope that some provision may be made for them, so that in case of sickness or death, they be not left to the mercy of strangers ...

Since they entered the hospitals ... they have in addition to the sufferings of disease, to submit to the torture of religious controversy, forced upon them by Christian clergymen, who are anxious "to save their souls."

On July 17, 1862, the United States Congress voted to change the words in the law pertaining to the appointment of military chaplains from "Christian denomination" to "religious denomination," leading to the official appointment of Rabbi Fischel as the first Jewish chaplain.

On December 17, 1862, General U. S. Grant issued General Order No. 11, expelling all Jews from the territory controlled by his army, which included the states of Mississippi, Kentucky, and Tennessee. The response from the Jewish community was immediate and furious. Parents of Jewish soldiers fighting for the Union joined community leaders in mass protests and petitions. The *New York Times* referred to the order as "one of the deepest sensations of the war." American Jews protested by sending letters and telegrams to Washington. Cesar Kaskel, a well-respected Jewish resident of Paducah, Kentucky, traveled to Washington and met with President Lincoln, who immediately rescinded the order.

On the Confederate side, Judah P. Benjamin, a former U.S. Senator from Louisiana, served as secretary of state and a close advisor to President Jefferson Davis. On the eve of the Civil War, Benjamin passionately delivered his farewell address to the Senate: "You never can convert the free sons of the soil into vassals paying tribute to your power, you never, never can degrade them to the level of an inferior and servile race—never, never." Benjamin's passion for the Confederate cause and his wise counsel to President Jefferson Davis was invaluable during the war, but anti-Jewish sentiments aimed at him even from former supporters surfaced openly as the Southern cause went down to defeat. Benjamin ultimately resettled in England, where he became a highly respected lawyer.

President Lincoln's assassination in April 1865 shocked the nation. For the first time since its founding, congregants of Shearith Israel in New York recited the *Hashkabah*—the Sephardic prayer for the dead—in memory of a non-Jew. In a

Judah Philip Benjamin

In an 1884 article in the *American Israelite*, Rabbi Isaac Mayer Wise described Benjamin as "undoubtedly the most successful statesman of the Jewish family in this century and country." Born in the West Indies in 1811, Benjamin and his parents moved to North Carolina in 1818. He attended Yale College but left after his sophomore year and settled in New Orleans, where he married a Catholic woman. He was a successful attorney and one-time sugar plantation owner who became known as a brilliant orator and debater.

Elected to the U.S. Senate, he resigned in February 1861 to accept President Jefferson Davis's invitation to join the Confederate government cabinet as attorney general. He served as secretary of war until 1862, when he was appointed secretary of state of the Confederacy, holding that position until the end of the Civil War. Facing certain imprisonment or death after the war, his property confiscated by the victors, Benjamin fled to the West Indies and ultimately settled in London, where he became a successful lawyer. He died and was buried in Paris, where his daughter lived, in 1884. Library of Congress

A Civil War Seder

Writing in the *Jewish Messenger* in April 1866, a former Union soldier named J. A. Joel recounted the seder he and his fellow Jewish soldiers arranged for themselves in West Virginia in 1861:

We obtained two kegs of cider, a lamb, several chickens and some eggs. Horseradish or parsley we could not obtain, but in lieu we found a weed, whose bitterness, I apprehend, exceeded anything our forefathers "enjoyed" ... The necessaries for the choroutzes we could not obtain, so we got a brick which, rather hard to digest, reminded us, by looking at it, for what purpose it was intended ...

The ceremonies were passing off very nicely, until we arrived at the part where the bitter herb was to be taken. We all had a large portion of the herb ready ... ; each eat his portion, when horrors! What a scene ensued ... The herb was ... fiery like Cayenne pepper, and excited our thirst to such a degree, that we forgot the law authorizing us to drink only four cups, and ... drank up all the cider. Those that drank the more freely became excited, and one thought he was Moses, another Aaron, and one had the audacity to call himself Pharaoh. The consequence was a skirmish, with nobody hurt, only Moses, Aaron and Pharaoh, had to be carried to the camp, and there left in the arms of Morpheus. This slight incident did not take away our appetite, and, ... we resumed the second portion of the service without anything occurring worthy of note.
(www.jewish-history.com).

fund-raising circular for a Springfield, Illinois, monument in Lincoln's memory sent to Jews, Julius Hammerslough, a local Jewish friend of Lincoln, wrote:

It is above all, fitting in this land where the Hebrews have won so proud a name and are so greatly respected and honored that they should thus show veneration for the fallen chief of the nation, whose wisdom, honesty and purity of purpose were so highly appreciated by foreign nations and who was so beloved at home.[29]

To His Excellency Abr. Lincoln ...

On January 5, 1863, members of the St. Louis B'nai B'rith wrote a letter to Abraham Lincoln requesting that he revoke General Order No. 11:

Sir

... In the name of the Class of loyal citizens of these U.S. which we in part represent.

In the name of hundreds who have been driven from their homes, deprived of their liberty and injured in their property without having violated any law or regulation.

In the name of the thousands of our Brethren and our children who have died and are now willingly sacrificing their lives and fortunes for the Union and the Suppression of this rebellion.

In the name of religious liberty, of justice and humanity—we enter our solemn Protest against this Order, and ask of you— the Defendor & Protector of the Constitution—to annull that Order and to protect the liberties even of your humblest Constituents.

(Abraham Lincoln Papers)

Post war Society

The small Jewish population in the United States grew in size and prominence after the Civil War. By the 1870s, many children of German-speaking Jewish immigrants had become successful in business and the professions; they created a close-knit culture heavily involved in community affairs and philanthropy, endowing large sums of money for public benefit. Social organizations offered ways to raise money while having fun and socializing. Beginning in 1861, annual Purim balls in New York were the height of the social calendar, mixing fund-raising with acknowledgment of the merry Jewish holiday.

The Young Men's Hebrew Association (YMHA) was founded in 1874, as an outgrowth of literary clubs for young Jewish men in the 1850s and 1860s. The YMHA served the cultural, entertainment, and social needs of young people outside of the synagogue and mirrored the popularity of the Young Men's Christian Association (YMCA). Indeed, rabbis welcomed the groups as educational vehicles that supported the dissemination of Jewish thought and culture. Since the YMHA was not affiliated with any specific branch of Judaism, it allowed young men of differing backgrounds to meet on neutral ground. An 1887 editorial in the *American Hebrew* stated that YMHAs "must supplement the pulpit, co-operate with it, and vigorously strive not only to Judaize the Jew, but to Americanize the Jew" (May 27, 1887, 42). Not to be outdone, Jewish women began organizing YWHAs during the first decade of the 1900s. Today, their descendants can be found in the many Jewish Community Centers (JCCs) throughout the United States.

A Reemergence of Anti-Semitism

In 1880, the first official census of Jews in America estimated their population at 250,000.[30] As Jews became more conspicuous, others began to view them as social and economic threats. An energized Christian lobby embarked on a variety of endeavors to formally institute Christianity as the state religion. They led efforts to amend the Constitution, enforce Sunday closing laws, and introduce Christian prayer and study into the public schools. The result was the beginning of a period

The Purim Ball
The Hebrew Purim Ball at the Academy of Music in New York City, April 1, 1865.
Library of Congress

of unprecedented anti-Semitism. Much of this was fueled by the stereotypes brought over from Europe by the large numbers of newly arrived Christian immigrants. Jews faced growing restrictions in housing, employment, and education. "Hebrew patronage not solicited" notices politely informed Jews that they were unwelcome at resorts. For several summers, Joseph Seligman—a well-known banker, friend of Abraham Lincoln, and leader of the American Jewish community—had brought his family on vacation to the Grand Union Hotel in Saratoga Springs, New York. On arriving by carriage from the train station in 1877 with his entourage, the financier was denied entry. A new owner had issued orders that "no Israelite shall be permitted in the future to stop in the hotel." "Outrage in Saratoga" was the headline in the *New York Times*.[31]

Responding to an accusatory letter in a magazine that denigrated Jewish service in the Union Army during the Civil War, Simon Wolf responded with an itemization of Jewish soldiers and their heroism. "My primary purpose has been to show that the Jewish people throughout the land not only took a share in the struggle which has ended so beneficently as to have brought prosperity to both antagonists and dispelled the cause of discord, but that they took their full share, and it is now conclusively shown that the enlistment of Jewish soldiers, north and south, reached proportions considerably in excess of their ratio to the general population."

Hanukkah Celebration, YMHA
The Hanukkah celebration by the Young Men's Hebrew Association at New York's Academy of Music on December 16, 1880. This scene depicts the sixth tableau, "the dedication of the temple." Holiday observances offered wealthy Jews an opportunity to proudly display their Judaism in a social setting while raising charitable funds. Library of Congress

During most of the 19th century, the steady trickle of Jewish immigrants from Eastern Europe had little effect on the established German Jewish community. The mainly Yiddish-speaking arrivals had little in common with their established coreligionists; the newcomers founded their own Orthodox synagogues and generally kept to themselves. Likewise, the established upper class of the German Jewish community tended to keep together. They worshiped in the same Reform temples, conducted business with one another, and established their own social and charitable institutions. By the end of the century, however, the secure, insular world of the German Jews would be rudely shaken by a virtual flood of Eastern European Jews, who by their sheer numbers altered the face of Jewish America.

1813–1880
A TIMELINE

1813
Mordecai Manuel Noah appointed consul at Tunis, the first Jew appointed to an American diplomatic position

1814
King Ferdinand VII of Portugal reestablishes Inquisition, six years after its abolition by Napoleon.

1819
Rebecca Gratz helps found Female Hebrew Benevolent Society in Philadelphia

1824
Isaac Harby establishes Reformed Society of Israelites in Charleston

1826
Maryland's "Jew Bill" adopted

1831
Isaac Leeser begins preaching in English

1838
Rebecca Gratz founds America's first Jewish Sunday school in Philadelphia

1840
Damascus Blood Libel spurs American Jews to rally

1842
Har Sinai in Baltimore established as first Reform congregation in America

1843
B'nai B'rith Organization established

1845
David Levy Yulee becomes first Jewish United States Senator

1849
California Gold Rush attracts Jewish merchants to West Coast

1852
First Eastern European Orthodox synagogue, Beth Midrash Hagadol, founded in New York

1859
Mortara Affair in Italy arouses international dismay

1860
Morris Raphall becomes first rabbi to open session of Congress

1862
Judah Benjamin named secretary of state of the Confederate States of America

1873
Founding of Union of American Hebrew Congregations

1877
New Hampshire is last state to eliminate religious test for elected office

1880
First official census of Jews in America estimates population at 250,000

81

1881–1913
The Great Wave

I t began with a trickle. The first Ashkenazic Jews from Eastern Europe arrived in America well before the end of the 18th century. Polish-born Haym Salomon, who helped to finance the American Revolution, was one of the better-known Ashkenazim. Those few Ashkenazic Jews who arrived in the 18th and early 19th centuries quickly adopted the rituals and customs of the Sephardic elite who preceded them. Through most of the 19th century, the relatively small numbers of Eastern European arrivals kept a low profile as they were absorbed into the mainstream American Jewish scene, which was dominated at first by the original Sephardic settlers and later by their German successors.

A Transatlantic Cargo of Old Hatred

As Jews grew in number and prominence in America following the Civil War, age-old stereotypes and hatreds began to flare up against them, fanned in part by a growing influx of European Christian immigrants who brought deep-seated anti-Jewish feelings across the Atlantic. At a time when American Jews were making

Anti-Semitic Cartoon of Jews at the Beach
Satiric cartoon that appeared in the British magazine *Punch* on May 11, 1881, with the caption "A Hint to the Hebrews: How They May Make Themselves Independent of the Watering Place Hotels." Note the flag on one balcony of the floating "Hotel de Jerusalem" that reads: "On his return from Florida this floor will be occupied by Isaacs the Hatter."
Library of Congress

unprecedented advances in their personal and economic lives, they began to face housing covenants, employment bias, and even violence. Major universities, including Harvard and Columbia, introduced quota systems limiting the number of Jewish students. While politicians and clergy denounced the discrimination, Jews throughout the country found themselves barred from jobs in major industries, hotels, social clubs, and private schools. "Hebrew patronage not solicited" was a polite way of announcing that Jews were not welcome. Financier Joseph Seligman's embarrassing experience at the Grand Hotel in 1877 was the public manifestation of the personal experiences of many Jews.

Reform rabbi Gustav Gottheil wrote that "when the Jew attempts to ... mix freely with his neighbors, he is repelled and unceremoniously shown back to his own tribe; and if he keeps there, he is accused of hereditary and ancestral pride."[1] Often, Jewish economic success was rooted in familial and social connections where trust was a major factor. It was that informal network that had allowed impoverished young immigrants from Germany to obtain loans, merchandise, and advice to begin their business careers in America as peddlers. Nonetheless, it was a time of important accomplishments for the Jews of America. They expanded their religious, social, and communal organizations even as they found ways to bypass the economic discrimination against them from financial institutions such as banks and insurance companies. By 1880, the United States was crisscrossed by a network of synagogues (mostly Reform), Jewish social clubs, self-help agencies, and newspapers.

85

Shifts and Tremors in Europe

In that bifurcated atmosphere of acceptance and rejection, the American Jewish community was about to face dramatic upheaval, triggered by events far across the ocean. In 1880, about 3 percent of the world's Jews were in the United States, while nearly 75 percent lived in—or, to be more specific, were confined to—a section of Eastern Europe known as the Pale of Settlement. For most of their history in Europe, Jews had been considered a people apart. Separated at first by religion, they were marginalized, subject to religious intolerance, persecution, and discrimination. As the most visible non-Christian group in Europe, they were looked upon with suspicion and hatred wherever they settled. Over the years, Jews had been expelled from one European country after another, while others restricted them to ghettos.

Yet things were improving somewhat for Western European Jews. Beginning with the French Revolution in 1789, a wave of freedom and enlightenment had descended upon the people of Western Europe. For Jews it was an impossible dream come true. The confining spirit of the ghetto was broken, and Jews could, for the first time, look forward to attaining rights of citizenship in the countries where they had lived for so long. Jews in the liberated countries could enter professions that were previously closed to them. They could attend public schools and gain admission to universities. Meanwhile, their brethren in Eastern Europe continued to suffer.

Pale of Settlement in the Russian Empire. www.berdichev.org

Bleak Realities of the "Old Country"

In Russia, the Pale of Settlement was a geographic area with a movable boundary that was first established in 1791 by Catherine the Great (1762–1796) as a result of the partition of Poland. Over time, with other partitions, Russia not only expanded its territory westward, but also inherited over 1,000,000 unwanted Jewish inhabitants of the region. Catherine and her successors decided to solve their "Jewish problem" by restricting Jews to the Pale of Settlement.

Czar Nicholas I (1825–1855) unleashed particularly harsh regulations on Jews in an attempt to "Russify" them, convert them, or reduce their numbers. In 1827 he ordered the conscription of Jewish boys as young as 12 to terms of 25 years of military service. The goal was to remove boys physically, religiously, and culturally from their families and cultural roots and force their conversions to Christianity. With a quota placed on each community, the local Jewish leaders were forced to appoint *khapers* (catchers) to kidnap boys for service. As the conscription pool tightened, younger children were targeted, as were unfortunate older men caught in heartless dragnets. Jewish families were torn apart and economically worse off than ever before.

Those charged with molding the unwilling conscripts into soldiers mistreated them badly. Away from home in so-called canton schools, many heartbroken, physically and emotionally assaulted young boys did not survive. Those who did faced long years of deprivation and hardship. Max Lilienthal, who later became an influential American rabbi, was invited by the Russian government in 1841 to oversee the reconfiguration of a Jewish educational system. He received a cold welcome from the Jewish community, who well understood the Russian government's real agenda. Lilienthal quickly fled when he saw through the government's plan to secularize and eventually convert Jewish students.

A Brief Glimmer of Hope

The next czar, Alexander II (1855–1881), brought a hint of hope to the downtrodden Jews. He instituted reforms to ease the lives of all Russians and displayed leniency in his treatment of Jews. He minimized the length of military service, abolished the "cantonist" schools, and permitted Jewish merchants, scholars, and artisans to reside outside the Pale of Settlement. The more liberal atmosphere under Alexander II nurtured a period of intellectual enlightenment—Haskalah—for the Jews of Russia. This movement produced Jewish intellectuals and writers who redeveloped the use of Hebrew as a modern written and spoken language and led to the awakening of Jewish nationalism in general and of Zionism in particular.

Nevertheless, at a time when Jews in Western Europe were enjoying new freedoms, life for the majority of Russian Jews, despite Alexander's refreshing benevolence, did not materially improve in any significant way. Most Russian Jews lived in the confined shtetls as workers or small merchants, surrounded by religious observance and the Yiddish language. In the larger cities were Jewish professionals,

---

Drafting Children for the Czar's Army

From a January 1863 article by Isaac Leeser in the *Occident and American Jewish Advocate*:

The accession of [Czar Alexander II] held out reasonable hopes that the time of Egyptian bondage would soon pass away ... The most cruel atrocities then yet practiced were:

The recruiting of infants, in the literal sense of the word ... [T]he Jews had to furnish four times as many recruits for the army as all other Russian subjects, the whole country being divided into western and eastern parts ... [T]he Jews ... were required to supply recruits annually and simultaneously with the east and the west, although in the east there are no Jewish inhabitants, and moreover, they were compelled to give ten per 1000 every time, instead of the other's five per 1000 ... [A]fter a lapse of some years—during which not one of the soldiers could return to his family, the Russian military service covering a period of 20 to 25 years—almost all the young men had been drafted away ... Yet the government ... issued orders that the boys should be ... brought up in the interior of Russia ... till their attaining the proper age for entering a regiment (eighteen years) ..., and then only began for them the period of regular military service ...

[A]lmost every day the synagogue resounded ... with the melancholy reading of the martyrs' prayers for one poor child or another, who had preferred submitting to all imaginable tortures rather than betray his religion.

87

Czar Alexander II

Alexander II (1855–1881) lifted much of the harsh official treatment of Russian Jews. Yet, his goal to assimilate the Jews of Russia only increased anti-Semitism there as Jews became more visible in Russian life. His assassination in 1881 led to the reimposition of restrictions on Jews, inciting violent *pogrom*s and ultimately spurring a mass emigration of Russian Jews to Western countries, particularly the United States. Library on Congress

students, and intellectuals who tried to assimilate into the greater Russian society. No matter where Jews lived, suspicion and hatred of them were never far below the surface. An especially bloody *pogrom* that took place in Odessa in 1871 heralded the violent resurfacing of anti-Jewish feeling.

Rise of the Pogrom

The assassination of Alexander II in 1881 and the ascendancy of Alexander III marked a grim turning point in the lives of Russian Jews. A harsh new era began that included, for the first time, government-sponsored physical violence—*pogroms*—and blood libels targeting Jews and their property. Local mobs indiscriminately attacked, raped, robbed, and pillaged Jews and their property, with government approval. The czar's ultimate goal, clearly described by Procurator-General Constantine Pobyedonostzev, was to force one-third of Russian Jews to emigrate, one-third to convert, and one-third to starve. With those goals firmly transformed into governmental will, Jews entered into a period of severe economic and political repression. Ensuing violence against Jews resulted in death and property destruction. *Pogroms* created an atmosphere of doom and fear among Russian Jews and hastened their flights to safer refuges.

The introduction of the "temporary" May Laws of 1882 removed any concessions previously granted to Jews. They were no longer permitted to hold governmental jobs, and low quotas were set for Jewish enrollment in high schools and universities. Jews were summarily expelled from areas in which they had lived for generations, ordered out of large cities such as Moscow, Kiev, and Saint Petersburg as well as little shtetls to be resettled in already-crowded towns within the loosely defined borders of the Pale. Further excessive rules and regulations were imposed that directly affected their quality of life. Jews were not allowed to open their shops on Sundays and Christian holidays even though they closed on the Sabbath and Jewish holidays. It was estimated that in some communities, up to 50 percent of the Jewish population depended on charity to survive. In the Pale, in 1898, 18.8 percent of the entire Jewish population applied for Passover charity.[2]

The excesses fomented by the Russian government created a furor of objection from other countries. While earlier *pogroms* had gone largely unnoticed in the outside world, faster communications technology in the early 20th century spread firsthand accounts of the events to newspapers around the world within days. Mass rallies and anti-Russian resolutions in the United States and Western European countries denounced the barbaric actions, even as thousands of unorganized Jews packed their belongings, said good-bye to friends and neighbors, and took the first steps toward America. Jews only recently arrived in America took advantage of their new political freedoms to influence American leaders. One petition drive addressed to President Theodore Roosevelt urged "your Excellency to employ the good offices of our government with the Imperial government of Russia … [with the goal] of securing more safety to Jews in Russia and making their existence there less wretched."[3]

Internationally sponsored charitable groups rallied as well, but despite their efforts, the Jewish masses in Russia continued to live in a state of near starvation. Many Jews did not have specific occupations. A contemporary report stated: "There are in Russia only 10,000 to 15,000 Jews who possess any certain means of existence. As to the masses, they possess nothing: and they are far poorer than the Christian populace, who at any rate own some land."[4] The reaction among more and more Russian Jews to the

The Protocols of the Elders of Zion

A forgery of the czar's secret police, the Protocols purports to be the original minutes of a Zionist plot for world power. Since its first appearance, it has become the most-disseminated piece of anti-Semitic literature ever. It was first translated into English by British journalist Victor Marsden. A few excerpts:

Our right lies in force. The word "right" is an abstract thought and proved by nothing. The words mean no more than: Give me what I want in order that thereby I may have a proof that I am stronger than you. (Protocol 1, Article 12)

In order to put public opinion into our hands we must bring it into a state of bewilderment by giving expression from all sides to so many contradictory opinions and for such length of time as suffice to make the goyim [Gentiles] lose their heads in the labyrinth and come to see that the best thing is to have no opinion of any kind in matters political, which is not given to the public to understand, because they are understood only by him who guides the public. This is the first secret. (Protocol 5, Article 10)

The Press, which with a few exceptions that may be disregarded, is already entirely in our hands. (Protocol 7, Article 5)

Russian May Laws of 1882

1. As a temporary measure and until a general revision of the laws is made regulating their legal status, Jews are forbidden to settle hereafter outside of cities and towns. Exception is made with regard to Jewish agricultural villages already in existence.

2. Until further orders, the issuing to Jews of mortgages or real estate deeds outside of cities and towns is forbidden. Equally void is the issuing to a Jew of any power of attorney for the administration or disposition of property of the above-indicated nature.

3. Jews are forbidden to transact business on Sundays and Christian holidays; the laws compelling Christians to close their places of business on those days will be applied to Jewish places of business.

4. The above measures are applicable only in the governments situated within the Pale of Settlement.

increase in violence, poverty, and uprooting was to vote with their feet. Between 1881 and the outbreak of World War I in 1914, nearly 2,000,000 freely abandoned their homes to seek new lives in other European countries, Palestine, and—most of all—America. "Although the Jews in Russia were less than one-twentieth of the total Russian population, they formed about half of the total Russian immigration [to America]."[5]

The Mass Exodus Begins

Jewish communities on Russia's borders and in the major European ports were inundated with thousands of Jews seeking their way out. Major philanthropic agencies such as the Alliance Israélite Universelle (founded in 1860) and the Baron de Hirsch Fund (1891) set up boardinghouses, food stations, and immigration advisers to ameliorate the condition of the refugees. But the onslaught was more than they could handle, and still the refugees came. From Romania, *fussgeyers* (travelers on foot) formed groups to pool expenses and protect one another while walking together through Europe to convenient ports. Whether by train, by

Satirizing Jewish Emigrants
Another cartoon from *Punch*, January 19, 1881, showing that this crowded "Hebrew Line" ship carrying Jewish emigrants is "For the Exclusive Use of 'The Persecuted.'" Library of Congress

wagon, or on foot, it is estimated that close to 30 percent of the Romanian Jewish population traveled to European ports between 1881 and the outbreak of World War I, on their way to the United States.[6]

For today's travelers, the journey taken by Eastern European Jews to America cannot be easily comprehended. People who lived their lives far from the ocean, in villages both culturally and geographically remote, braved long and hazardous trips to major European ports—sometimes even on foot. Once there, they exhausted their funds booking ship passage, usually in steerage class where the accommodations were both confining and unhealthy.

The journey was not easy. In a Yiddish booklet distributed in Europe, one writer advised those about to embark that the difficult trip to America was "a kind of hell that cleanses a man of his sins before coming to the land of Columbus."[7]

The "Tempest-Tossed" Arrive in Droves

Compelled by the events in Europe and the sudden increase in arrivals to New York and other East Coast ports, immigrant aid organizations such as the Hebrew Emigrant Aid Society (1881) and the United Hebrew Charities in New York (1874) took

> ### Advice to New Immigrants
> A popular immigrant guidebook advised:
>
> Hold fast, this is most necessary in America. Forget your past, your customs and your ideals. Select a goal and pursue it with all your might. No matter what happens to you, hold on. You will experience a bad time but sooner or later you will achieve your goal. If you are neglectful, beware for the wheel of fortune turns quickly. You will lose your grip and be lost. A bit of advice for you: do not take a moment's rest. Run, do, work and keep your own good in mind ... A final virtue is needed in America—called cheek ... Do not say, "I cannot: I do not know." (Riis 1892, 35)

shape in America. But American Jewish philanthropists were conflicted in their welcome to Eastern European Jews. The United Hebrew Charities stated in its 15th Annual Report, "European almshouses and infirmaries were not to be relieved at the expense of American Jewry." Attempts by European-based agencies such as the Alliance Israélite Universelle to send over only skilled workers and tradesmen failed. In a letter sent in 1881, the Russian Emigrant Relief Fund in New York complained, "We are overrun with peddlers already, who have become a source of much annoyance to us ... Some of the emigrants whom we placed in this city at trades, requiring only light manual labor, remained at work only a day or two, declaring that the work was too hard and too confining to them."[8]

The Hebrew Emigrant Aid Society was founded specifically to provide aid for the masses of impoverished refugees who fled *pogroms* and persecution in 1881 and 1882. The society opened a refuge and labor bureau on Ward's Island to house newcomers and help them find employment and housing. Patience was a necessary component of good will. The lack of skills and cultural ignorance of the newcomers sometimes led to frustration on the part of those seeking to help them. The society's secretary, Augustus A. Levy, quit, saying with finality that since "the mode of life of these people in Russia has stamped upon them the ineffaceable marks of permanent pauperism, only disgrace and a lowering of the opinion in which American Israelites are held … can result from the continued residence among us … of these wretches."[9] The work was overwhelming and the charity disbanded in 1883, but not before helping tens of thousands.

Still Neighbors, Far from Home

As newcomers gravitated toward New York City's Lower East Side, they settled near others from their own village or region. In the early days of mass immigration, a map of the area would indicate the specific blocks that housed majority Hungarians, Poles, or former neighbors from Kovno or Minsk. As the flood of new arrivals reached a crescendo, those artificial borders evaporated and the entire Lower East Side became a melting pot where Yiddish predominated, with Russian, Polish, or Hungarian accents. In other arrival cities such as Boston or Philadelphia, the same scenario prevailed but on a smaller scale. *Landsmanshaften* (organizations loosely based on geographic ties to home villages) were the first sources of aid for immigrants in need. There were few government programs in place, and these mutual aid societies were lifelines. The *landsmanshaften* provided members with health insurance, no-interest loans, and medical and burial assistance. They assumed the role of an extended family, outside of the synagogue, whose language and customs were familiar and comforting. Other organizations also tried to ameliorate the harsh lives of the newcomers and help ease them into American life.

Still, the nation's relief system was far from coordinated. Those who arrived at the beginning of the mass migration relied on themselves or on the rather haphazard patchwork of relief organizations. It was a time of industrial expansion in the United States, and immigrants were needed to keep the economic fire burning. On the other side of the Atlantic, steamship and railroad companies eager to tap into the transportation needs flooded the Jewish communities with newspaper advertisements and handbills extolling the wonders of the New World, omitting any hints of the wretched steerage conditions that awaited the poor travelers, let alone the hardships most of them would face in America.

The Russian Jew in America

Writing in the *Atlantic Monthly* in July 1898, Abraham Cahan described the importance of the community synagogue for Russian Jewish immigrants:

The Russian Jew brings with him the quaint customs of a religion full of poetry and of the sources of good citizenship. The orthodox synagogue is not merely a house of prayer; it is an intellectual centre, a mutual aid society, a fountain of self-denying altruism, and a literary club, no less than a place of worship.

The study-rooms of the hundreds of synagogues, where the good old people of the Ghetto come to read and discuss "words of law" as well as the events of the day, are crowded every evening in the week with poor street peddlers, and with those gray-haired, misunderstood sweat-shop hands of whom the public hears every time a tailor strike is declared. So few are the joys which this world has to spare for these overworked, enfeebled victims of "the inferno of modern times" that their religion is to many of them the only thing which makes life worth living. In the fervor of prayer or the abandon of religious study they forget the grinding poverty of their homes.

Many impoverished immigrants depended on charity for survival. When the Baron de Hirsch Fund undertook a survey of the slum dwellers to ascertain the depth of need, rumors spread that the good Baron intended to give anywhere from $100 to $500 to each Jewish family, leading some immigrants to hold false expectations.[10] The survey indicated that a majority of jobholders in the Lower East Side worked as tailors, as cloakmakers, or in related garment industry work.

Clashes and Commonalities

At first, a clash of cultures separated the newcomers not only from the established German Jewish elite, but even from each other. Lithuanian *Litvaks*, Russian *Russische*, Polish *Polakin*, and Hungarian *Galitzianer* spoke their common Yiddish with recognizable variations and thought of "the other" as being beneath them, intellectually and culturally. Each group created its own synagogues, social clubs, and newspapers.

Regardless of where in the Pale of Settlement they came from, the Yiddish language united nearly all of the Jewish immigrants. Some came with Orthodox religious backgrounds; others were actively secular, embracing the spirit of Haskalah, the Jewish enlightenment. Still others were Zionist in orientation. *Hovevey Zion*, Lovers of Zion, attracted those who believed that the only solution for Jews was the restoration of a

Lower East Side—Garment Seller
For newly arrived immigrants with scanty dollars and even fewer English words, street selling offered one of the few ways to earn a pittance. Library of Congress

Jewish homeland in Palestine. Their major goals were to develop organized Jewish immigration to Palestine and to revive Hebrew language and culture.

Zionism

For most of the 19th century, outside the small and closely knit Zionist community, few paid attention to the utopian hope of reestablishing the Jewish homeland after a 2000-year exile. The publication of a little book in 1896 by Dr. Theodor Herzl, a Viennese journalist, revolutionized the Jewish world. This book, *The Jewish State*, was a call to action. "The Jews who wish for a State shall have it, and they deserve to have it," he declared. Of the delegates to the First Zionist Congress in 1897, convened by Herzl, only one was an American. Three years later, three delegates represented the small American Zionist community. One was a young activist Reform rabbi, Stephen S. Wise, who helped forge disparate American supporters into a cohesive and energetic Zionist Organization of

America. He was, ironically, an "uptowner," a Reform rabbi and the son of German immigrants. At a time when the Reform movement was nearly unanimous in its opposition to Zionism, viewing America as their Promised Land, Wise joined with the "downtowner" Russian immigrants, who were nearly unanimous in their support. The official Reform stand was: "We are unalterably opposed to political Zionism. The Jews are not a nation but a religious community ... America is our Zion."

Socialism

Some immigrants were radical Socialists who had joined with non-Jewish Russians to bring about changes in the repressive government. Others formed uniquely Jewish organizations such as the *Arbeiter Bund* (Worker's Union), which shared Socialist principles with other Russians while asserting Jewish claims as a distinct nationality within Russia. The aim of the Bundists was to place Jews on an equal footing with all Russians. Bundists were not among the earliest Eastern European immigrants to arrive in America. Only after the failed Russian Revolution of 1905 did they lose hope in ever democratizing Russia and begin to leave the country in larger numbers.

Stephen S. Wise

Born in Budapest in 1874 and arriving in America when he was an infant, Wise grew up to become an activist Zionist, serving as president of the Federation of American Zionists (1898) and as a delegate to the Second Zionist Congress. He was a noted orator and served as a Reform rabbi in Portland, Oregon, before being offered the pulpit of Temple Emanu-El in New York, perhaps the most prestigious pulpit in the country. There, after a debate with the lay leadership on freedom of the pulpit, he left to found the Free Synagogue of New York in 1907. He was one of the original 1909 founders of the National Association for the Advancement of Colored People. In response to what he perceived as the undemocratic manner in which the American Jewish Committee operated, he founded the American Jewish Congress in 1918. He died in 1949.

Here for Good

"Between 1908 and 1914, when for every hundred of all immigrants [to America] who arrived nearly thirty-one departed, the number of Jews who left the country was only seven out of every hundred."[11] Newly arrived Jews, experiencing the strangeness of the New World and barely able to survive themselves, wrote back glowing accounts extolling their new homes to their left-behind relatives and friends and urged them to come. Between 1881 and 1890, 3.7 percent of all immigrants to the United States were Jews. By the first decade of the 20th century, that figure had

Henrietta Szold

Born in Baltimore in 1860, the daughter of a respected rabbi, Szold founded a night school for Russian immigrants. She was a founder of The Jewish Publication Society and Hadassah, the Women's Zionist Organization of America. In 1918, she organized a mission of medical practitioners to Palestine, where she founded the Hadassah Hospital. She died in 1945.

jumped to over 10 percent. The Jewish exodus from Russia, unlike much other migration of the time, was a movement of families. They came to America to stay. They had no reason to return. If the czar's legal movements to restrict and impoverish Jewish life did not compel Jews to leave, then the increasing number of *pogroms* certainly did. "In 1880 close to 6 million of the world's 7.7 million Jews lived in Eastern Europe and only 3% lived in the United States. By 1920 … 23% of world Jews called America home."[12] Eastern Europeans "only numbered ten percent of the total Jewish population in the United States in 1880. By 1906 it was estimated that they constituted seventy-five percent of American Jewry."[13] Beyond the statistics were the individual stories of heroic people who willingly left behind their medieval ghettos and survived long, often humiliating sea journeys to start life anew in a totally foreign land.

Abraham Cahan

Born in Russia in 1860, Cahan came to America where he became a labor activist. He honed his writing skills as a journalist for the Yiddish press. He wrote a number of popular books, including *The Rise of David Levinsky*, a story of Russian Jewish immigration to America in which the protagonist, much like the author, quickly learned the ways of America. When the Yiddish newspaper *Jewish Daily Forward* was founded in 1897, he became its first editor, and through its pages he shaped, educated, and persuaded generations of Yiddish-speaking immigrants. The newspaper, with its Socialist leanings and labor support, quickly became the home of the best Yiddish writers of the time and set the standard for Jewish newspapers in the United States. Cahan died in 1951.

Most newcomers settled close by their arrival sites, with New York, as the busiest port, accounting for the largest numbers. By 1895, the *New York Times* reported that the Lower East Side was more densely populated than Bombay, India. Earlier Jewish settlers from Central Europe had gravitated there and created a Jewish milieu, which attracted the later Eastern Europeans. The newcomers came with little secular education or industrial experience and highly unrealistic expectations of America. Some had worked in the garment business in the large cities, but most arrived with no trade. By the time of their arrival, the legendary profession of rural peddling that had empowered earlier German Jewish immigrants was no longer an option. The descendants of those peddlers had ultimately forsaken the wilderness for the cities. The newcomers quickly discovered that to survive, they needed to depend on their own wiles. But first they needed help, and the uptowners—the acculturated, wealthy German Jews of the previous immigration wave—came to the rescue, although reluctantly at first.

Uptowners versus Downtowners

The cultural and economic gaps between the acculturated uptown Jews and the poor downtown Jews were glaring ones. While the Yiddish-speaking masses on the Lower East Side concerned themselves with basic issues of daily survival, uptowners could plan for their annual Purim balls, begun as "a good fancy dress ball, the proceeds to be donated to charity." In 1881, as Eastern Europeans clamored for dingy living space and ways to make a living, the new constitution of the Purim

Association of the City of New York saw their annual ball as "... a refined way, which should fittingly represent the social side of New York Judaism ..." The cultural divide between rich and poor Jews was too great to significantly bridge. The uptowners feared "that the distinction between the 'better class of Jews' and the 'vulgar Jews' would collapse and that everything they had worked for would be destroyed."[14]

In an effort to exclude *luftmenschen* (people without a trade who "lived on air"), Jewish leaders asked European organizations to carefully screen emigrants. But the numbers were too great to manage, and refugees—skilled or not—continued to pour out of Europe. With slight panic, the *American Israelite* reported, "These newcomers must be turned into useful Americans or they will upset our position in the community. The thoroughly acclimated American Jew ... has no religious, social or intellectual sympathies with them. He is closer to the Christian sentiment around him than to the Judaism of these miserable darkened Hebrews."[15]

Lillian Wald

Lillian Wald was born in Cincinnati in 1867 but raised in Rochester, New York. First a reporter and later a social activist, she attended nursing school in New York. While studying to become a doctor, she volunteered to provide medical aid to the poor immigrants on the Lower East Side, ultimately deciding to put her efforts there instead of continuing toward a medical degree. With help from financier Jacob Schiff, she founded the Henry Street Settlement in 1893, also known as the Visiting Nurse Society of New York, which became a model for cities throughout the country. She died in 1940. Library on Congress

The life experiences of each group created a real divide between them. English-speaking, Reform-minded, university-educated, and culturally advantaged uptown Jews had little in common with their poorer brethren except for the tenuous link to a common religious tradition. Initial reaction was to ignore the newcomers. Gradually, however, as important members of the established uptown community reached out to help their impoverished brethren, attitudes toward the new arrivals softened. When restrictive legislation before Congress (beginning in 1882) threatened to curtail immigration, both uptowners and newcomers joined together to successfully battle the restrictions. Over several years, legislation that was often vaguely written began limiting immigrants for medical and economic reasons.

Jacob Schiff was at the forefront of those whose philanthropy bettered the lives of poor Eastern European immigrants. As a member of the New York Board of Education, he was instrumental in abolishing the practice that segregated students by race. Working with Lillian Wald to provide medical care to the poor of the Lower East Side, he helped her found the Henry Street Settlement House in 1893. Wald realized that nursing services alone could not solve the underlying social problems of the poor and with Schiff's help established kindergartens, mothers' clubs, safe milk stations, summer camps, and educational classes for adults and children.

Motivations for Philanthropy

Schiff described philanthropy "as the aim and ideal of Judaism."[16] But the altruism of Schiff and other wealthy uptowners was sometimes viewed as self-serving, masking attempts to Americanize the newcomers as quickly as possible. A writer for the *American Hebrew* put it this way: "All of us should be sensible of what we owe not only to those … coreligionists, but to ourselves, who will be looked upon by our gentile neighbors as the natural sponsors for these, our brethren."[17] Besides, as with the descendants of the original Sephardic settlers, who were lost to Judaism after several generations, rising rates of assimilation and intermarriage by the grandchildren of German immigrants were already casting doubt on the longevity of Judaism in America. In fact, were it not for the unanticipated arrival of the Yiddish-speaking masses, the chances are quite good that Jewish culture in America would ultimately have disappeared.[18] So, for various reasons, uptown Jews soon recognized the need to help the newer immigrants become part of American culture in general and Jewish American culture in particular.

Jacob Schiff

Born in Frankfurt in 1847, Schiff became one of America's best-known financiers, helping to bankroll America's industrial growth through his firm, Kuhn, Loeb & Company. He was active in the Reform movement, but when he thought the movement had become too liberal, he helped found the Jewish Theological Seminary of America. He was one of the most notable philanthropists of the early 20th century, with a special interest in the well-being of Jewish immigrants. He supported Lillian Wald's Henry Street Settlement and was one of the founders of the American Jewish Committee. He died in 1920.

97

Diversionary Tactics

Alarmed by the large number of newcomers crowding Atlantic ports, charitable organizations devised plans to divert some immigrants to less crowded cities. Established Jews feared that the massive crowding of poor, culturally disadvantaged, Socialist-leaning immigrants into unsanitary urban conditions would lead to the stereotyping of all American Jews and an increase in anti-Semitism. They also feared that anti-alien feelings would result in legal restrictions on immigration just when Congress was debating a literacy bill in 1891, ultimately vetoed by President Ulysses S. Grant, that would have limited immigration from Southern and Eastern Europe. With assistance from the Industrial Removal Office (I.R.O.), thousands of immigrants were diverted successfully from New York to other cities around the country. By the start of World War I, the I.R.O. had diverted 70,000 immigrants from New York.[19] For the major New York Jewish relief agency, the United Hebrew Charities, the removal plan freed up dwindling resources to help the remaining Jewish poor with needed services. For a time, the removal effort relied on B'nai B'rith lodges throughout the country to welcome newcomers and find them housing and work, but the enterprise faltered when large numbers of Eastern Europeans overwhelmed small Jewish communities.

Because of an existing relationship between a German shipping line and I.R.O. officials, some immigrants bypassed New York and were sent directly to Galveston, Texas, which became a gateway to Middle America. The Galveston Committee in New York, directed by Jacob Schiff, coordinated the immigration details with organizations in Europe. Schiff wanted immigrants to think of America as being more than New York. By opening up ports away from the East Coast, he hoped to increase the number of immigrants and decrease the financial and institutional demands on New York Jews. The Galveston Plan was selective in choosing who would come by focusing on younger skilled workers. Between 1907 and 1914, that southern port welcomed 10,000 immigrants on their way to find homes in America's interior. The Galveston Plan did not dramatically affect the continued flow of immigrants to East Coast cities but did foster a Jewish presence in the southern and central United States.

The Shmatte Business

German Jews who preceded the Eastern European arrivals had established themselves in garment-manufacturing businesses. It was natural for newcomers with garment-making experience to gravitate toward the clothing industry in America,

> ### The Tenement Sweatshop
>
> In his book *How the Other Half Lives*, Jacob Riis gives this eyewitness description of a tenement sweatshop:
>
> *But the tenement has defeated its benevolent purpose. In it the child works unchallenged from the day he is old enough to pull a thread. There is no such thing as a dinner hour; men and women eat while they work, and the "day" is lengthened at both ends far into the night. Factory hands take their work with them at the close of the lawful day to eke out their scanty earning by working overtime at home. Little chance on this ground for the campaign of education that can alone bring the needed relief: small wonder that there are whole settlements on this East Side where English is practically an unknown tongue, though the people be both willing and anxious to learn. "When shall we find time to learn?" asked one of them of me once. I owe him the answer yet.* (Riis 1890, chapter 11)

but large numbers of unskilled new arrivals ended up there as well. Quite simply, many Eastern European immigrants found that the only jobs available were in the garment factories created by their predecessors. Some "factories" were nothing more than sectioned-off rooms in walk-up tenement buildings, but many consisted of large buildings packed with employees.

Cold in winter, hot in summer, these factories were dirty, noisy, and unhealthy. Windows and doors were often locked to prevent thefts. The closed windows also kept out fresh air, and as a result many workers developed lifelong sicknesses, including tuberculosis. For most, "streets paved with gold" turned out to be dirty, crowded roads to the grimy sweatshops where they toiled in miserable conditions to keep their families alive. "Their sweatshops," wrote Jacob Riis, "and their starvation wages, are the faithful companions of their dire poverty."[20] Workers could be—and were—fired at the boss's whim. "In the shops we don't have names, we have numbers," one woman said. Yet workers were afraid to complain publicly at first. They were fortunate just to have jobs.

Whether or not they had prior experience in garment making, however, many new immigrants brought with them a legacy of Socialist and revolutionary activism. The immigrants who arrived after the failed Russian Revolution of 1905 brought to garment workers the intellectual and radical leadership they had developed while trying to overthrow the czar. Only now, the targets of their militancy were other Jews, the shop bosses.

Meyer London

Born in Poland in 1871, London arrived on the Lower East Side in 1888, where he became active in Socialist politics. He became a lawyer and represented the interests of labor unions. The residents of the Lower East Side respected him and, in a milestone election, sent him to Congress in 1914 as the only Socialist Party candidate elected to the United States House of Representatives. He served three terms, supporting liberal legislation to aid workers and voting against United States entry into World War I. He died in 1926.

Labor Strife

The tradition of social activism that new workers brought with them led to the country's fledgling labor unions. In 1888, the United Hebrew Trades joined together a number of smaller Jewish unions to bolster their position during strikes. "In unity there is strength" was the slogan that led to the founding of the International Ladies Garment Workers Union (ILGWU). In 1909, the downtrodden workers, mostly young Jewish women, would no longer tolerate the terrible working conditions. The strike began with one factory and quickly spread to include nearly every shirtwaist factory in New York. Day after day, strikers picketed their factories and fought to keep scab workers from entering. They faced violence, which the police did little to prevent, from gangs hired by the factory owners to intimidate the pickets. Many strikers were hurt, but the picketing continued until the strike was settled in February 1910 with an agreement on a shorter workweek. Union solidarity had held, and the strike, "The Uprising of the 20,000," changed the role of women and Jews in American labor politics. Later that year a larger strike of 60,000 mainly male cloakmakers, known as "The Great Revolt," nearly shut down the American garment industry.

Samuel Gompers

Born in London in 1850, Gompers learned the trade of cigar making from his father. When he immigrated with his family to New York during the Civil War, he continued working in the cigar industry and joined the local union. Rising in labor union circles, he avoided the radical elements within the unions to maintain a steady conservative course, which ultimately helped to make unions acceptable to the business world. In 1886, Gompers became the founder and first president of the American Federation of Labor, the most powerful national organization of labor unions in America. With the exception of a few years, he served in that high-profile presidency until his death in 1924.

On the Picket Line
Two women strikers during the "Uprising of the 20,000" garment workers' strike in New York City. The call for the strike came from Clara Lemlich, a 15-year-old Yiddish-speaking immigrant, at a mass meeting of union members. No longer able to tolerate the harsh working conditions, the workers unanimously ratified the strike vote and within days, despite picket line attacks by police and goons hired by the bosses, succeeded in closing down New York's shirtwaist factories. Library of Congress

Leaders of the American Jewish community were concerned by the bitter confrontations between Jewish bosses and Jewish workers. Boston lawyer Louis Brandeis, later to become the first Jew appointed to the United States Supreme Court, worked out a settlement. The "Protocol of Peace" called for joint worker and owner committees to settle grievances and marked a milestone in labor history. Unions had become a force in American life.

The Triangle Shirtwaist Company fire on March 25, 1911, put a human face on union demands for safe working conditions. One hundred forty-six workers, mostly young Jewish and Italian women, died because of locked doors, lack of fire-extinguishing resources, and an indoor fire "escape" that was useless as an escape route. The *Ladies Garment Worker* of April 1911 righteously complained:

Is it not strange that in this most democratic of all countries in the world the employers can so easily use the arm of the law to protect themselves against any inconveniences which their work people may cause them, but the law is nowhere when the life and limb of the worker is to be protected.

The national outrage energized unions and led to the enactment of state and national legislation to improve the safety of American workers.

Seeking Escape from the Ghetto

For "the people of the Book," education, education, education became the mantra for pulling oneself out of the ghetto. Coming, as most did, with no trade or profession, the first step out of poverty was often vocational training tinged with Americanism. In 1884, the United Hebrew Charities founded the Hebrew Technical Institute to encourage immigrants away from the garment trade. Organizations founded and funded by uptown Jews, such as the Educational Alliance, offered a variety of training programs. However, these were not universally accepted by Yiddish speakers, as the courses were deliberately taught in English.

Baron Maurice de Hirsch, perhaps the wealthiest Jew of his time, also founded the Jewish Colonization Association in England to encourage healthy young Jews to join rural agricultural colonies and stay away from crowded and unhealthy cities in the United States and elsewhere. The first colony in the United States was established on Sicily Island, Louisiana. Several others followed in such widely dispersed places as New Jersey, Colorado, and Oregon. Colonies founded by the Baron and others quickly failed, since the new farmers were not accustomed to life on the farm. Shaky finances, poor climate, and unsuitable land did not help matters. Not the least of the problems was the dislocation many new farmers felt from the larger Jewish communities. Many left the farms and rejoined their *landsleit* (countrymen) in the big cities. Nonetheless, some agricultural communities proved more successful in providing an alternative to urban life in America, such as the National Farm School (now Delaware Valley College), established in 1896 in Doylestown, Pennsylvania, by Rabbi Joseph Krauskopf as a nonsectarian, nondenominational school.

> ### The Door of Paradise
>
> For many immigrants, the public library was more than a haven from the tumult of the street; it was its own little university where an education could be obtained one book at a time. In her book *The Promised Land*, Mary Antin describes that passion for the library:
>
> *Long before one o'clock I was to be seen on the library steps, waiting for the door of paradise to open. I spent hours in the reading-room, pleased with the atmosphere of books, with the order and quiet of the place ... Anything so wonderful as a library had never been in my life. It was even better than school in some ways. Once could read and read, and learn and learn, as fast as one knew how, without being obliged to stop for stupid little girls and inattentive little boys to catch up with the lesson.* (Antin 1912, 256)

Many immigrant parents quickly realized that while they were limited by cultural, linguistic, and educational handicaps in the New World, for their children nothing would be impossible. The route out of the Lower East Side was education, and for the children of immigrants, enrolling in New York's public schools began the journey. The school system, under the leadership of Superintendent William Maxwell, saw as its mission "to bring all social classes together in a common effort for improvement ... it is the melting pot which converts the children of the immigrants of all races and languages into sturdy, independent American citizens."[21] In 1908, when Jews were about 2 percent of the population, they made up nearly 8.5 percent of all college students, including 13 percent in law schools and 6 percent in dental schools.[22]

The Lure of Education

Author Mary Antin neatly summed up education's strong appeal for immigrants desperate to transcend, through and for their children, the crushing realities of their lives:

If education, culture, the higher life were shining things to be worshipped from afar, he had still a means left whereby he could draw one step nearer to them. He could send his children to school, to learn all those things that he knew by fame to be desirable. The common school, at least, perhaps high school; for one or two, perhaps even college! His children should be students, should fill his house with books and intellectual company, and thus he would walk by proxy in the Elysian Fields of liberal learning. As for the children themselves, he knew no surer way to their advancement and happiness. (Antin 1912, 204)

In the "Old Country," highest praise was given to the Torah scholar. Even for those not destined for yeshivah life, religious education was a part of growing up. For the youngest children, it took place in the *heder*, a one-room school usually situated in the teacher's house. In America, the transplanted *heder* could not succeed. The grimy *heder* in the back room of a tenement on Ludlow Street overseen by a teacher with sometimes questionable credentials could not compete with the American public school.

In America, the chaider *[sic] assumes a position entirely subordinate. Compelled by law to go to the American public school, the boy can attend* chaider *only before the public school opens in the morning or after it closes in the afternoon … Contempt for the* chaider*'s teaching comes the more easily because the boy rarely understands his Hebrew lessons to the full. His real language is English, the teacher's is commonly the Yiddish jargon and the language to be learned is Hebrew.*[23]

Generational Changes

The first generation of any immigrant group is by nature bipolar; one foot still in the cultural memory of the Old Country, the other trying to gain a foothold in a strange society, with unfamiliar customs and an unrecognizable language. The new arrivals tried to transplant their Eastern European culture on American soil, with limited success. Yiddish culture flourished for a time, with a large array of Yiddish newspapers and theatrical productions that nurtured memories of the Old Country with an American twist. And guiding the immigrants through the maze of everyday life were their children, raised in the public school system as absorbent sponges of American life and language.

Abraham Goldfaden

Although he was not musically trained, Goldfaden transformed folk songs and cantorial melodies into popular Yiddish music that became famous throughout Europe. Known as "the father of Yiddish theater," he was born in Russia in 1840 and came to America first in 1887 and again in 1903. Many of his 400 plays and operas became the mainstays of the Yiddish theaters that proliferated in America to serve the immigrant community. His bittersweet "Rhozinkes mit Mandlen" (Raisins and Almonds), originally written for his play *Shulamit* (1880), became the best-known Yiddish melody of the early 20th century and a staple at Jewish weddings and bar mitzvahs. He died in 1908.

By the second generation, those same children—born or raised in America—had thrown off Yiddish and the traditional religious practices of their parents. They were not abandoning Judaism; they were developing new ways of expressing themselves as Jews in English-speaking, multicultural America. They could still speak Yiddish with their parents, but their native tongue was English, making them linguistically indistinguishable from other Americans.

The taunt of "greenhorn" greeted newcomers whose strange clothes and appearances marked them and their immediate shtetl past. Most immigrants tried to "look American" as quickly as possible, but others never reached that goal. In Anna Yezierska's story "Fat of the Land," she captures one girl's image of her mother: "God knows how hard I tried to civilize her so as not to have to blush with shame when I take her anywhere. I dressed her in the most stylish Paris models, but Delancy Street sticks out from every inch of her. Whenever she opens her mouth, I'm done for."

Mary Antin

Mary Antin was born in Russia in 1881 and immigrated as a child with her parents to America, where her thirst for learning flourished in the free public schools and libraries. At age 15, her first poem was published in a Boston newspaper, and three years later her first book, *From Plotzk to Boston*, appeared. Her classic book, *The Promised Land*, was published to critical acclaim in 1912 and depicts her quest for realizing the immigrant dream.
Chicago History Museum: DN-0067276

Life on the Street

While the public schools provided formal education for the young, it was on the streets that they learned the truth about life. All too often, the children became the parents to their own parents, who were overwhelmed by bureaucracy and language barriers. Young people sought respite from their families' crowded tenements and the "old-fashioned" ways of their parents by hanging out in the streets with peers. Sometimes they got into trouble. A rising juvenile delinquency rate among young Jews led to the founding of institutions to stem the tide. The Hawthorne School of the Jewish Protectory and Aid Society was established in 1907, followed by the Lakeview Home for unwed Jewish mothers. The Hebrew National Orphan Home was founded on the Lower East Side in 1912 to meet the increasing needs of children, either truly orphaned or unable to be cared for by their indigent parents.

Freedom from Religion?

As previous Jewish arrivals had before them, most newcomers learned to adapt their religious lives to fit the demands of America. Survival depended on work, and with

Poster for Yiddish Theater
Yiddish theater was a prominent force in the lives of Jewish immigrants. In this poster from New York's Thalia Theater, patrons are invited to a series of Yiddish plays featuring "first-class actors and actresses." The advertised plays include *King Solomon, Bar Kokhba, Kol Nidrei,* and *Hannah the Finisher,* a play based on the garment industry, which employed many of the theatergoers. Library of Congress

Sunday being a legal day of rest with all commerce prohibited in most places, it became necessary for bread-winners to work on Saturday. For those newcomers for whom Judaism was just a cultural identifier and not a religious marker, the freedoms of America allowed for sometimes outlandish rebellion. Flaunting their pious neighbors, freethinkers organized Yom Kippur feasts and balls. Others, not so brazen, became three-day-a-year Jews, if only to retain a religious connection to their heritage. Some nonreligious Jews created an ad hoc belief system rooted in Socialism and labor activism. The *Arbeiter Ring*, later known as the Workmen's Circle, became the focal point for Yiddish-based, nonreligious liberal activity infused with Jewish culture and secular tradition.

A Chief Rabbi for New York

The burgeoning numbers of Orthodox synagogues in New York created a dilemma of organization. Unlike in Europe, where local *kehillah* organizations governed Jewish communities, America had no single governmentally recognized umbrella organization to represent Jewish communities. Rabbi Isaac M. Wise had tried to

Fathers and Sons

Adjusting to life in America was difficult. The cultural gap between immigrants and their American-born children sometimes led to tension between the generations, as in this letter written by Judah David Eisenstein to his father in Chicago about his son, Isaac, in 1886:

You reprimand me that it is improper to teach him to play the piano, and maintain that it is useless to know the language of the land grammatically. You support your argument by our fathers and their fathers, forgetting that they lived in the past: the present requires other measures ... There are many things which we did not do then, but nevertheless do so now in broad daylight. For necessity impels us, so that we may mingle with the people among us. (quoted in *American Jewish Quarterly*, September 1962-June 1963, 243)

create such a group earlier based on the then-majority Reform movement, which had not anticipated the flood of Yiddish-speaking, religiously observant Jews. By the mid-1880s, Eastern European Orthodox Jews had become the new majority in New York City and sought to re-create a European model of community. Among other factors, they were concerned about the varying standards for kashrut that resulted from a lack of central authority to supervise the *shochtim* (ritual slaughterers). Furthermore, there was no universally accepted *beit din* (rabbinic court), so every synagogue community was free to set its own standards and practices.

A consortium of Orthodox congregations offered the position of chief rabbi of New York to a number of prestigious European rabbis. Most viewed the offer as an affront and declined to travel to the "unkosher" land. One who accepted the invitation was the scholarly, saintly Rabbi Jacob Joseph from Vilna, who arrived to a warm welcome in 1888. But even saints needed street smarts in America. Although initially successful in bringing order to unsupervised kosher slaughtering, his attempt to fund kashrut supervision by imposing a tax on slaughtered chicken and matzot resulted in personal attacks from butchers, grocers, and consumers who had quickly absorbed the ideals of American freedom and independence. In a Yiddish handbill for a mass meeting opposing the imposition of the "tax," the rabbi was accused of "making too much *business* for the sake of heaven," with the English word *business* transliterated into Yiddish. The constant infighting fatally diminished Chief Rabbi Joseph's popularity and effectiveness. In 1895, the good rabbi suffered a stroke and spent the last five years of his life paralyzed, ignored, and in abject poverty.

Other Orthodox rabbis arrived in New York seeking their own place in the sun. "In 1892, Rabbi Chayyim Ya'akov Vidrowitz came to New York from Moscow, gathered a few small Hassidic *shtibalech*—small prayer houses—under his control, and hung out a shingle which bore the legend 'Chief Rabbi of America.' When asked: 'Who made you Chief Rabbi?' he replied with a twinkle in his eye: 'The sign painter.'"[24] Like their earlier Sephardic coreligionists, the newcomers had swiftly grasped the concept of "land of the free" and rebelled against the hierarchical communal discipline that had governed the lives of European Jews. As the earlier German Reform rabbis had sadly learned, in America the power of congregational lay leaders trumped the scholarship, piety, and authority of rabbis.

The Commissioner's Lament

In a September 1908 *North American Review* article, New York Police Commissioner Theodore Bingham wrote:

It is not astonishing that with a million Hebrews, mostly Russian in the city (one quarter of the population) perhaps half of the criminals should be of that race when we consider that ignorance of the language, more particularly among men not physically fit for hard labor, is conducive to crime . . . they are burglars, firebugs, pickpockets and highway robbers—when they have the courage; but though all crime is in their province, pocket-picking is the one to which they take most naturally . . . Among the most expert of all the street thieves are Hebrew boys who are brought up to lives of crime. (Bingham 1908, 383)

A Reform View on a Chief Rabbi

"Rabbi Joseph is unfamiliar with the language of this country and is therefore unfitted to exercise authority or influence over American Jews. The Jews of this country do not need a Grand Rabbi and one from a Foreign country: one who is reared among the prejudices and bigotries of the Eastern countries will certainly prove an obstacle to the people over whom he is expected to exercise control." (Rosenberg 1954, 68)

Seeking a Religious Compromise

With a main goal of bringing the newcomers solidly into the larger society of American Jewry, the established Jewish community could not ignore the importance of religion. Children of immigrants did not feel at home in the Yiddish-speaking, "old-world" Orthodoxy of Europe, but neither were they comfortable in what was to them the alien Reform Judaism of America. There was a fear that either extreme might drive children of immigrants from Judaism entirely. Indeed, the appearance of Christian missionaries on the Lower East Side made the fear immediate, although their success in wooing Jews to Christianity was far from notable.

As if on command, a middle road to Jewish religious observance appeared. Its roots were established in 1883 at a banquet marking the first graduation of American-trained Reform rabbis from Hebrew Union College in Cincinnati. The menu was varied and, to many in attendance, shocking. Shrimp and crabmeat appetizers were followed by meat and ice cream courses. Some bewildered guests left the room in disgust, while others sat stunned in their places, not daring to touch the food before them. The liberals of the Reform movement had made their point. There was no place in their vision of Reform Judaism for those who wanted to hold onto old traditions. The "*Treif* (unkosher) Banquet," as it became known, directly triggered the development of Conservative Judaism. The ascendant liberal wing of the Reform movement institutionalized their views in the Pittsburgh Platform of 1885. Other more traditional rabbis within the movement withdrew to form the Jewish Theological Seminary of America.

In 1902, a group of wealthy Reform Jews invigorated this small struggling seminary with sizeable contributions for the training of American rabbis. Their foresight established the seminary as the fountainhead of Conservative Judaism. This American-born Judaism offered a new generation of children of Yiddish-speaking immigrants a way to preserve their religious heritage without doing away with the familiar traditions of *halakhah* (Jewish religious law) as the Reform movement had done. The die was cast for the religious division of American Jewry into three distinct parts: Reform, Conservative, and Orthodox.

The second generation of Orthodox Jews likewise was not immune from the Americanization trends adopted by Reform and Conservative movements. In 1912, a small group founded the National Council of Young Israel to advance "traditional Torah-true Judaism." Their attempt to create a "modern Orthodoxy" in America succeeded in stemming the flow away from traditional Judaism by preserving traditional practices while providing a decorous service, congregational singing, and English sermons.

Organizing for Self-Help

The period from 1881 to the outbreak of World War I marked a period of organization in general for the Jews in America. The sheer increase in Jewish population, with unprecedented social, religious, and economic needs, required a new model of communal leadership. The European autocratic model of community leadership would not work in a democratic society. The fragmented delivery of social services to the ballooning immigrant community led to duplication and contention.

With the turn of the century, aid came from a large number of philanthropic agencies, at first from those set up by wealthy, established Jews and later by Eastern Europeans who had begun to succeed in America. Once they felt established and comfortable in their new homeland, they united to help their newly arrived brethren. They created their own institutions in New York, including the Hebrew Sheltering Home and Beth Israel Hospital.

Outside New York, debates about servicing the needs of immigrants consumed Jewish communities throughout the country. To what extent were existing Jewish communal organizations responsible for the needs of newcomers? In Boston, the ability of the United Hebrew Benevolent Association to provide meaningful financial aid was quickly exceeded by the number of immigrants, which by 1900 had nearly tripled the

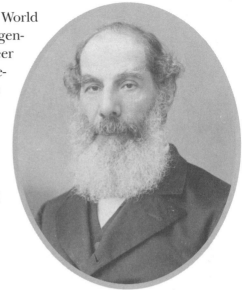

Sabato Morais
The longtime *hazzan* of Philadelphia's Congregation Mikveh Israel was a descendant of a Portuguese family and was born in Leghorn, Italy, in 1823. He arrived in Philadelphia in 1851. Throughout his life, Morais thought of himself primarily as a teacher and served as a professor at Maimonides College in Philadelphia. Alarmed at the liberal trend at the newly established Hebrew Union College in Cincinnati, he supported the founding of the Jewish Theological Seminary in 1886 and served as its president until his death in 1897.
Courtesy of the Ratner Center for the Study of Conservative Judaism, Jewish Theological Seminary.

107

Religious Division

When an ad hoc committee of Orthodox rabbis in New York issued a resolution denying the rabbinic legitimacy of graduates from the Jewish Theological Seminary, an editorial in the *American Hebrew* (June 17, 1904) offered a response:

... we would like to know who appointed the members of the Union of Orthodox Rabbis ... as authorities to lay down the law in regard to the appointment of rabbis? These men desire to transplant here conditions which, even for one moment, cannot be allowed to exist. Are these rabbis so senseless as to believe that their methods and ideas can possible have any weight or influence with the growing generation of Jews in this country?

Solomon Schechter

A child prodigy who became a noted rabbinic scholar and historian, Schechter was born in Romania in 1847. During his studies at the University of Vienna, he formed his own vision of a "Catholic Israel," embracing all Jews in consensus religious practice. In 1890 he became a lecturer at Cambridge University, where his responsibilities included maintaining the university library's Hebrew manuscript collection. His reputation as a scholar grew when his discovery of ancient manuscript fragments in a Cairo synagogue *genizah* led to new understanding of the development of Jewish tradition. (*Genizah*, Hebrew for "hidden away" and typically found in a synagogue's attic or basement, is a storage space where sacred Hebrew books containing God's name await proper interment per Jewish law.)

From 1902 until his death in 1915, Schechter held the presidency of the fledgling Jewish Theological Seminary in New York. Under his leadership, the seminary developed into a major institution of scholarship and the Conservative movement in America was reorganized and rejuvenated. Courtesy of the Ratner Center for the Study of Conservative Judaism, Jewish Theological Seminary.

city's Jewish population. Working together, the established German Jewish population and earlier landed Eastern Europeans established agencies that cooperated with one another to aid new arrivals. The growing fund-raising and coordination needs of disparate aid agencies led to the formation of the Jewish Federation movement in Boston (in 1895) and in other cities.

The most prominent of the self-help organizations was the founded in 1909. Branches of the organization opened in major cities, with HIAS representatives at the docks and train stations to welcome immigrants and guide them through the often confusing and sometimes dangerous bureaucracy. David Alpert, the Boston HIAS director, "cultivated good relations with the immigration officials, and in one year, 1913, reported that of 5,386 Jewish immigrants to Boston only 148 were excluded."[25] The society provided safe temporary shelter, a kosher meal, and more important, the ability to represent newcomers before immigration authorities.

In New York, Reform rabbi Judah Magnes led the fight to "develop a real Jewish community." The name of the umbrella organization that eventually emerged was the Kehillah (the community), based on the *kehillah* model of many Eastern European Jewish communities familiar to recent immigrants. This attempt joined uptowners and downtowners in an uneasy alliance to provide a governance structure for the New York Jewish community. Of prime concern at the time was the frightful condition of newly arrived indigent Jews from Europe, who came to America with dreams of better lives but found themselves instead in situations that imperiled not only their health, but their very

Boston's Jewish Quarter, 1899
Ghetto life duplicated itself in major American cities with the arrival of masses of immigrant Jews. As in New York's Lower East Side, newcomers who were poor, unskilled, and unfamiliar with American ways tended to gravitate toward neighborhoods filled with familiar sights and sounds. In Boston, Jews first settled in the North End before "bettering themselves" and moving on to other areas such as Chelsea, Dorchester, and Roxbury. Library of Congress

Young Israel

From the founding statement of Young Israel:

The appeal is to all Jewish young men and women, whatever be their views of Judaism, whatever be their social or economic statues. The movement is not Orthodox or Reform. It is not Zionistic or Socialistic. It intends to awaken Jewish young men and women to their responsibilities as Jews, in whatever form these responsibilities are conceived. Young Israel believes in the old-Jewish doctrine: all Israel are brothers. We are convinced that through a broad, earnest appeal to the Jewish spirit of our young men and women, the Jewish people will be strengthened and Judaism made a living force.
(Quoted in Kaufman 1999, 201–02)

Judah Magnes

Magnes was a Reform rabbi, born in 1877, and an early Zionist who helped establish the New York Kehillah. Through his activism, he tried to bring responsible leadership to the fragmented Jewish community with the Kehillah plan. When the concept of a centralized self-government structure for New York failed, later to be absorbed into a federation structure, he moved his family to Palestine, ultimately becoming president of the Hebrew University. His views on closing the gaps between Arabs and Jews in Palestine met with Jewish opposition. He died in New York in 1948 on one of his many fund-raising trips, as Israel was born. He was reburied in Israel in 1955.

survival. In 1917, after some initial success, particularly in reforming education and fighting crime, the Kehillah was absorbed into the Federation for the Support of Jewish Philanthropic Societies of New York.

It was in the area of Jewish education that the Kehillah left a lasting mark by hiring educator Samson Benderly to direct its Bureau of Jewish Education. "What we want in this country," declared Benderly, "is not Jews who can successfully keep up their Jewishness in a few large ghettos, but men and women who have grown up in freedom and can assert themselves where they are."[26] Supporting the nearly universal view of the uptown founders of the Kehillah, Benderly urged parents to support the public schools and to consider day schools as a detriment to strengthening the Jewish experience in America.

In some ways, the New York Kehillah had drawn on the American model of Jewish community federations first organized in Boston. The purpose was to provide a single fund-raising agency in each community to eliminate the duplication of efforts by disparate charitable and cultural organizations that had arisen over the years. The local federation not only reduced the fund-raising costs of individual charities, but also led to the formation of an umbrella organization to coordinate the good works of separate groups. All the local federations that formed throughout the country "could do what no single agency could do; they could jointly examine the requirements and assess the services of all the participating agencies and assign the funds where the needs were most urgent and where the greatest impact could be made."[27] Early federation leaders developed unique fund-raising methods that relied on personal solicitation by friends and business colleagues—methods still in use today. Within decades, federations had become the "central addresses" for their respective Jewish communities.

Taking Defensive Measures

The founding of Jewish "defense" agencies such as the American Jewish Committee, Anti-Defamation League, and American Jewish Congress mirrored a growing anti-Semitism both in America and Europe. The treason trial of French Army captain Alfred Dreyfus in 1894 unleashed a decade of anti-Jewish hate, splitting the French nation in two and capturing world attention. For Jews, the Dreyfus Affair struck a warning bell. The first trial and surrounding anti-Semitism directly affected Theodor Herzl, a totally assimilated Viennese journalist who covered the trial. He understood that if Jews could not enjoy liberty in France, their lives in other countries were certainly in jeopardy. He began mobilizing and politicizing the Zionist movement to reestablish a Jewish homeland in Palestine. While the American Jewish Committee's original role was to safeguard the civil rights of Jews in Russia, its work broadened to include the legal and social conditions of Jews and other American minorities.

Louis Marshall

A founder of the American Jewish Committee, Louis Marshall was the foremost champion of Jewish rights in America for the first three decades of the 20th century. He was born in Syracuse, New York, in 1856 and graduated from Columbia University Law School. He lived and worked in New York City, where he served as president of Temple Emanu-El and was active in Jewish affairs. He was a founder of the National Association for the Advancement of Colored People (NAACP). Speaking in 1911, he explained that the fight for Jewish rights was no more or less a fight for the rights of all Americans.

Although a prominent leader of Reform Judaism, he said "nothing Jewish is alien to me" and was a founder of Conservative Judaism's Jewish Theological Seminary. He died in 1929. American Jewish Historical Society

The Kishinev Massacre

When a particularly deadly three-day *pogrom* was inflicted on the Jews of Kishinev (the capital of Bessarabia) in April 1903, American Jews, both native and newly arrived, organized protests that affected American public opinion. Just two months later, President Roosevelt addressed the executive committee of the B'nai B'rith Organization: "I have never in my experience in this country known of a more immediate or a deeper expression of sympathy for the victims, and of horror for the appalling calamity that has occurred."[28] In response to the continuing violence against Jews in Russia, a number of prominent Jewish Americans, including Jacob Schiff; Louis Marshall, a noted lawyer; Julius Rosenwald, the president of Sears, Roebuck and Company; and Cyrus Sulzberger, publisher of the *New York Times*, formed the American Jewish Committee in 1906, America's first civil-rights organization to "take concerted action against the constant and ever increasing efforts to traduce the good name of the Jew."

Violence against Jews did not abate, and after other massacres in 1905 resulting from a failed Russian Revolution, the United States Congress passed a joint resolution,

Lady Liberty Chastises the Czar

Titled "The Crime of the New Century,"the cartoon shows the figure of a young woman, wearing a dress decorated with stars and sash labeled "Columbia," rebuking Czar Nicholas II of Russia, who appears embarrassed and dismayed. A poster shows several skulls and bones and reads "Kishinef—Massacre of 400 Jews—700 Jewish Homes Looted—Dead Left Bleeding in the Streets. Tirospol—General Slaughter of Jews—Young and Old Killed and Wounded." Jews in Imperial Russia were subject to *pogrom*s in the late 19th and early 20th centuries. Especially brutal were the 1903 massacres in Kishinev and Tirospol, now part of Moldova. They aroused widespread indignation in the United States. A petition signed by thousands of outraged citizens was sent by the United States government to the czar, but the Russian government refused to receive it. Library of Congress.

signed by President Roosevelt on June 26, 1906, condemning the "massacre of the Hebrews in Russia, on account of their race and religion …" With the continued mistreatment of and discrimination against Jews in Russia, including American Jewish visitors, a campaign began to annul an 1832 trade treaty. After intense and successful lobbying in Congress, the treaty was abrogated on December 18, 1911, sending Russia an important message. In part to convey the freedom Jews enjoyed in America, President Roosevelt appointed Oscar Straus as secretary of commerce and labor, the first Jew to hold a cabinet position.

The Leo Frank Case

The founding of the Anti-Defamation League of B'nai B'rith in 1913 resulted from a home-grown event, the lynching of Leo Frank. Frank, who was raised in Brooklyn, came to Atlanta to manage his family's pencil factory. When a young woman worker, Mary Phagan, was found brutally raped and bludgeoned to death at the factory in April 1913, Frank was charged with her murder. Despite less-than-convincing evidence in the courtroom and amid rampant anti-Semitic demonstrations outside, Frank was convicted and sentenced to death. While national news coverage of the trial focused on the inconsistencies of the accusation and trial, Southerners were quick to

Mr. and Mrs. Julius Rosenwald
Born in 1862 in Springfield, Illinois, Julius Rosenwald went from manufacturing men's clothing to becoming a partner in Sears, Roebuck and Company, and ultimately its president and then chairman. Active in his own synagogue and in Reform movement affairs nationally, he was a patron of Jewish institutions and causes, helping to found the Chicago Federation of Jewish Charities and giving financial support to Hebrew Union College and the American Jewish Committee. His philanthropic efforts, which translated into tens of millions of donated dollars, did not stop at Jewish organizations but went on to include museums, schools, libraries, and universities. He is best remembered for his work on behalf of African Americans. Through the Julius Rosenwald Fund, which he established in 1917, he was responsible for building over 5,000 schools for African American children in the South. Library of Congress.

113

A Leo Frank Detractor

The anti-Semitism that swirled around the Leo Frank case surfaced in newspaper letters to the editor. Here is a segment written by Bob Munroe of Arkansas in the March 25, 1915, edition of the *Jeffersonian*:

If the big Jew editors, bankers and others don't look out they will fan into flame the smoldering embers of that old-ground-in-the-bone prejudice from which even the double eagle may be unable to save them.

assume the worst about the "Yankee Jew" and the perceived Jewish cabal to free Frank. Georgia governor Frank Slaton was not fully convinced of Frank's guilt and commuted the death sentence to life imprisonment, an act of bravery that ended the governor's political future and endangered his own life. On August 16, 1915, a raiding party calling itself the Knights of Mary Phagan descended on the prison, overpowered the guards, and kidnapped Frank. Early the next morning, they lynched him. The Frank case had a profound effect on American Jews. No longer could they view a *pogrom* in Russia or the Dreyfus Affair in France as remote events that could never take place in America.

Oscar Straus

A member of a noted merchant family (Macy's), Straus was born in 1850. He studied law and embarked on a diplomatic career at a time when few Jews were involved in such pursuits. He was active in the work of the American Jewish Committee and was a founder and first president of the American Jewish Historical Society in 1882. In 1887, President Cleveland appointed him minister to Turkey, and his success there led to other appointments. In 1906, Theodore Roosevelt named him to his cabinet as secretary of commerce and labor. Three years later, President Taft appointed him as the first ambassador to Turkey. He returned to become a candidate for governor of New York, and although his party went down to defeat, respect for him grew. He used his diplomatic and political influence to aid Russian Jews. He died in 1926.

A Population Forever Altered

By World War I, the United States contained the second-largest Jewish population in the world next to Russia itself, which by then had lost a third of its Jews to immigration. "What Russia achieved with persecution, America achieved with indifference."[29] The Jewish population of New York City had mushroomed from an estimated 60,000 in 1880 to more than 1.5 million by 1914.[30] But although Eastern European Jews continued to emigrate to America during World War I, increasingly restrictive U.S. immigration laws gradually decreased their numbers. The floodwaters were receding.

It had been a chaotic, almost surreal experience in acculturation and adaptation for the masses of arrivals. In a generation, they had changed the tone, direction, and intensity of the American Jewish experience. Never completely cohesive, the Jewish community found itself divided. The well-to-do established German pioneers, largely Reform and acculturated, found themselves outnumbered by Socialist, Zionist, Yiddish-speaking Eastern Europeans. The time had now come to regroup, build, and grow.

1881–1913
A TIMELINE

1881
Assassination of Alexander II; *Pogroms*; beginning of mass exodus from Russia

1882
First Yiddish play produced in New York by Boris Tomashefsky

1885
Pittsburgh Platform adopted by Reform Judaism; first Yiddish newspaper, *Tageblatt*, published in America

1888
Founding of The Jewish Publication Society of America; Jacob Joseph assumes position as chief rabbi of New York

1889
Isaac M. Wise establishes Central Conference of American Rabbis; Union of Orthodox Jewish Congregations formed

1893
Hannah Solomon forms National Council of Jewish Women

1894
Nicholas II assumes power; *Protocols of the Elders of Zion* published; Spanish-American War. American armed forces include 4,000 Jews

1897
First Zionist Congress in Basel, Switzerland; founding of Rabbi Isaac Elchanan Theological Seminary, precursor to Yeshiva University

1899
First National Conference of Jewish Charities

1900
The *Arbeiter Ring* (Workmen's Circle) is organized; International Ladies Garment Workers Union (ILGWU) formed

1903
Kishinev Massacre; outbreak of massive *pogroms* throughout Russia

1906
Oscar Straus is first Jew appointed to president's cabinet; founding of American Jewish Committee

1907
Albert Michelson is first American Jew to win Nobel Prize

1909
The Kehillah of New York organized to oversee Jewish life; Hebrew Immigrant Aid Society founded; uprising of 1909 by garment workers in New York

1911
Congress abrogates 1832 treaty with Russia; Triangle Shirtwaist Company fire

1912
Founding of Hadassah, the women's Zionist organization; publication of *The Promised Land* by Mary Antin

1913
Leo Frank arrested and put on trial; founding of Anti-Defamation League of B'nai B'rith

1914–1948

From Home to Homeland

5

On the eve of world war, most American Jews lived in urban ghettos, surrounded by the sounds of *mameloshen*—their Yiddish mother tongue. Little more than 30 years earlier, before the onslaught of Eastern European immigrants began, American Jews were predominantly Reform and English speaking. The sheer volume of newcomers had created tensions not only between Jews and non-Jews in America, but also within the different segments of American Jewry itself. And as tensions in Europe escalated into war, Yiddish-speaking Jews continued to flee Eastern Europe, bound for America's ports.

From a Torrent to a Stream

World War I was a catastrophe of the first order for the Jews of Eastern Europe, bringing the nightmare of military occupation along with expulsions, hunger, and fear into their lives. Jews and other civilians suffered as opposing armies scourged the shtetls and villages along the Polish and Russian borders, causing dislocation and economic ruin. Families were stranded and divided. Some families tried to reunite by emigrating to America, and some just wanted to leave situations that had become untenable. So the wave of immigrants continued—but at a slower pace. Ever since 1882, concerned with the rising number of "undesirable" immigrants, the United States had been gradually tightening immigration requirements, first by instituting regulations to prevent paupers, criminals, or diseased persons from entering. In 1891, new laws discouraged the admission of "assisted immigrants" who were encouraged or supported by organizations, counteracting efforts by immigrant aid societies such as the Joint Distribution Committee and HIAS to assist would-be immigrants. In 1917, a head tax of $8 was imposed, together with a requirement that arrivals be literate in English or some other language. Interestingly, the only other languages specifically mentioned were Hebrew and Yiddish.

The Joint Distribution Committee

In America, Jews who only a generation earlier would have been in Eastern Europe joined with established American Jews to raise money to help those left behind. The major vehicle for relief was the American Joint Distribution Committee (JDC), organized in 1914 by philanthropists Jacob Schiff and Louis Marshall to provide aid for Palestinian Jews, then under Turkish rule, and Jews in war-torn Europe. The JDC today remains the major aid clearinghouse for needy overseas Jews.

Yiddish Culture in Wartime America

In urban America, it was Yiddish—despite differences in regional inflections and pronunciations—that united recent Jewish immigrants of all classes and backgrounds, more so even than their common religion. Yiddish was the language of the street, the home, and the marketplace. First-generation immigrants were comforted by the familiarity of Yiddish culture that surrounded them in the cities. Yiddish theater in America provided an escape for immigrant audiences, with plays rich in melodrama and comedy. Although translations of classical works by

Shakespeare offered uplifting fare, most theatergoers preferred the less cerebral entertainment of vaudeville. Yiddish vaudeville began in the 1890s and served as a training ground for ambitious young men and women who went on to success in the great American vaudeville circuits. Vaudeville was a tough business. Those who were not quick on their feet, clever, and tenacious quickly fell by the wayside. The best performers eventually graduated to acts of their own. Jewish entertainers, many with Yiddish vaudeville experience, included Groucho Marx, Walter Winchell, and George Jessel. Their careers began on the streets of the Lower East Side and led them from Yiddish vaudeville to iconic fame, first in films and later on radio and television. Yiddish theater in America was not a lasting phenomenon and began to disappear as newer generations of young Jews further assimilated into American culture.

A Lower East Side Reflection

Anna Yezierska included this description of New York's Lower East Side in her book, *Salome of the Tenements*:

... she went to the window, looking out on a fire-escape where she kept her can of milk and groceries for her breakfast. The roaring tumult of the noises from the street below woke her from her dreams. Wedged in, jumbled shops and dwellings, pawnshops and herring-stalls, strained together begging for elbow room. Across the alley a second-hand store protruded its rubbish. Broken stoves, beds, three-legged chairs sprawled upon the sidewalk. The unspeakable cheapness of a dry goods shop flared in her face—limp calico dresses of scarlet and purple, gaudy blankets of pink and green checks. From the crowded windows hung dirty mattresses and bedding—flaunting banners of poverty. (Yezierska 1923, 5)

By 1920, there were more than 20 Yiddish newspapers published in New York reflecting a variety of religious, cultural, and political views, in addition to numerous other journals. Perhaps the most important was the *Jewish Daily Forward*, a newspaper with Socialist underpinnings edited by Abraham Cahan. The *Forward* was more than a disseminator of current news. Its legendary "Bintel Brief" column was a forerunner of the "Dear Abby" columns of a later generation, answering questions from bewildered immigrants trying to make sense of their Americanized children and their new circumstances in a strange world. With a national readership, photographs of missing husbands were prominently featured to counteract an epidemic of men who deserted their families. Instructional articles on the English language and American institutions (including an illustrated primer on baseball) helped newcomers understand the sometimes arcane foreign culture that surrounded them.

Molly Picon

The First Lady of the Yiddish theater was born in 1898 and began her acting career at age five in Philadelphia. For Yiddish-speaking immigrants and their children, she brought joy and entertainment with familiar words and music. During her long acting career she performed on stage and in films, radio, and television. Her roles, both Yiddish and English, included serious plays, musicals, and comedies. She starred in such well-known Broadway plays and Hollywood films as *Milk and Honey*, *Funny Girl*, and *The Front Page*. In 1981, she became the first Yiddish actress to be elected to the Theatre Hall of Fame. She died in 1992.

George Gershwin

Gershwin, the son of Russian Jewish immigrants, was born in 1898 in Brooklyn, two years after his famous older brother, Ira. While Ira was the studious brother, reading and writing, George spent his time on the streets, where he was introduced to music, particularly jazz and ragtime. George was first to enter the music business, writing his first song in 1914 and launching a career that produced popular hits, Broadway shows, and classical pieces such as *Rhapsody in Blue,* which have become iconic examples of American popular music. Ira joined him in the music business, his sophisticated lyrics enhancing George's music. Together they wrote Broadway musicals, including *An American In Paris, Porgy and Bess,* and *Girl Crazy.* But while Ira lived into his late 80s, George died unexpectedly at age 38 as a result of a brain tumor, at the height of his musical success. Library of Congress

From the "Bintel Brief"

Dear Mr. Editor,
I was born in a small town in Russia, and until I was sixteen I studied in *Talmud Torahs* and yeshivas, but when I came to America I changed quickly. I was influenced by the progressive newspapers, the literature. I developed spiritually and became a free thinker ... but the nature of my feelings is remarkable. Listen to me: Every year when the month of *Elul* rolls around, when the time of *Rosh Hashanah* and *Yom Kippur* approach my heart grows heavy and sad. A melancholy descends on me, a longing gnaws at my breast. At that time I cannot rest, I wander about through the streets lost in thought, depressed.

When I go past a synagogue during those days and hear a cantor chanting the melodies of the prayers, I become very gloomy and my depression is so great that I cannot endure it ...

These emotions and these moods have become stronger over the years and I decided to go to the synagogue. I went not in order to pray to God but to heal and refresh my aching soul with the cantor's sweet melodies, and they had an unusually good effect on me.

Sitting in the synagaogue among *landsleit* [people from the same village or town] and listening to the good cantor, I forgot my unhappy weekday life, the dirty shop, my boss, the bloodsucker, and my pale sick wife and my children. All of my America with its hurry-up life was forgotten. (Unkown man from New York City, Metzker 1990, 101).

Fighting for America

World War I officially began in July 1914, but America did not enter the fray until April 1917. For young male Jewish immigrants, the war provided a way to hasten their Americanization. Ironically, many of them had left Eastern Europe to avoid service in the czar's army, yet nearly 200,000 Jews served in the U.S. military during the war. Living and fighting together provided an opportunity for large numbers of young men of different religions and backgrounds to discover each other and to become Americans in a far swifter and more visceral way than civilian life might have allowed. Three days after the United States entered the war, the Jewish Welfare Board (JWB) was organized. As an agency officially recognized by the

War Department, the JWB supported Jewish soldiers by training and furnishing chaplains and organizing religious services at military bases and hospitals. With government support, it co-published with The Jewish Publication Society the *Abridged Prayer Book for Jews in the Army and Navy of the United States*, a prayer book that could be accepted by all Jewish soldiers whether they identified with Reform, Conservative, or Orthodox traditions. In June 1917, Rabbi Mordecai Kaplan rallied American Jews to enlist: "The ideal for which we are fighting is to suppress the great bully and outlaw among the nations—the German government … As Jews … we owe it to America to stand by her in her hour of trial."[1] Some Jews did not support the war, notably Emma Goldman, who believed that militarism in all forms needed to be defeated to achieve freedom. She was imprisoned for two years and deported to Russia in 1919.

> ## The *Jewish Daily Forward* on Elections
>
> In November 1914, the *Jewish Daily Forward* put forth an optimistic view on the power of annual elections to affect the course of human events:
>
> *When the founders of this Republic established the annual elections, they believed that this custom would achieve wonders. They thought that it would put an end to all bitter struggles among the citizens; that it would render unnecessary a bloody revolution, like the one they had experienced; that it would end forever oppression and injustice, against which they had fought so bitterly. For Election Day will make it possible for the citizen to abolish every evil which oppresses, calmly, quietly, without shedding a drop of blood, without firing one shot. The greatest revolutions, the most fundamental changes would be effected by means of the elections....* (Translated in Masserman and Baker 1932, 415).

The Rise of American Zionism

As Europe was igniting into war in August 1914, American Zionists held an emergency meeting at New York's Hotel Marseilles and elected Louis D. Brandeis, the Boston lawyer who had designed the "Protocol of Peace" in 1910, to be president of the Provisional Executive Committee. In his acceptance speech, Brandeis said, "I find Jews possessed of those qualities which we of the twentieth century seek to develop in our struggle for justice and democracy." Brandeis's election marked a turning point in the American Zionist cause. His vast experience as a reformer and organizer led him to emphasize the democratic aspects of Zionism, making the fledgling movement more compatible with American ideals. He succeeded in bringing together existing Zionist-oriented groups under the umbrella of the Zionist Organization of America. "Let no American imagine that Zionism is inconsistent with patriotism," he admonished Reform rabbis. Judge Julian Mack, also a Reform Jew, echoed Brandeis's thoughts: "To be good Americans, we must be better Jews, and to be better Jews, we must become Zionists."

At the beginning of the war, there were fewer than 20,000 Zionist members in America. By the end of the war, that number had jumped to 125,000. One reason for growth was the large number of recent immigrants who brought with them an emotional and religious fervor for the cause. Brandeis's equating of Zionism with Americanism nullified previous fears of dual loyalties. In a 1915 speech to the

Emma Goldman

From her childhood years in Lithuania where she was born in 1869, Emma was cognizant of the social injustices that surrounded her. She fled to America as a teenager, only to discover that injustice also flourished on this side of the Atlantic. She became active in the anarchist movement and founded a political magazine, *Mother Earth*, which increased her reputation in leftist political circles. She was an ardent lecturer who traveled the country espousing her causes. Often arrested, she used her times in jail to broaden her own education.

During World War I, she became one of the most visible opponents to the war and the drafting of young men. Accused of conspiracy, she was sentenced to two years in jail and eventual deportation. She had never become an American citizen. During her exile from the United States, she settled for short periods in European countries, continuing to write and advocate for her beliefs. After her death in 1940, her body was returned to the United States for burial in Chicago.

American Zionist convention, Brandeis stated, "The highest Jewish ideals are essentially American in a very important particular. It is Democracy that Zionism represents. It is Social Justice which Zionism represents, and every bit of that is the American ideal of the twentieth century."[2]

Many non-Jews also supported Zionist goals. Early Christian activity to help Jews return to Palestine was motivated by the theological conviction that when Jews were once again living in their Promised Land, the "second coming" of Jesus would occur. President Woodrow Wilson, son of a Protestant minister, was strongly attracted to the Zionist cause on these religious grounds and told a delegation of American Jewish Congress leaders on March 2, 1919, that "our own government and people are agreed that in Palestine there shall be laid the foundation of a Jewish commonwealth."[3] In 1916, President Wilson nominated Brandeis to the U.S. Supreme Court. Never before in America had a Jew held such a highly visible and important government position. His nomination unleashed anti-Semitic rhetoric in newspapers, social clubs, and the halls of Congress, but ultimately he was confirmed by the Senate.

The Balfour Declaration

Zionist hopes worldwide were raised during the war by the Balfour Declaration of 1917. Lord Balfour, the British foreign minister, supported the establishment of a Jewish national homeland, in part to fulfill his own religious beliefs but also to influence American public opinion in favor of entering the war on Britain's side against

The Balfour Declaration of 1917

Succinct and significant, the declaration reads in its entirety:

His Majesty's Government view with favor the establishment in Palestine of a national home for the Jewish people and will use their best endeavors to facilitate the achievement of this object, it being clearly understood that nothing shall be done which may prejudice the religious rights of existing non-Jewish communities in Palestine or the rights and political status enjoyed by Jews in any other country.

Germany, perhaps overestimating the real political power of American Jews.

The words of the Balfour Declaration were carefully crafted to satisfy Jews while not alarming Arabs. Nonetheless, for Zionists it represented a significant success. For the first time, a major international power had officially recognized the right of the Jewish people to reestablish its homeland in Palestine. Jews in America's largest cities celebrated with parades and rallies. Justice Brandeis and Rabbi Stephen S. Wise spent the summer of 1918 convincing President Wilson to support the declaration. (For decades, Rabbi Wise was the unofficial spokesman of the American Jewish community and founder of the American Jewish Congress.) Finally, as Rosh Hashanah approached, the president wrote to Rabbi Wise:

I welcome the opportunity to express the satisfaction I have felt in the progress of the Zionist movement in the United States and the Allied countries since the declaration of Mr. Balfour on behalf of the British Government, of Great Britain's approval of the establishment in Palestine of a national home for the Jewish people.[4]

Two Jewish Justices

Benjamin Cardozo, born in 1870 and descended from Colonial Jewish families, was the second Jew appointed to the U.S. Supreme Court. After graduating from the Columbia School of Law, he embarked on a successful private practice before his election to the New York Supreme Court in 1913 and his appointment as a regular member of the state's court of appeals in 1917. He was unanimously confirmed to the U.S. Supreme Court in 1932 and died in 1938. "No judge in his time was more deeply versed in the history of the common law or more resourceful in applying the living principles by which it has unfolded than Mr. Justice Cardozo."

That tribute came from Felix Frankfurter, appointed to the U.S. Supreme Court by President Roosevelt in 1939. Frankfurter was born in Vienna in 1882 and came to America when he was 12. He was editor of the Harvard Law School's law review and after graduation served in several government positions before returning to teach at the school. His liberal views on the Constitution mirrored his long-standing support of social interests, and during his tenure as Supreme Court Justice, he became known for his positions on civil rights law. He died in 1965.

While President Wilson was in favor, Secretary of State Robert Lansing was anxious not to deviate from American neutrality in the war, which it had maintained until it joined the Allied forces in 1917. Lansing wrote to the president, "… We should go slowly in announcing a policy … we are not at war with Turkey and therefore should avoid any appearance of favoring taking territory from that Empire by force … [also] many Christian sects … would resent turning the Holy Land over to [Jews]."[5] Supporters of the Zionist cause viewed the overthrow of the Ottoman Empire as a milestone toward the ultimate reestablishment of the Jewish homeland. While European Jews viewed a Jewish homeland in Palestine as a necessary option to escape the palpable anti-Semitism that surrounded them, American Jews displayed no such desire to leave their homes. They considered America their Zion. Louis Marshall prayed that American Jews should remember "the gratitude that we owe to the God of our fathers, Who has led us out of Egypt into this land of freedom."[6]

In 1918, Rabbi Wise founded the American Jewish Congress to counteract the perceived elitism of the older American Jewish Committee. Wise envisioned an organization that would attract a broad representation of American Jews. At the conclusion of World War I, all interested parties prepared for a peace conference in Paris. The American Jewish Congress sent Rabbi Wise and a delegation to Paris on a mission to convince the conference to "recognize the aspirations and historic claims of the Jewish people with regard to Palestine…" The delegation went with the blessing of President Wilson, who, before their departure, assured them that "in Palestine there shall be laid the foundation of Jewish commonwealth."[7]

Competing Factions within Zionism

Zionists saw the end of the Great War as an opportunity to raise world consciousness about their struggle for the reestablishment of the Jewish homeland. The nascent Zionist movement in the United States was a mix of ideologies and temperaments. Reform Judaism and the American Jewish Committee institutionally opposed Zionism, fearing charges of disloyalty by non-Jewish Americans. Yet, ironically, Zionism in America would not have succeeded in the end were it not for those crucial American Jewish Committee and Reform leaders who championed the Zionist cause early on.

> ### Another Jewish View on Zionism
>
> Congressman Julius Kahn of California made a statement to the *New York Times* before his departure for the Paris Peace Conference after World War I, where the topic of Zionism was to be discussed. In it he voiced his opposition to Zionism:
>
> **It creates a divided allegiance, as between our country and its Stars [sic] and Zion with its white flag with the blue star. The Zionists in this country are bent upon following their flag. The real American Jew knows but one flag, the Stars and Stripes. The American Jew sings "The Star Spangled Banner" as his national anthem. The Zionist sings "the Hatikvah."** (The *Current Opinion*, May 1919, 315–16)

During the 1920s, the Zionist movement in the United States was torn by internal debate. Assimilated Jewish leaders such as Brandeis and Wise competed with the Yiddish-speaking Eastern Europeans immigrants allied with respected scientist Dr. Chaim Weizmann, successor to Theodor Herzl as head of the World Zionist Organization. In 1921, Weizmann visited the United States. In a grueling fund-raising tour of major American cities, he stirred audiences to action. He understood that American Jews were not about to move to Palestine, so he focused instead on the importance of a Jewish state for all Jews. "If you want your position to be secure elsewhere," he said repeatedly, "you must have a portion of Jewry which is at home, in its own country." Zionist advocacy grew into political action. On September 22, 1922, President Harding signed a Joint Congressional Resolution supporting the Balfour Declaration. He was the first in a long line of American political leaders to officially support the establishment of a Jewish homeland in Palestine. In spite of such outward displays of support, membership in Zionist groups declined during the 1920s.

Damming the Flood

The era between the two world wars saw an increase in anti-Jewish feeling in the country. With the Russian revolution of 1917, a "Red Scare" had enveloped America, and fears of spreading Bolshevism led to anti-Jewish propaganda. Even as the children of immigrants were insinuating themselves into the fabric of American life, public displays of intolerance continued to buffet their full acceptance into the larger society.

The strict immigration laws of the 1920s put an end to mass immigration to the United States and directly affected Jewish life in America. The Immigration Acts of 1921 and 1924 reflected a growing American distrust of immigrants after World War I, and effectively shut down new arrivals from Eastern and Southern Europe by instituting harsh quotas. New York Congressman Emmanuel Celler declared during congressional debate in 1924, "It is the most vaunted purpose of the majority of the Immigration Committee to encourage assimilation, yet this bill has already done more than anything I know of to bring about discord among our resident aliens."[8]

The nonstop replenishment of a "greenhorn" society was replaced by a new generation of acculturated Jewish Americans. Effectively closing America's borders to new arrivals hastened the Americanization and assimilation of earlier immigrants. It disintegrated the ghetto. It gave a death blow to the Yiddish press. It weakened Orthodoxy. It practically destroyed the Yiddish stage. "Most important of all, it [took] from thousands of Jews in Eastern Europe the last hope of Freedom."[9] Although Jewish groups fought against the anti-immigrant regulations, they did not do so vigorously. Newer issues at home required more attention, and the focus of the Jewish community turned inward.

From the *Dearborn Independent*

The Jews [sic] determination to wipe out of public life every sign of the predominant Christian character of the United States, is the only active form of religious intolerance in the country today ... Not content with the fullest liberty to follow their own faith in peace and quietness, in a country where none dares make them afraid, the Jews declare ... that every sight and sound of anything Christian is an invasion of their peace and quietness, and so they stamp it out whenever they can reach it through political means. (March 12, 1921)

Chief among the B'nai B'rith's activities ... is the work of the Anti-Defamation League. This inside committee in every lodge attends to the espionage work necessary to keep the Grand Lodges informed as to what is going on with reference to Jewry in the United States. In its work, the Anti-Defamation League always takes the offensive ... (March 19, 1921)

The question arises whether it is patriotic for Mr. [Louis] Marshall to implant into the minds of his foreign-born co-religionists the idea that this is not a Christian country, that Sunday laws should be opposed, and that the manners and customs of the native-born should be scorned and ridiculed. The effect has been that thousands of immigrant Jews from Eastern Europe are persistently violating Sunday laws in the large industrial centers of the country, that they are hailed to court, lectured by judges, and fined. American Jews are carrying into practice the teachings of Mr. Marshall and his followers are reaping the whirlwind of natural resentment. (November 26, 1921)

125

The Public Face of Anti-Semitism

The African American *Cleveland Advocate* Responds to Mr. Ford

Mr. Ford and His Anti-Jewish Campaign

Henry Ford of the Dearborn Independent—better known as Henry Ford of "Tin Lizzie" fame—is making a vigorous attack on our friends, the Jews, in the columns of his personally conducted organ.

While it is understood that Mr. Ford runs the "Independent" for recreation, the fact remains that thousands of its readers will take "The Independent" seriously. Hence it is very necessary for us to throw some light on the errors of the "Ford way."

Undoubtedly, the attempt of the Ford weekly to "throw mud" on the Jews, is akin to the attempt of a small boy to bale [sic] the Pacific Ocean with a quart bottle.

The contribution made by the Jews to civilization and to human progress stands "Gibraltar-like" against the paper darts of the "Dearborn Independent," and its angel—the man who in all earnestness told a jury in Judge Sessions' court during his famous libel suit "that Benedict Arnold was famous writer." (November 27, 1920; 8)

In sheer numbers, the new immigrants, with their Old World looks and mannerisms, greatly outnumbered the descendants of German immigrants who had been largely absorbed into American culture. But the growing anti-Semitism in America did not distinguish immigrant pedigrees and affected fifth-generation Jews as well as recent arrivals. Perhaps the best-known purveyor of anti-Semitism in the 1920s was the American industrial icon Henry Ford. Through his widely distributed newspaper, the *Dearborn Independent*, Ford published articles attacking Jews, their patriotism, and their character. He disseminated the discredited *Protocols of the Elders of Zion*, a czarist forgery that "proved" the existence of a secret international Jewish plot to control the world. The newspaper constantly accused the New York Kehillah and newly created defense organizations such as the Anti-Defamation League and the American Jewish Committee of nefarious plots to "Judaize" American society. He theorized that the "meaning of the heavy migration of Jews all over the world toward New York" was an engineered plan to transfer the center of Jewish world power to the United States. While Ford's theories of Jewish world domination provided a source of ironic comedy to Jews whose families had escaped Russian *pogroms*, other Americans seriously accepted the anti-Jewish rants as truthful.

Quotas

In the 1920s, some prestigious universities established quotas limiting the number of Jewish students. The president of Harvard University explained that "the anti-Semitic feeling among students is increasing, and it grows in proportion to the increase in … Jews." While Ivy League schools limited the number of Jewish students, Jewish graduates also faced discrimination as they sought admission to graduate schools. Quotas at medical schools forced otherwise talented Jewish students to enter foreign medical schools or change their career goals. Some changed their names and hid their Jewish background to gain admission.

Discrimination in housing and accommodations was even more blatant. "Hebrew patronage not requested" frequently accompanied newspaper advertisements for resort hotels. Classified employment ads commonly added that the openings were for white Christians only. Discrimination continued against Jews in private clubs and private schools. At the same time that Jews were charged by anti-Semites with controlling American business, they were systematically excluded from management positions in such important fields as banking, insurance, and public utilities. Jews were largely confined to small businesses and to those large industries that they had helped create, including films, broadcasting, and retailing. Although weak civil rights laws at the state level provided some minimum protections in housing and employment, widespread discrimination continued unabated.

Father Coughlin
One of the most popular radio personalities of the period was Roman Catholic priest Charles Coughlin, shown here speaking at Madison Square Garden in 1935. Coughlin's messages were often marked by anti-Semitic charges and attracted a huge audience nationwide. He continued the work of Henry Ford in disseminating the *Protocols*. "I emphasize once more that I am not interested in the authenticity of the *Protocols*," he said. "I am interested in their factuality." (Quoted in Finkelstein 1997, 108) Library of Congress

Economic Successes

Despite frequent stumbling blocks, increasing numbers of Jews succeeded in improving their economic conditions. Labor unions strengthened the economic position of factory workers, and white-collar workers and professionals made advances as well. American Jews were quickly becoming the richest and most influential Jewish community in the world. At the same time, a smaller but highly visible minority of immigrant children achieved success in less conventional ways. No single group of ghetto graduates gave more pride to their immigrant parents and neighbors than the popular singers, actors, and comedians of the 1920s such as Eddie Cantor, Sophie Tucker, and George Burns. Another unconventional way in which some Jews found success was in sports.

Richard Rodgers
Born in New York in 1902, composer Richard Rodgers, in collaboration with Oscar Hammerstein and Lorenz Hart, is credited with changing the face of American musical theatre by making songs an integral part of the play's message. In such plays as *South Pacific*, *Oklahoma*, and *Sound of Music*—later turned into successful films— Rodgers created songs that have become indispensable parts of the American songbook. He died in 1972.

127

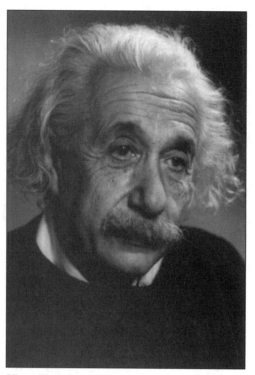

Albert Einstein
In 1921, while American universities were limiting Jewish applications, Swiss citizen Albert Einstein was winning the Nobel Prize in Physics for his special theory of relativity. Born in Germany in 1879, Einstein was in California in 1933 when Hitler came to power. He never returned to Germany, instead becoming an American citizen (while retaining his Swiss citizenship) in 1940. He was offered the presidency of the new State of Israel in 1948 but declined. Library of Congress.

128

Rose Schneiderman

Schneiderman, born in Poland in 1882, was a labor activist and political leader who worked tirelessly to improve working conditions. A friend of Eleanor and Franklin Roosevelt, she spoke with them often about labor issues. As a teenager, she helped organize women into labor unions and actively supported worker legislation. In 1933, President Roosevelt appointed her as the only woman member on the labor advisory board of the National Recovery Administration. She died in 1972.

A Song in Their Hearts

American popular culture of the 20th century was improbably spawned in the Jewish ghettos of America's large cities. Today, it is difficult to imagine American writing, music, and theater without the works of Roth, Ozick, Berlin, Gershwin, and Hammerstein. The work of the composers inadvertently created a climate in which patriotism prevailed, religious separatism disappeared, and multiculturalism flourished. Irving Berlin's "God Bless America" bestowed a blessing on all the country's inhabitants, and Rodgers and Hammerstein's *South Pacific* enshrined the noble theory of brotherhood.

Technology in the form of film and radio brought Jewish entertainers to previously *Judenrein* (Jewish-free) America where, for most people, little personal contact with Jews existed. *The Jazz Singer*, famous as the first talking picture, introduced movie audiences to *Kol Nidrei* and Jewish tradition, albeit in a story line that touted assimilation and intermarriage. The universality of the film's content—the alienation of children from their parents—played well to Middle America. The themes of assimilation were displayed on stage and film and later in radio and television programs. Depictions of authentic Judaism could not win out against stories in which Jewish characters identified their Americanization through assimilation.

Less Admirable Successes

The children of immigrants were less bound by Old World traditions than their parents. Most were born into lives of poverty and were quickly influenced by the behavior of the streets.

Rising out of the urban ghettos, neighborhood toughs expanded their influence by involving themselves in labor union issues. Hired as *shtarkes* (thugs) by both labor and management to physically threaten strikers and strike-breakers, they soon realized the power—and profit potential—they had in controlling diverse Jewish-oriented institutions, ranging from the garment industry to kosher meat slaughtering. It was not a quantum leap from breaking arms and legs of picketing workers to the realization that profits could be made in other illegal areas. The Volstead Act of 1919, which introduced the Prohibition Era, enriched bootleggers and expanded their business horizons.

Just as those ghetto graduates who succeeded in fields like entertainment or sports gave their parents tremendous pride, no group provided more embarrassment than headline-grabbing gangsters such as "Bugsy" Siegel, "Dutch" Schultz, and the Purple Gang. Their exploits (and killings) were avidly followed by millions in the daily newspapers. It is important to note, though, that the era of Jewish gangsters lasted but one generation. Like their more respectable peers, they too dreamed of leading their families into middle-class acceptability and encouraged their children to pursue honest work and lead socially acceptable lives. By the end

Irving Berlin

Born Israel Baline in Siberia in 1888, Irving Berlin was brought to America as a young child, where he grew up poor on the streets of the Lower East Side. As a young man, he left school and became a singing waiter and eventually, despite his lack of education or formal musical training, began composing music. His first success, "Alexander's Ragtime Band" (1911), launched his career as the preeminent composer of American popular music.

Through the years, Berlin's songs for stage and screen have become iconic representations of American culture. "White Christmas" and "Puttin' on the Ritz" are only two of the thousands of songs Berlin created over his long and productive life. His musical comedies, such as *Annie Get Your Gun* and *Call Me Madam*, continue to be performed today. He is shown here in a scene from a 1943 World War II film, offering his rendition of "Oh, How I Hate to Get Up in the Morning." He died in 1989.
Library of Congress

Henry "Hank" Greenberg

At a time with when American Jews had few heroes to emulate, baseball star Hank Greenberg energized the Jewish community. Born in New York in 1911, Greenberg became—as it says on his plaque at the National Baseball Hall of Fame in Cooperstown, New York—"one of baseball's greatest right-handed hitters." "Hammerin' Hank" won numerous baseball awards and broke several long-standing records. Although he encountered anti-Semitism during his career, his decision not to play in a crucial game scheduled for Yom Kippur 1934 endeared him to Jews and non-Jews alike. He died in 1986.

Fanny Brice
Like many children of Jewish immigrants, Fania Borach knew she wanted to become an entertainer. Born on the Lower East Side in 1891, she began her career in the chorus line of a burlesque show. She changed her name to Brice and, using an exaggerated Yiddish accent, rose to fame in the Ziegfeld Follies of the 1920s and '30s. Her problematic marriage to gangster Nicky Arnstein attracted public attention. Brice found success in broadcast radio with her portrayal of Baby Snooks. The film *Funny Girl*, starring Barbra Streisand, was based on Brice's life. Library of Congress

of World War II, due to their high educational levels, most Jews had established themselves firmly into the middle class, with large numbers employed in "economically secure" jobs as civil servants, teachers, accountants, lawyers, and medical professionals.

Moving to Middle-Class America

By the 1930s, Yiddish culture was in decline. The Americanized children of the immigrant generation spoke English and associated with non-Jews. Their psyche was fully entrenched in American culture, with the Yiddish world of their fathers only a nostalgic memory. One of the few connections joining the generations was food, which provided a shared emotional link to their Jewish heritage. "Knishes, blintzes, bagels, bialys, herring—in all forms—had little or nothing to do with Judaism but were regional dishes enjoyed, in variation, by Jews and non-Jews in the Old Country."[10] Too often, an individual's connection to Judaism was through one's stomach rather than one's mind.

A major manifestation of acculturation between the two wars was that as economic conditions improved, immigrants born or raised in America moved out of the ghettos and into middle-class neighborhoods not far from the inner city. From the Lower East Side of New York, families sought out new homes in Brooklyn and the Bronx. In Boston, Jews moved from the North End and lower Beacon Hill to Roxbury and Dorchester. The trailblazers often found themselves unwelcome in their new communities. Building owners refused to rent to Jews, and threatening neighbors occasionally required them to leave their new homes. But the volume of Jews emerging from the ghettos was too great to be intimidated by such obstacles. They created their own insulated environment, which—although a part of their new communities—was often apart from their non-Jewish neighbors. Jews clustered together and created their own cultural and religious institutions. If fancy resorts would not welcome them, they vacationed in Jewish-operated hotels. The Catskill Mountains, within driving range of New York's Jewish suburbs, became a popular destination with their large collection of Jewish-owned resorts where Jews could feel "at home." Settlement houses across the nation, with their recreational, social, and educational offerings, were open to the general public but attracted many Jewish immigrant families and benefited from Jewish philanthropy.

Poster for Multiethnic Carnival
Settlement houses played an important role for Jewish immigrants and their families in many communities across America, providing recreational and educational facilities for young and old. This poster advertises a carnival sponsored by Pittsburgh's Kaufmann Settlement House in 1923.
Rauh Jewish Archives, Pittsburgh

In short order, away from the teeming ghettos, they began re-creating Jewish cultural and religious life, with an American touch but still within an environment that was predominantly Jewish and traditional. They built impressive synagogues, hired American-born rabbis, and began the process of commercializing the Jewish experience. The result was the growth of *Yiddishkeit*—Jewish sensibilities rooted in nostalgia, tradition, behavior, and culture rather than devout religious observance. The rise of the Jewish Federations, led by community professionals and large donors, centralized the authority of the numerous self-help and charitable organizations. Unlike the European model, community leadership in

The New Jew

The new Jew is entirely an American product. He is not only different from but the very antithesis of his forefathers who dwelt in the European ghettos. In essential respects he is more American than Jewish. He devotes his energies to American rather than Jewish causes. His mode of life in relation to Judaism is centrifugal rather than centripetal. He will not and cannot exist among the institutions created by Old World Jewry. At best he gives only lip service to these, and then usually for the sake of not offending his elders. His interests are primarily non-Jewish: he knows little, and cares less, about Jewish affairs, either in this country or abroad. (Masserman and Baker 1932, vii)

Reconstructing Judaism

Reconstructionist Judaism is based on the teachings of Rabbi Mordecai Kaplan, who viewed Judaism as a constantly evolving civilization. "The past has a vote, not a veto," Kaplan taught. As a progressive movement with Judaism, it integrates tradition and culture with modern scientific knowledge. In his *Sabbath Prayer Book*, published in 1945, Rabbi Kaplan wrote:

Jews are not a divinely chosen race ... the Torah is a human document and not one supernaturally inspired and ... modern Jews no longer look forward to the advent of a personal Messiah.

Rabbi Kaplan recorded his inner struggle with Jewish traditions in this diary excerpt from January 15, 1931:

After all the years of thinking on the problem of religion, I am still at a loss how to connect the conclusions I hold with the actual situation in which we find ourselves. I know very well what I mean by God. God to me is the process that makes for creativity, integration, love and justice. The function of prayer is to render us conscious of that process ... But how shall I relate all these ideas to the problem of Jewish religion?

By 2003, Reconstructionist Judaism had grown to include 16,000 households and 103 affiliated congregations. (Jewish Reconstructionist Federation Growth Fact Sheet)

America, which had begun in the 19th century with religious leadership, rested securely by the 20th century with lay leadership.

As has so often been the case in American Judaism, the views and needs of the lay leadership influenced changes in traditional observance. The previously simple bar mitzvah ceremony, which in an earlier age would have consisted of calling a boy to the Torah and, following that, a simple libation of kichel, herring, and wine, was transformed into an elegant social event with fully catered meals, and music. In keeping with the democratic spirit of America, the first recorded bat mitzvah can be traced back to 1922, when Rabbi Mordecai Kaplan, the founder of Reconstructionist Judaism, called his daughter Judith to the Torah on a Saturday morning.

The Looming Nazi Threat

Two disparate events of the 1930s left an indelible mark on American Jews. The first was the rise of Nazism in Germany. Writing of that period, Rabbi Wise said, "I cannot remember Jewry being so wrought up against anything happening to American Jews as the sudden reversion on the part of a great and cultured and liberty-loving people [the Germans] to practices which may be mildly characterized as medieval." The second was the Great Depression (1929–1939). The election of President Franklin D. Roosevelt and the creation of the New Deal reshaped the country's economic and social policy. American Jews embraced Roosevelt and his ideas and became stalwarts of the Democratic Party. The Socialist ideals brought over by Jewish parents transformed into the liberal politics of their children. Unlike other American groups, which turned more conservative as they got wealthier over the years, Jews have remained loyal to the Democratic Party.

To React Publicly or Not

After the German elections of 1933, which put the Nazis in power, the Jewish defense organizations in America debated about possible actions to take but

Anti-Nazi Rally
A mass demonstration, "Boycott Nazi Germany," filled Madison Square Garden in New York City on March 15, 1937. Library of Congress

could not come to a consensus. The American Jewish Congress and the Jewish War Veterans favored loud and public demonstrations, while the American Jewish Committee feared that such tactics could backfire and "kill Jews in Germany."[11] When the question of boycotting German goods arose, B'nai B'rith, the American Jewish Committee, and the American Jewish Congress feared that such action would further inflame the Nazis and lead to severe repercussions for German Jews. And in fact, leaders of the Jewish community in Germany, fearing retribution, had urged the Americans not to protest. Yet in New York and in 80 other American cities, Jews and non-Jews rallied. The American Jewish Congress, founded by Rabbi Wise, worked to focus public attention on Germany. On March 27, 1933, over 25,000 people filled Madison Square Garden while thousands more jammed the surrounding streets, as speaker after speaker rose to condemn the anti-Jewish actions in Germany. The next day's front page headline in the *New York Daily News* declared, "40,000 ROAR PROTEST AGAINST HITLER." Bernard Deutsch, president of the American Jewish Congress, spoke for all who gathered to protest Germany: "We are overwhelmed with grief as we behold a situation, which if permitted to continue, would result in the descent of a great nation from a high state of enlightenment to a position of barbaric medievalism."[12] Other mass rallies during the 1930s, including another major Madison Square Garden gathering in 1937, marshalled American Jewish opposition to the worsening condition of Jews in Germany.

Lindbergh's Isolationist Stance

Charles A. Lindbergh was an outspoken proponent of American isolationism. In this speech given on behalf of the America First Committee, just months before Pearl Harbor, he laid part of the blame for eventual American involvement in World War II on Jews.

The three most important groups who have been pressing this country toward war are the British, the Jewish and the Roosevelt administration ... It is not difficult to understand why Jewish people desire the overthrow of Nazi Germany. The persecution they suffered in Germany would be sufficient to make bitter enemies of any race.

No person with a sense of the dignity of mankind can condone the persecution of the Jewish race in Germany. But no person of honesty and vision can look on their pro-war policy here today without seeing the dangers involved in such a policy both for us and for them. Instead of agitating for war, Jews in this country should be opposing it in every way, for they will be the first to feel its consequences ... Their greatest danger to this country lies in their large ownership and influence in our motion pictures, our press, our radio and our government. (Lindbergh 1941)

While American Jewish organizations disagreed on appropriate public response to the Nazis, they agreed on the need for diplomatic efforts. Representatives of the groups met frequently with officials at the State Department to urge an American response, but these private appeals produced little in the way of direct results. Responses from members of Congress were more forthcoming. After a series of particularly bloody riots against Jews in 1935, Congressman Emmanuel Celler spoke out: "When are these brutalities to end? When will Germany cease her cowardly and diabolical attacks against a defenseless race? Surely the civilized nations cannot remain complacent while the Jews in Berlin live in constant terror of the Nazi raids."[13]

The American Jewish community was largely silent, invoking the "Sha! Sha! (Shhh! Shhh!) Syndrome": keeping out of the public limelight and not offering enemies a target for attack. For many, their religion had become a source of anxiety and discomfort. The *B'nai B'rith Magazine* described the effect in 1936: "During this election campaign just over we heard a great deal to this effect: that the Jew efface himself as much as possible from public life lest he appear too prominent and make himself a shining mark for enemies."

There was no lack of enemies. Anti-Jewish feelings in America were at a fever pitch just prior to the outbreak of World War II. "At no time in American history has anti-Semitism been as strong as it is today. At no time has that particularly smug mealy-mouthed, 'some-of-my-best-friends-are-Jews' type of anti-Semitism received such widespread public utterance on political platforms, in the houses of Congress and in the news."[14] In 1938, 50 percent of Americans said they had a low opinion of Jews.[15] It was an era of "America First" attitudes that drew to its leadership a number of influential people who, under the guise of isolationism, accused Jews of leading the United States into war. Rabbi Wise responded to the America Firsters by declaiming, "We are Americans first, last and all the time. Nothing else that we are, whether by faith or race or fate, qualifies our Americanism."[16]

Resurgence of Zionism

Meanwhile, as people grew more alarmed at the threats to Jews around the world, American Zionism began to make a strong comeback from its fragmented past. With America basically off-limits because of restrictive immigration policy, nearly half of the Jewish population of Germany had left for Palestine in the 1930s, directly bolstering the Zionist dream of a Jewish homeland. Jewish organizations that had previously opposed the movement now joined with the Zionists. In early 1935, over 1,500 delegates attended the first National Conference for Palestine, which the *London Times* referred to as "the most representative Jewish gathering which has ever assembled in the United States."[17] Harold Ickes, the secretary of the interior, told the delegates, "America has nothing but good will for the reborn Jewish nationalism," and while conceding that prejudice against Jews existed in America, he remarked that "the Jew has had in this land opportunities equal to all others." At their 1937 conference, Reform rabbis, in spite of their movement's long-standing opposition to Zionism, declared "the obligation of all Jewry to aid in [Palestine's] upbuilding as a Jewish homeland."

Abba Hillel Silver

An influential American Reform rabbi, Silver (1893–1963) was born in Lithuania and came to America as a child. He was an ardent Zionist and used his brilliant oratorical skills to promote the cause. One of the first Reform Zionists, he helped the movement change its anti-Zionist stance to one of official support in the Columbus Platform of 1937. At odds with the quiet diplomacy mode of the American Jewish Committee and Rabbi Stephen S. Wise, he mobilized public opinion on behalf of the Jewish state. In a particularly contentious meeting in the White House in January 1948, Silver grew angry and pounded on President Truman's desk. Truman's response was furious and immediate: "No one, but no one, comes into the office of the President of the United States and shouts at him, or pounds on his desk!" (Truman 1948)

One Goal, Two Philosophies

In 1935, Rabbi Wise was elected leader of the Zionist Organization of America. Wise strongly believed in the power of quiet diplomacy and relied on his friendship with President Franklin Roosevelt and the State Department to rescue the endangered Jews of Europe. He was too optimistic. The failure of quiet diplomacy led to the rise of a new leader of American Zionists, who, like Wise, was a Reform rabbi. But unlike Wise, with his belief in quiet interaction, Abba Hillel Silver urged American Jews to go public with "loud diplomacy." While Wise was willing to postpone the struggle for a Jewish state to get Jews to safety in Palestine, Silver viewed implementation of the Balfour Declaration as imperative.

Deadly Obstruction of Immigration

Despite increasingly ominous news from Europe, fear of newcomer competition for American jobs during the Depression years prevented any changes in immigration laws. This dramatically limited the options for Jews seeking to escape the growing Nazi threat in Europe. The previously complacent views of American Jews toward their government's strict quota system changed as they began realizing the plight of European Jews. Although reports of Nazi excesses against Jews appeared periodically in American newspapers, there was little editorial response until 1938. On November 9 and 10, violence against Jews broke out all over Germany in what came to be known as Kristallnacht (the Night of Broken Glass). The next day, American newspapers widely reported beatings of Jews, burnings of synagogues, and imprisonment of innocent people.

National Jewish organizations lobbied Congress with the aim of loosening the strict immigration policy, but with little success. Meanwhile, Hitler was imposing new laws on the Jews of Germany that deprived them of the most elemental rights, in addition to the Nuremberg Laws of 1935 already in place. As the situation in Germany darkened, the humanitarian Wagner-Rogers bill was introduced in Congress in 1939. While not changing the quota regulations, the bill would have allowed 20,000 Jewish children from Germany into the United States by applying that number to future years' quotas from Germany. But the bill failed to pass. To make things worse, in May 1939, as Jews desperately sought refuge from Hitler's Germany, the British bowed to Arab demands and issued a White Paper— an official policy statement—limiting Jewish immigration to Palestine and stopping it completely in 1944.

Obstructionist Immigration Policies

Excerpt from a memo written in 1940 by Assistant Secretary of State Breckinridge Long to State Department officials, describing ways to avoid granting U.S. visas to desperate European Jews:

We can delay and effectively stop for a temporary period of indefinite length the number of immigrants into the United States. We could do this by simply advising our consuls, to put every obstacle in the way and to require additional evidence and to resort to various administrative devices which would postpone and postpone and postpone the granting of the visas. However, this could only be temporary. In order to make it more definite it would have to be done by suspension of the ruled under the law by the issuance of a proclamation of emergency— which I take it we are not yet ready to proclaim. (June 26, 1940)

Even in the face of the British White Paper and new reports of Nazi atrocities, the State Department continued its strict immigration procedures, going so far as to obstruct legal visa applications. The continued obfuscation of Assistant Secretary of State Breckinridge Long raised the ire of Congressman Celler, who said, "If men of the temperament and philosophy of Long continue in control of immigration administration, we may as well take down that plaque from the Statue of Liberty and black out the 'lamp beside the golden door.'"

The organized Jewish community in the United States was by now working diligently to save European Jews, but their ability was hampered by certain realities. First, American Jews at the time did not have an important political voice. They feared being thought of as "too pushy." Even Rabbi Wise, when he expressed support for the Wagner-Rogers bill, had been nervous about taking too partisan a position lest he appear unpatriotic. Prior to Pearl Harbor, American sentiment was set against intervention in another "European war," and Jews did not want to be cast as warmongers. Second, after the United States entered the war, the entire country focused on the main business of winning the war. Jews wanted to be viewed as loyal Americans. They did not want to appear overly critical about the lack of world action on behalf of Europe's Jews while millions of young Americans, Jewish and non-Jewish, were heading overseas to fight.

The Biltmore Conference

In May 1942, American Zionists held a conference at New York's Biltmore Hotel and produced the "Biltmore Program," condemning the British White Paper as "cruel and indefensible" and calling for immediate and unrestricted Jewish immigration to Palestine. The delegates, including for the first time those from previously non-Zionist Jewish organizations, also adopted a resolution, anticipating the eventual end of the war, which called for Palestine to be declared "a Jewish Commonwealth, integrated in the structure of the new democratic world."

> ### The MacDonald White Paper, 1939
>
> Issued by the British government on May 17, 1939, the White Paper seemed to negate the intent of the Balfour Declaration of 1917 by proposing a single Palestinian state within 10 years in which the Jewish population would be relegated to minority status. At the same time it seemed to ignore the pressing immigration needs of European Jews:
>
> *For each of the next five years a quota of 10,000 Jewish immigrants will be allowed on the understanding that a shortage one year may be added to the quotas for subsequent years, within the five year period, if economic absorptive capacity permits. In addition, as a contribution towards the solution of the Jewish refugee problem, 25,000 refugees will be admitted as soon as the High Commissioner is satisfied that adequate provision for their maintenance is ensured, special consideration being given to refugee children and dependents ... After the period of five years, no further Jewish immigration will be permitted unless the Arabs of Palestine are prepared to acquiesce in it.*

Riegner Telegram Confirms "Final Solution"

On November 28, 1942, Rabbi Wise held a news conference in New York where he publicly revealed the Nazi plan to exterminate all the Jews of Europe. His information had come from Gerhardt Riegner, the Swiss representative of the World Jewish Congress, of which Wise had been president since 1936. Three months earlier, Riegner had received unimpeachable confirmation from anti-Nazi German industrialist Eduard Schulte, with impeccable sources, about Nazi plans to exterminate millions of Jews—Hitler's Final Solution for the "Jewish question" in Europe. Riegner immediately sent a telegram to Rabbi Wise through the State Department's private communications system, to which President Roosevelt had given Wise access. Rumors about death camps had surfaced earlier, but this was the first credible report to reach the Allies. Officials at the State Department thought the report unbelievable, however. The American Embassy cautioned that "the report has earmarks of war rumor inspired by fear…" Afraid of hysterical public reaction, the State Department did not pass the telegram on to Wise. But Riegner, anticipating State Department inaction, had sent a duplicate message to the World

Jewish Congress office in London, which in turn notified Wise by telegram on August 28. Wise, furious that the original message had not been forwarded to him, confronted Undersecretary of State Sumner Welles, who apologized and finally produced the telegram. Welles asked Wise not to publicize the contents of the telegram until the charges could be confirmed by independent sources. By November, the information was confirmed and Wise held the news conference. The next day, news of the mass murder of Jews received short shrift in the American press: a short piece appeared on page 10 of the *New York Times*. It seemed that no one could—or would—comprehend the scale of Hitler's murderous plans.

Text of Riegner Telegram

```
RECEIVED ALARMING REPORT THAT IN FUHRERS HEAD-
QUARTERS PLAN DISCUSSED AND UNDER CONSIDERATION
ALL JEWS IN COUNTRIES OCCUPIED OR CONTROLLED
GERMANY NUMBERING 3 ? TO 4 MILLION SHOULD AFTER
DEPORTATION AND CONCENTRATION IN EAST AT ONE
BLOW EXTERMINATED TO RESOLVE ONCE FOR ALL JEWISH
QUESTION IN EUROPE STOP ACTION REPORTED PLANNED
FOR AUTUMN METHODS UNDER DISCUSSION INCLUDING
PRUSSIC ACID STOP WE TRANSMIT INFORMATION WITH
ALL NECESSARY RESERVATION AS EXACTITUDE CANNOT
BE CONFIRMED STOP INFORMANT STATED TO HAVE CLOSE
CONNECTIONS WITH HIGHEST GERMAN AUTHORITIES AND
HIS REPORTS GENERALLY RELIABLE STOP ...
```

Even after the release of the Riegner Telegram, American newspapers were guarded in reporting news about what was happening to the Jews of Europe. The *New York Times* headlines below provide a glimpse as to how news about the ongoing Holocaust was treated.

On November 25, 1942, the following headline appeared on page 10:

HIMMLER PROGRAM KILLS POLISH JEWS;

Slaughter of 260,000 in Plan to Wipe Out Half in Country
This Year is Reported ...

On August 8, 1943, page 11 carried this headline:

2,000,000 MURDERS BY NAZIS CHARGED;

Polish Paper in London Says Jews Are Exterminated
in Treblinka Death House ...

And on November 29, 1943, page 3:

50,000 KIEV JEWS REPORTED KILLED;

Soviet Atrocity Group Hears Nazis Machine-Gunned Victims in Sept., 1941;

BODIES LATER BURNED

Prisoners of War Forced to Build Pyres Were Shot to Destroy All Evidence

Religious Services in Berlin in 1945
World War II was just one of the wars covered by photojournalist Robert Capa, who was born Endre Friedmann in Budapest in 1913 and eventually became an American citizen. Perfecting a unique photographic style, Capa was best known for the intensity of his war photographs and his skill in putting a human face on violence. He was a founder of the Magnum Agency, representing the work of the world's best photographers. He died in Vietnam in 1954 while covering the French-Indochina war.

This Capa photograph, taken in 1945, depicts the first Rosh Hashanah service held in Berlin since 1938. Photograph by Robert Capa © 2001 by Cornell Capa/Magnum Photos

Rabbi Wise and others made frequent contact with the White House. In 1942 Wise led a delegation to speak with the president about the atrocities in Poland: "We appeal to you, as head of our government, to do all in your power to make an effort to stop it." Roosevelt replied that the government was aware of the killings and then added, "We are dealing with an insane man—Hitler—and the group that surrounds him represents an example of a national psychopathic case… It is not our purpose to fight for greater rights for anyone at the expense of another group. We are for the freedom for all and equal rights for all. We consider the attack on the Jews in Germany, in Poland, as an attack upon our ideas of freedom and justice, and that is why we oppose it so vehemently." As the group left the president's office, Roosevelt told them, "We shall do all in our power to be of service to your people in this tragic moment." Unfortunately, his words never translated into direct action.

Increasing Calls for a Homeland

In 1943, Rabbis Silver and Wise, with their contrasting approaches to leadership, were appointed cochairmen of the American Zionist Emergency Committee. In a fiery speech that year, Silver told a meeting of the American Jewish Committee:

We cannot truly rescue the Jews of Europe unless we have free immigration into Palestine. We cannot have free immigration into Palestine unless our political rights are recognized there. Our political rights cannot be recognized there unless our historic connection with the country is acknowledged and our right to rebuild our national home is reaffirmed. These are inseparable links in the chain. The whole chain breaks if one of the links is missing.[18]

Henry Morgenthau Jr.

Born into a wealthy German Jewish family in New York in 1891, Morgenthau's interest in agriculture led him to become a farmer and later a publisher of an influential farm journal. He was active in Democratic party politics and was a friend of nearby neighbors Eleanor and Franklin Roosevelt. With Roosevelt's election as president, Morgenthau assumed appointed positions within the government, ultimately becoming secretary of the treasury in November 1934. As the Nazis rose to power in Germany, Morgenthau's influence increased as he developed plans to finance the war and prepare the world for postwar rebuilding. He was instrumental in convincing Roosevelt to form the War Refugee Board. Here are excerpts from his missive to the Foreign Funds Control Unit on January 13, 1944:

One of the greatest crimes in history, the slaughter of the Jewish people in Europe, is continuing unabated.

This Government has for a long time maintained that its policy is to work out programs to serve those Jews of Europe who could be saved.

I am convinced on the basis of the information which is available to me that certain officials in our State Department, which is charged with carrying out this policy, have been guilty not only of gross procrastination and willful failure to act, but even of willful attempts to prevent action from being taken to rescue Jews from Hitler.

After the war, Morgenthau took leadership roles in the United Jewish Appeal and Bonds for Israel. He died in 1967.

Silver energized Zionist public relations with limitless press releases, mass demonstrations, letter-writing campaigns, and political activism. The cause was embraced by state legislatures, labor unions, churches, and news organizations. Fueling support for a Jewish state were reports filtering out of Europe about the indiscriminate murder of Jews by advancing German forces. The quiet diplomacy espoused by Rabbi Wise seemed to garner fine words of support from American leadership, but very little action. With the European war winding down, President Roosevelt called Rabbis Wise and Silver to the White House to reassure them that "full justice will be done to those who seek a Jewish National Home, for which our Government and the American people have always had the deepest sympathy, and today more than ever, in view of the tragic plight of hundreds of thousands of homeless Jewish refugees."[19] But eloquence like this was not saving Jewish lives. Zionists adopted an active public relations campaign to pressure the U.S. government into a more proactive stance to rescue European Jews and at the same time plan for the creation of a Jewish homeland after the war. A small Zionist group led by a Palestinian Jew known as Peter Bergson (in reality Hillel Kook, nephew of Jerusalem's chief rabbi) staged successful plays, pageants, and rallies to call American attention to the plight in Europe. Bergson, frustrated with the reluctance of the mainline

Jewish organizations to openly push elected officials to take meaningful steps to save Jewish lives, organized public relations efforts to keep the plight of European Jews in the public eye.

One example was a dramatic pageant, "We Will Never Die: A Memorial to the Two Million Jewish Dead of Europe," written and produced in 1943 by such well-known theatrical personalities as Kurt Weill, Moss Hart, and Ben Hecht. Performed first in Madison Square Garden, it traveled to Washington and other cities, with famous actors including Edward G. Robinson and Paul Muni and a cast of hundreds. In the audiences were diplomats, members of Congress, and molders of public opinion, including Eleanor Roosevelt. The intense public lobbying by the Bergson Group and the private arguments by the president's secretary of the treasury, Henry Morgenthau, produced limited results. In January 1944, Roosevelt signed Executive Order 9417 establishing the War Refugee Board, whose efforts were too little and too late but did succeed in saving 200,000 Jews through its limited rescue efforts.

Reorganizing Jewish Leadership

The wall of self-created anonymity that Jews had defensively thrown around themselves began to crumble during the Holocaust. The horrors that emanated from Nazi Europe shocked American Jews into the realization that they had to actively combat hatred, discrimination, and prejudice at home. By 1945, Jews had become the most "racially liberal of all white groups." They began by strengthening their own existing defense organizations. The leaderships of the Anti-Defamation League, American Jewish Committee, and American Jewish Congress passed from the older generation of philanthropists to a younger group of professionally trained social workers and lawyers.[20]

141

The Time Had Come

When World War II ended, the horrors of the revealed Holocaust led Jews to the inescapable conclusion that it was time for a Jewish state. The Zionist movement now overshadowed other major American Jewish organizations, and its dream of establishing an independent Jewish nation seemed closer than ever to realization: "Zionism resolved the dilemma of American Jewry; it provided a home for the remnants of European Jewry without incurring an immigrant exodus to the United States."[21] After the deaths of 6,000,000 Jews, the world sympathized with the plight of desperate survivors. Hundreds of thousands, with no

An Alternative to Zionism

Not all American Jews were Zionists. A small but influential group composed mostly of Reform rabbis and successfully assimilated lay people were concerned with the effect of political Zionism on American Judaism and in 1942 had organized the American Council for Judaism. One of the founders, Rabbi Morris Lazaron, stated that Zionism only delayed Jewish integration into American life, made impossible a peaceful resolution of the Palestine question, and challenged the universalist values of prophetic Judaism (quoted in Penkower 1998, 167). While the council's agenda often found support in the White House and State Department, it did not represent the vast majority of American Jews. Twenty-five years after its founding, it largely disappeared from view.

homes to which they could return, languished in Displaced Persons camps as pressure mounted on Great Britain to lift the strict immigration rules it had imposed on Palestine. While diplomatic efforts continued, a highly organized large-scale movement began of illegal Jewish immigrants to Palestine. Jewish defense groups escalated violence against the British, while Arab attacks on Jews grew in intensity. The British, unable to control the situation, announced plans to withdraw from Palestine effective in May 1948. Attention turned to the United Nations.

American Jews and Zionist leaders mobilized yet another public relations campaign to influence governmental leaders. Since the Holocaust, American Zionists had firmly renounced the quiet diplomacy of Rabbi Stephen Wise in favor of the public activist stance of Rabbi Abba Hillel Silver, who declared, "If our rights are denied to us, we shall fight for them with whatever weapons are at our disposal."[22] Thousands of letters and telegrams from Christians as well as Jews flooded Washington. Governors of 37 states, 33 state legislatures, 54 U.S. senators, and 250 congressmen all notified the president of their support for a Jewish homeland.

Resistance from Truman

Inheriting the presidency from Roosevelt in 1945 was Harry Truman, largely unknown to the Jewish community. Truman was a stubborn personality who never hid his opinions. As American Jews grew ever more relentless in their campaign for his support, Truman grew testy on the explosive issue of Palestine. In November 1947, with the United Nations set to vote on a final partition plan that would divide Palestine into two states, one Jewish and one Arab, the decision fell on President Truman to declare the official U.S. policy. Anti-Zionist, pro-Arab officials in the State Department opposed the partition plan, fearing that U.S. support of partition would anger Arab countries who might cut off supplies of oil. Furthermore, a long tradition of ingrained anti-Semitism at the State Department precluded any objective assessment. It was clear, however, that the U.S. government would not provide any military or economic assistance. Jews would have to rely on themselves. Membership in the Zionist Organization of America rose to 500,000 by 1948, and financial contributions exceeded $200 million. The number of Jews in the United States in 1950 was approximately 5,000,000 out of a total population of 146,571,000.[23] Underground activities in the United States raised additional money for the purchase of military equipment that would be necessary for the survival of a Jewish state.

The King's Ear

For hundreds of years, as Jews fashioned lives for themselves in the Diaspora, their voices in the chambers of power belonged to well-connected *shatdlanim,* individuals who had the ear of the appropriate king, prince, or potentate. In democratic America, where Jews enjoyed only limited access to the inner circles of political power, American presidents relied on trusted Jewish political supporters for advice regarding Jewish issues. President Wilson had Louis Brandeis; President Roosevelt had a number of Jewish advisors, including Rabbi Wise; but it was unclear who spoke for Jewish interests in the Truman White House.

When a B'nai B'rith official in Washington realized that one of their members in Kansas City was actually an old friend of the president, he telephoned the friend, Eddie Jacobson, with a request. Could Jacobson speak with his friend in the White House about seeking the admission to Palestine of 100,000 desperate displaced Jews still languishing in Europe? "Harry Truman will do what's right if he knows the facts," Jacobson told his caller. "If I can help supply them, I will. But I am no Zionist, so first I need the facts from you." Fully briefed, Jacobson wrote a letter to Truman "in behalf of my people,"[24] and as the United Nation's vote

Letter from Eddie Jacobson to Harry Truman

This excerpt from Jacobson's letter to Truman demonstrates clearly the close friendship between the two men:

The future of one and one-half million Jews in Europe depends on what happens at the present meeting of the United Nations ... I think I am one of few who actually knows and realizes what terrible heavy burdens you are carrying on your shoulders during these hectic days. I should, therefore, be the last man to add to them: but I feel you will forgive me for doing so, because tens of thousands of lives depend on words from your mouth and heart. Harry, my people need help and I am appealing to you to help them. (October 3, 1947)

on partition approached he made several private visits to the White House. On November 29, 1947, the United Nations General Assembly voted 33 for, 13 against, and 10 abstaining for the partition of Palestine into two states. "It was because the White House was for it that it went through," one insider said. Eddie Jacobson later recounted that Truman said, "he [Truman] and he alone was responsible for swinging the votes of several delegations." In his diary, Jacobson wrote two words for November 29: "Mission accomplished."

The battle was won, but as Truman himself remarked, "The vote in the United Nations is only the beginning." As British troops were preparing to leave Palestine, the U.S. ambassador to the United Nations declared that once the British left, the partition plan would crumble and the combined Arab armies of five neighboring countries would "drive the Jews into the sea." The Jews of Palestine prepared for the consequences, but went ahead with plans to proclaim an independent Jewish state the moment the British left on May 15, 1948.

Without international recognition, that state could not survive. While the president fought his own diplomats, pressure on him from American supporters of a Jewish state increased his own stubbornness. He refused to meet with Jewish leaders or hear out anyone on the Palestine issue. "I do not think that I ever had so much pressure and propaganda at the White House as I had in this instance," Truman later noted. In a personal letter to a friend, he wrote:

The main difficulty with our friends, the Jews in this country, is that they are very emotional ... the President of the United State has to be very careful not to be emotional or to forget that he is working for one hundred and forty-five million people primarily and for peace in the world as his next objective.[25]

143

Supporters of a Jewish state felt that all might be lost unless Chaim Weizmann could meet with the president, but no one could convince Truman to see him. Once again, Eddie Jacobson received a call from Washington, this time from Frank Goldman, the national president of B'nai B'rith. Jacobson wrote another letter to his friend in the White House, urging Truman to meet with Weizmann. When Truman refused, Jacobson packed a suitcase and headed for Washington.

An Argument Between Friends

On arriving at the White House on March 12, 1948, Jacobson entered the president's office, as he often did, without an appointment. After some casual and

Old Friends Truman and Jacobson

The friendship of Eddie Jacobson and Harry Truman is credited by some with the United State's quick recognition of the new State of Israel in 1948. In this photograph, both men are leaving a Kansas City, Missouri, synagogue after the former president was presented with a certificate signifying trees planted in his honor in Israel. Truman Presidential Library [75-497]

friendly banter, Jacobson brought up the subject of Palestine. Truman's demeanor immediately changed. His words were few, his manner angry. "He never talked to me in this manner or in any way even approaching it," Jacobson later recounted. Jacobson reminded Truman "of his [Truman's] feelings for Dr. Weizmann." Jacobson raised one argument after another but to no avail. Truman spoke only about the "disrespectful and mean" way certain Jews had treated him in their zeal for a Jewish state. Jacobson thought sadly to himself that his "dear friend, the President of the United States, was at that moment as close to being an anti-Semite as a man could possibly be."[26]

With nothing more to add, Jacobson noticed a bronze statue of Andrew Jackson against the wall. "Harry," Jacobson said, "all your life you had a hero. You are probably the best read man in America on the life of Andrew Jackson ... Well, Harry, I too have a hero, a man I never met, but who is, I think, the greatest Jew who ever lived ... he is a sick man, almost broken in health, but he traveled thousands and thousands of miles just to see you and plead the cause of my people. Now you refuse to see him because you were insulted by some of our American Jewish leaders. It doesn't sound like you, Harry... I wouldn't be here if I didn't know that if you will see him, you will be properly and accurately informed on the situation as it exists in Palestine, and yet you refuse to see him." The room was silent.

Through tear-filled eyes, Jacobson noticed that the president was drumming on his desk with his fingers. The president then turned his swivel chair toward the window and stared out into the rose garden for what seemed like an eternity to Jacobson. Suddenly the president turned his chair around, looked directly at his old friend, and blurted, "You win, you bald-headed son of a bitch. I will see him. ..."[27]

One Last Cliff-Hanger

For days, no one knew what the response of the United States would be. At the United Nations the American ambassador, without White House approval, recommended abandoning the partition plan. Truman was livid; Jacobson and American Jewish leaders were confused. But finally, 11 minutes after David Ben Gurion proclaimed the birth of the Jewish state on May 14, the United States officially recognized the State of Israel.

The government has been informed that a Jewish state has been proclaimed in Palestine, and recognition has been requested by the provisional government thereof. The United States recognizes the provisional government as the de facto authority of the new State of Israel.

Later that evening, President Truman received a telegram from Eddie Jacobson. "Thanks," the message read, "and God bless you."

145

1914–1948
A TIMELINE

1914
Outbreak of World War I; opening of Grossinger's resort in Catskill Mountains of New York; founding of Joint Distribution Committee; socialist Meyer London elected to U.S. House of Representatives

1915
Lynching of Leo Frank in Georgia; founding of Joint Distribution Committee to aid impoverished Jews abroad

1916
Louis Brandeis is first Jew appointed to United States Supreme Court

1917
United States enters World War I; Balfour Declaration marks first international recognition for Zionist movement; founding of National Jewish Welfare Board; The Jewish Publication Society's English translation of the Jewish Bible

1918
Founding of American Jewish Congress

1920
Henry Ford launches *Dearborn Independent*

1921
Hebrew Teachers College founded in Boston

1922
Judith Kaplan is first bat mitzvah

1926
Synagogue Council of America founded, bringing together Orthodox, Conservative, and Reform rabbis

1927
The Jazz Singer is first "talkie" film; Charles Levine flies across Atlantic, beating Charles Lindbergh's distance record

1929
Stock market crashes; Great Depression begins; Joel Spingarn elected president of National Association for the Advancement of Colored People (NAACP)

1933
Hitler comes to power in Germany

1937
Columbus Platform adopted by Reform movement recognizes Palestine as Jewish homeland

1939
Outbreak of World War II and beginning of Holocaust

1941
The United States enters World War II

1942
Formation of anti-Zionist American Council for Judaism; Riegner telegram confirms Hitler's plan for "Final Solution"

1943
Bergson Group marshals 400 Orthodox rabbis to Washington to focus attention on Holocaust

1948–present
Into the Mainstream

6

In the aftermath of World War II, as the new State of Israel began its struggle to survive, Jews in America were discarding the remaining vestiges of shtetl imagery to recreate themselves religiously, culturally, and socio-economically. The rich Yiddish culture of the first generation was reduced to nostalgic memory as their children and grandchildren assimilated American cultural and social values into their Jewish lives. In the next generation, their children took a more dramatic route to assimilation. A breakdown in overt anti-Semitism, hastened by events of the Holocaust and the overall positive interaction of Jewish and non-Jewish soldiers, made it easier for Jews to abandon the cities of their parents and grandparents. In a significant shift away from the inner cities after World War II, the descendants of ghetto dwellers embraced the fresh air of suburbia and set out to establish their own vision of Jewish life, with memories of a Yiddish-inflected world fresh in their minds.

Saving Yiddish

In 1980, 23-year-old graduate student Aaron Lansky embarked on a seemingly impossible mission: to save Yiddish books from oblivion. As the number of grandparents who spoke and read Yiddish grew smaller, their children and grandchildren couldn't read or understand the Yiddish books left behind and saw no purpose in keeping them. Lansky created an organization with like-minded individuals to collect (or as he put it, to "rescue") the books. Since its inception, the National Yiddish Book Center (now located in Amherst, Massachusetts) has collected over 1.5 million Yiddish books. Today, with a small but growing number of Yiddish language courses in colleges, these books are available to scholars and libraries and, with financial backing from Steven Spielberg, are being digitized to assure the continuation of Yiddish literature.

Patricia Williams/National Yiddish Book Center

Into Suburbia

From downtown Baltimore and Pittsburgh to Pikesville and Squirrel Hill and from Roxbury and Brooklyn to Newton and Long Island, the move to "the country" quickly became a migration. Later, Jews also spread geographically beyond the urban/suburban centers of the East Coast to establish footholds in Sunbelt communities in California, Florida, and Arizona. Returning soldiers, starting up their own families, took advantage of generous government-assisted mortgages to reestablish themselves in the housing subdivisions sprouting on the peripheries of major urban centers. They were drawn to the suburbs by the promise of safe streets, better schools, and the image of an idealized lifestyle for the American family. For young Jewish families, migrating to suburbia also meant being uprooted from the familiar womb of the inner cities where they were surrounded by Jewish culture. Even though most young Jews were not overly religious, living in a concentrated urban environment provided Jewish identity by osmosis. Wherever one turned there were Yiddish conversations, synagogues, kosher restaurants, and Jewish neighbors. No one needed to belong to a synagogue or check a calendar to know it was Shabbat or Yom Kippur or Passover.

The move from urban to suburban living heightened the role of the synagogue in the lives of American Jews. In the brand-new suburbs, with no traditions in place, young families faced the challenge of reinventing their Jewish selves. They wanted to live side by side with their non-Jewish neighbors but still maintain connections to Jewish life. In the suburbs where they were no longer a majority, one's Polish, Russian, or Lithuanian background mattered little. Jewish self-identity began to evolve from newly organized synagogues that superseded the old immigrant identities. In short, joining a temple defined one's Judaism. Reform and Conservative temples flourished: many people flocked to them not only to fulfill religious needs, but also to provide for their social needs.

Isaac Bashevis Singer

Winner of the Nobel Prize for Literature in 1978, Isaac Bashevis Singer garnered a long-overdue recognition for Yiddish literature. Born in Poland in 1914, he received a religious education. His interest in writing was nurtured early in life, and he began writing seriously in the 1920s. He emigrated to the United States in 1935 and began writing for the Yiddish-language *Jewish Daily Forward*, which printed many of his stories and books in serial form. The English translation of *The Family Moskat* and other novels resulted in fame beyond the Jewish world. Singer died in 1991. Library of Congress (cph3c02541)

Restructuring Jewish Connections

Suburban Jews quickly established other local institutions, such as B'nai B'rith lodges, Hadassah chapters, and scout troops. None was more important than the religious school, which parents hoped would instill Jewish values and tradition in children who were becoming even more assimilated than their parents. The month of December and its siren song of Christmas was too great a lure to ignore. Enter an invigorated version of the minor Jewish holiday of Hanukkah, which in Europe had been marked in low-key fashion and now was elevated to popular status, eclipsing all other Jewish holidays in commercial and psychological appeal. Suburban life also provided an opportunity for women, most of whom in the 1950s did not work outside the home, to participate creatively in Jewish affairs through volunteer organizations. Sisterhood, Federation, and specific groups such as the National Council of Jewish Women; Women's American ORT, which supported a global network of schools and training institutions; and Pioneer

Women (today's Na'amat) offered vehicles for talented women to meet one another while actively contributing to Jewish life nationally and in their own communities.

Strengthening the Role of Jewish Federations

The Federation movement's role grew and evolved as it assumed the responsibility of being the "address" for local communities, carrying on a long-standing tradition of lay leadership that embodied the American principle of separation of church and state. Whether known as The Associated in Baltimore, United Jewish Federation in Pittsburgh, or Combined Jewish Philanthropies in Boston, the local federation evolved into more than just a fund-raising organization. It became the major policy-setting umbrella under which other community groups gathered. No longer limited to the largest Jewish population centers, federations sprang up wherever Jews were, whether in Sarasota (1959), Orange County (1964), or Las Vegas (1973). Local federations, in turn, were loosely connected through the national organization, United Jewish Communities.

Jews on the Move

A significant geographic shift has occurred in the past few decades among American Jews. In 1960, according to data in the *American Jewish Year Book*, 67 percent of American Jews lived in the Northeast, 14 percent in the Midwest, 9 percent in the South, and 11 percent in the West. By 2000–2001, according to the *National Jewish Population Survey* (NJPS), the percentage of Jews in the Northeast had declined to 43 percent, while the percentage in the Midwest had dropped slightly to 12 percent. In contrast, the percentage of Jews living in the South and West had each increased to 22 percent. Additional data from NJPS 2000–2001 indicate regional population movements by showing that two-thirds of all Jews living in the South and nearly half of all Jews residing in the West were born in either the Northeast or Midwest (*Report Series on the National Jewish Population Survey 2000/01*, October 2004, 7).

Organizing to Serve

In 1900, representatives from 40 cities met to organize the National Conference of Jewish Charities, a forerunner of today's United Jewish Communities, the umbrella organization of American Jewish federations. President Max Senior of Cincinnati stated, "Through the length and breadth of the land the conviction has spread that better methods of administering charity must prevail; that above all else the manhood of the poor must be recognized, and every effort made not break down character. Open-handed but indiscriminate alms-giving and a cordial but unthinking welcome to the stranger within your gates have ceased to be the be-all and end-all of charity" (Senior 2000).

Growth of Conservative Judaism

In the 20 years after World War II, the number of Conservative congregations grew by almost 450, more than Reform and Orthodox congregations combined. The Conservative movement had won by default. The children and grandchildren of East European immigrants saw Reform as too far removed from familiar religious traditions, while the Orthodoxy of their parents seemed arcane and did not fit into their assimilationist worldview. Conservative Judaism, which followed traditionalist thought, interpreted *halakhah* according to the needs of a changing world. With Jews in larger numbers living in the sprawling suburbs, the Conservative movement

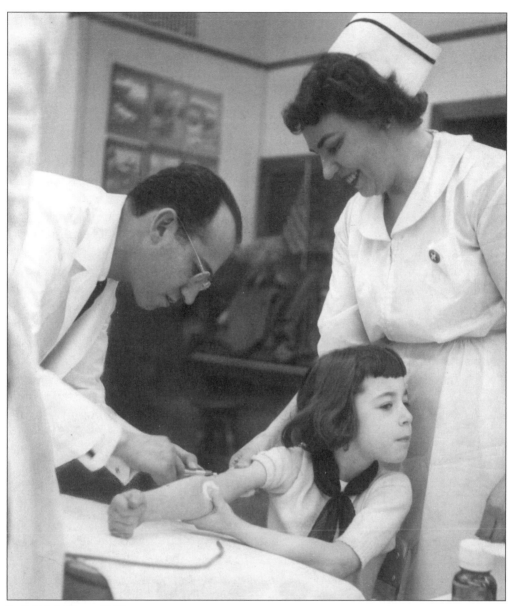

151

Dr. Salk Injecting a Child

In the 1950s, the polio epidemic was striking fear into parents across the country. When Dr. Jonas Salk's research resulted in an effective polio vaccine in 1955, he was hailed as an international hero. Salk, a child of Russian Jewish immigrants, was born in Harlem in 1914. The first of his family to attend college and medical school, he received his MD degree in 1939, and his interest in microbiology led him to the University of Michigan to work on developing flu virus vaccines. In 1947 he moved to the University of Pittsburgh, where his work soon drew attention from the National Foundation for Infantile Paralysis, which largely funded his development of a vaccine to combat polio.

Salk never patented his discovery, preferring to make it as widely available as possible. By the end of 1955, over 7 million children had been inoculated with the vaccine, marking the beginning of the end to the polio threat to children. To continue his vaccine research, he founded the Salk Institute for Biological Studies in La Jolla, California, in 1963, and hired renowned American Jewish architect Louis Kahn to create its spare, exquisite design. In 1977, Salk received the Presidential Medal of Freedom. He died in 1995, working on a vaccine against AIDS.

National Archives

Sandy Koufax

Sanford "Sandy" Koufax was born in Brooklyn in 1935 and grew to fame as a baseball player. The best-known pitcher in the National League in the early 1960s, his earn/run average led the entire league. For American Jews, he will always be remembered for choosing not to pitch on the opening day of the 1965 World Series because it coincided with Yom Kippur. He was a recipient of the Cy Young Award and was named to the Baseball Hall of Fame in 1972.

ruled in 1950 that it was permissible to use an automobile to drive to Shabbat services. It was better, the rabbis reasoned, that Jews ride to synagogue than not attend at all. Further liberalization allowed for limited uses of electricity—previously forbidden—and a greater involvement of women in ritual, beginning with mixed seating of men and women in religious services. Ramah summer camps provided a way to provide informal education and Jewish immersion to the children of Conservative parents. But members of Conservative temples did a certain amount of liberalizing on their own. Although they chose to affiliate with the Conservative branch of Judaism, many ignored the norms of kashrut and ritual practice ordained by their own movement. "By far, the most common expression of Jewishness in suburbia was membership in a synagogue."[1] The synagogue provided for social and communal needs of middle-class suburbanites, even eclipsing the obvious religious function for which it was ostensibly created. Synagogue attendance, with the exception of the High Holidays, revolved around the celebration of life-cycle events, especially bar and bat mitzvah observances.

Changing Religious Directions

Even before World War II, both the Reform and Orthodox communities had also begun to evolve in response to internal pressures. Reform congregations began a shift to the right and the inclusion of rituals and ceremonies discarded in the 19th century. In 1937, the movement had met in Columbus, Ohio, and superseded the Pittsburgh Platform of 1885 with the Columbus Platform, "The Guiding Principles of Reform Judaism." More moderating in tone than the Pittsburgh Platform, the changes called for all Jews to assist in rebuilding Palestine as the Jewish homeland and to increase the use of Hebrew language in prayer. Previously discarded symbols and ceremonies of Sabbath and holiday observance were reemphasized. *Kippot* (skullcaps) and *tallitot* (prayer shawls) became more visible at services. In 1999, a second Pittsburgh Platform emerged, which moved Reform Judaism toward increased observance while promoting Shabbat observance and the study of Hebrew and Torah. Unlike the 1885 Platform, it strongly supported the State of Israel.

Orthodoxy Takes a Right Turn

Orthodoxy also turned to its right, with a more stringent observance of rules and behavior. This was largely in response to the arrival in the United States of European rabbis just before and after the Holocaust, heads of traditional Hasidic congregations who encouraged stricter adherence to religious observance. They brought to America a tradition of delegitimizing more liberal branches of

Judaism by avoiding any interaction with them. Once established in America, they opened their own day schools and yeshivot. Although the number of Orthodox Jews in the United States showed no great rise (comprising about 7 to 9 percent of the Jewish population by the year 2000), their shift to the right marginalized modern Orthodox Jews, who were equally comfortable as observant Jews and as active participants in the secular world that surrounded them. In some instances, following the example set by more zealous teachers, modern Orthodox children became even more observant than their parents.

From the other end of the religious spectrum, disaffected young Jews from Reform and Conservative homes began turning to the Orthodox and Hasidic worlds. These *baalei teshuvah*, penitent returnees similar to born-again Christians, viewed the "Torah True" values of the Orthodox as more authentic and personally meaningful than the liberal, assimilationist Judaism of their parents. The new adherents joined other Orthodox Jews in creating an increasingly inward-looking society, with its own schools and communities and defined behavior.

Chaim Potok
With his first novel, *The Chosen* (1967), Chaim Potok, born in 1929, opened the heretofore little-known world of American Hasidism to the larger world. More important, his work drew movingly on his own experiences to describe personal conflicts with religious identity. Other novels included *The Promise* (1969), *My Name is Asher Lev* (1972), and *Davita's Harp* (1985). For many years he served as editor-in-chief of The Jewish Publication Society. He died in 2002.

A major Hasidic group that defied the increasing insularity of other traditional Jews was the Chabad Lubavitch movement, known for its missionary outreach work with other Jews. Reconstituted in America after the Holocaust, the seventh Lubavitcher Rebbe, Menachem Mendel Schneerson, embarked on a campaign to reach disaffected and unconnected Jews through education and social action. Today, Chabad centers are scattered over the globe, staffed by 4,000 emissary families. The movement makes up with its fervor and highly public image for its small percentage of American Jewish adherents.

Reconstructionist Judaism, with roots in the Conservative movement, became a distinct ideology in 1934 with the publication of Rabbi Mordecai Kaplan's book, *Judaism as a Civilization: Toward a Reconstruction of American Jewish Life.* Unlike Orthodox and Conservative Jews, Reconstructionists do not accept *halakhah*, traditional Jewish law, as binding but believe it is open to contemporary interpretations. And unlike Reform, they emphasize the importance of religious community. Until

1961, Reconstructionists required members to also belong to another movement. In 1967, Reconstructionist Jews opened their own rabbinical seminary. By 2000, according to the National Jewish Population Survey, there were approximately 180,000 members, accounting for 3 percent of all Jews who identified with a specific religious group.

As Judaism was changing from within, relations with Christians, in particular the Catholic Church, improved. In 2000, a group of 200 rabbis and Jewish scholars issued a national statement on Christians called *Dabru Emet* (Speak the Truth). Although dissenters argued that the statement blurred religious distinctions, *Dabru Emet* mirrored the release of *Nostra Aetate* by the Catholic Church. Here is the first paragraph of *Dabru Emet*:

In recent years, there has been a dramatic and unprecedented shift in Jewish and Christian relations. Throughout the nearly two millennia of Jewish exile, Christians have tended to characterize Judaism as a failed religion or, at best, a religion that prepared the way for, and is completed in, Christianity. In the decades since the Holocaust, however, Christianity has changed dramatically. An increasing number of official Church bodies, both Roman Catholic and Protestant, have made public statements of their remorse about Christian mistreatment of Jews and Judaism. These statements have declared, furthermore, that Christian teaching and preaching can and must be reformed so that they acknowledge God's enduring covenant with the Jewish people and celebrate the contribution of Judaism to world civilization and to Christian faith itself.

Menachem Mendel Schneerson

The leader of the worldwide Chabad Lubavitch movement, Menachem Mendel Schneerson, upon the death of his father-in-law in 1950, became the seventh rebbe of the Lubavitch Hasidic movement. Hasidim were nearly decimated by the Nazis during World War II. Of those who immigrated to the United States, perhaps no group rebuilt itself as successfully as the Lubavitchers under Schneerson's leadership. In his youth, Schneerson had studied at universities in Berlin and Paris and had developed a worldview not typical of other Hasidic leaders. He reached out to secular and unaffiliated Jews and spread the Lubavitch message by establishing Chabad centers in communities large and small, not only in the United States, but also around the world. The rebbe, who guided the Chabad Lubavitch movement from 1950 until he died in 1994, is credited with reinvigorating it. After his death, some followers proclaimed him the Messiah, thereby creating dissension within the movement. A successor to lead the Lubavitch movement has not been chosen.
Michelle Studio/Chabad.org

Equality for All

Even as suburban life was luring Americans away from large cities in increasing numbers, many Jews were active participants in the Civil Rights movement, working to end discrimination not only for African Americans, but also for themselves. The fight against racial segregation in the United States peaked in the 1950s. National Jewish organizations were highly visible in the courts and on the streets. Working with the National Association for the Advancement of Colored People (NAACP)—led consecutively from 1930 to 1966 by two Jewish brothers, Joel and Arthur Spingarn, who each took a stint as president—and other African American civil rights groups, lawyers for the American Jewish Committee, the Anti-Defamation League, and the American Jewish Congress won landmark court cases.

A New Church View

On October 28, 1965, the Second Vatican Council issued a historic proclamation, *Nostra Aetate*, which was confirmed on December 8 by Pope Paul VI. After 2000 years of Church-inspired hatred, bigotry, and persecution of Jews, the document "reminds us of the bond with which the people of the New Testament are spiritually tied to the descendants of Abraham." In a succinct but forceful document, the Council repudiated two points that had been the roots of persecution: the accusation that Jews were collectively and forever responsible for the death of Christ, and anti-Semitism:

Furthermore, in her rejection of every persecution against any man, the Church, mindful of the patrimony she shares with the Jews and moved not by political reasons but by the Gospel's spiritual love, decries hatred, persecutions, displays of anti-Semitism, directed against Jews at any time and by anyone.

Mordecai Kaplan

Born in 1881, Kaplan arrived in the United States as a child to join his father, an Orthodox rabbi in New York who had emigrated from Lithuania a year earlier. Mordecai Kaplan attended the Jewish Theological Seminary and earned a bachelor's degree in 1900 from City College of New York. He attended graduate school at Columbia University, where his thinking developed on his idea of Judaism as an amalgam of religions, ethnicity, and culture. "I believe that Judaism need not and must not be afraid to meet and absorb all that is good in modern culture," he wrote in 1904. He began teaching at the Jewish Theological Seminary in 1909, developing his ideas about American Judaism during his 50-year tenure there. His thinking was cogently revealed in his classic book, *Judaism as a Civilization* (1934), which led to the development of the Reconstructionist movement. His view of the synagogue as not only a place of prayer, but also the center of Jewish cultural and ethnic life, resonated strongly enough even with non-Reconstructionist American Jews that many incorporated Kaplan's teachings within their own congregations. Kaplan died in 1983. Courtesy of the Reconstructionist Rabbinical College

Brown v. Board of Education

On May 17, 1954, the U.S. Supreme Court issued a unanimous decision in the historic *Brown v. Board of Education* case, declaring as unconstitutional the "separate but equal" practice that had effectively limited African Americans to second-class status in American life. The Court urged that integration be implemented throughout the country "with all deliberate speed." The Anti-Defamation League and the American Jewish Committee had long been involved in the legal process of eliminating discrimination. With the *Brown* decision, religious groups also got involved. The Reform Union of American Hebrew Congregations issued a statement exhorting all members to use "their influence to secure acceptance and implementation of the desegregation decisions in every community in our land." Conservative rabbis meeting in convention that year stated that the "unanimity of their act and its courage will leave its indelible stamp not only on our country but on the entire world."[2]

The Spingarn Brothers

The Spingarn brothers, both civil rights activists, were early leaders of the National Association for the Advancement of Colored People (NAACP). Joel, a literary critic and scholar who was born in 1875, became president of the NAACP in 1930. Upon his death in 1939, he was succeeded by Arthur (born in 1878), who served until 1966. Arthur was an outstanding lawyer whose legal work on seminal civil rights cases led to the Brown v. Board of Education decision of 1954. He died in 1971. Each year, the NAACP honors the brothers with the awarding of the Spingarn Medal to an outstanding African American.

Reaction from the South was immediate. Hate groups such as the Ku Klux Klan and newly spawned White Citizens' Councils went into action. Bigots of every stripe surfaced to foment hatred against blacks. Jews, a vulnerable minority comprising less than 1 percent of the population in the South and visible as Main Street merchants or professionals, were also targeted. As during the Civil War era, most southern Jews tended to identify publicly with the views of their white, non-Jewish neighbors. Whatever inner feelings on segregation they may have had, they wanted nothing more than to blend into the background and not call attention to themselves. But a revival of anti-Jewish sentiment among hard-core segregationists made it difficult for Jews to remain anonymous in the hate-filled atmosphere.

Rabbis in the North and South used their influence to strengthen convergent support of civil rights. A year after *Brown v. Board of Education,* the fight for civil rights took a dramatic step out of the courtroom and into the streets. Nonviolent tactics, symbolized by Rosa Parks and the Reverend Martin Luther King Jr., included marches; testing of desegregation laws on buses, trains, and planes by Freedom Riders; and sit-ins, pray-ins, and even swim-ins. Many young Jews actively participated in these activities. Prominent among the large number of Jewish activists who shared Dr. King's vision was Rabbi Abraham Joshua Heschel of the Jewish Theological Seminary, who marched alongside King in the South.

Martin Luther King Jr. with Rabbi Eisendrath
During America's civil rights struggles of the 1950s and '60s, many Jews were active participants in public demonstrations and marches. Here, Rabbi Maurice Eisendrath of the Union of American Hebrew Congregations bears witness to racial equality while holding a Torah in the presence of Rev. Martin Luther King Jr. American Jewish Archives

Segregationists responded to the nonviolent approach with bombings, beatings, and killings. The 1964 murders of three young civil rights workers in Mississippi—two Jewish and one African American—sickened the country.[3] President Lyndon Johnson signed into law the Civil Rights Act of 1964, banning discrimination in places of public accommodations and empowering the federal government to actively defend the rights of all citizens. A year later, the Voting Rights Act of 1965 provided all Americans with easy access to the ballot box, without recourse to the arcane tests and requirements previously used to intimidate blacks and prevent them from exercising their right to vote. In 1968, the Fair Housing Act eliminated yet one more stumbling block to equality.

Powerful Foreign Influences

On the home front following World War II, issues such as the migration to the suburbs and the Civil Rights movement were changing the experience of Jews in America and even the face of American Judaism. But it was three foreign issues that largely shaped the self-identity of American Jews in the second half of the 20th century: Israel, Soviet Jewry, and the memory of the Holocaust. Together, these concerns became "substitute religions" that American Jews used to define themselves.[4] The causes also provided a positive common ground for individuals from the various religious streams of Judaism.

Fighting for Israel

Danger surrounded the new State of Israel from the first moments of its founding in 1948, as armies from five Arab nations and supporting groups prepared to attack. The chances of Israel's survival were less than promising. In the United States, Israeli operatives used innovative, if sometimes illegal, methods to obtain American arms and funding. Help came from unlikely sources, including organized crime and organized labor. And when the dust cleared following Israel's War of Independence, the fledgling Jewish state was in control of 25 percent more land than originally specified in the United Nations partition plan.

The vast majority of American Jews were committed to the survival of the new Jewish state. They drew the line, however, at "making aliyah," or returning to their ancient homeland. They may not have emigrated to Israel, but in economic and political ways, their support was invaluable. Within a decade of Israel's founding, there were no less than 18 major American Jewish organizations dedicated to Israel's support. To coordinate activities and avoid duplication of efforts, three "umbrella" organizations were created: the American Zionist Council, the National Community Relations Advisory Council, and the Conference of Presidents of Major American Jewish Organizations. In effect, they created a politically powerful network to advocate for Israel in Washington. The fact that American Jews were concentrated in major population areas such as New York, Baltimore, Boston, Chicago, and Los Angeles, and that they tended to vote in greater proportion than most other citizens, contributed to the myth of an all-powerful "Jewish vote." In actuality, Jews comprised less than 3 percent of the American population, but politicians decided they could not ignore Jewish concern for Israel. Fund-raising for Israel became a primary concern of the American Jewish community. Between 1946 and 1962, United Jewish Appeal (UJA) raised more than $1 billion. Israel Bonds were established in 1951, and since then more than $10 billion worth has been sold.

Abraham Joshua Heschel

Dr. Heschel was the Jewish conscience of the American Civil Rights movement. Born in Warsaw in 1907 into a family of Hasidic scholars, he was ordained before moving to Berlin, where he received his Ph.D. from the University of Berlin. At the beginning of World War II he escaped to England and made his way to the United States, where he became an instructor at Hebrew Union College in Cincinnati. Unhappy at the central institution of Reform Judaism, he was hired in 1943 by the Conservative movement's Jewish Theological Seminary in New York and remained there for the rest of his life. His writings, including *God in Search of Man* (1955), *Between God and Man* (1959), and *Who is Man* (1965), made him highly visible in religious circles. Many thought him one of the most important Jewish thinkers of the 20th century. To Heschel, fighting for the rights of others was simply an extension of his religious obligations. He died in 1972.

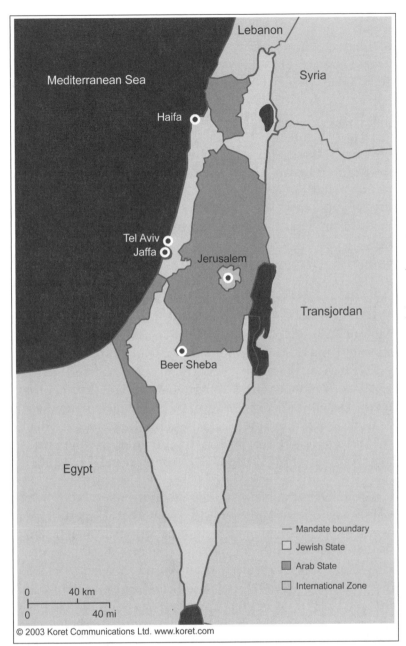

1947 UN Partition Plan
On November 27, 1947, the General Assembly of the United Nations accepted a resolution that partitioned the Land of Israel into two states, a Jewish state and an Arab state, with Jerusalem to be under international supervision.
www.israelinsider.com

159

Despite constant military and political threats to Israel's very existence, the world seemed largely indifferent to the new country's problems. American Jews were particularly frustrated by the American government's lack of understanding of the dangers Israel faced from its neighbors. The Eisenhower administration did not initially grasp the deep feelings most American Jews held for Israel. The views of the president and his advisers were colored by their close ties with supporters of the anti-Zionist American Council for Judaism. In addition, the fight against communism and America's dependence on oil tilted American foreign policy in favor of Arab countries, as the Cold War escalated between the United States and the Soviet Union. American Jews protested, but to little avail.

The Suez War

Ongoing skirmishes with Arabs escalated into an all-out war in 1956. Egypt, whose king had been overthrown by a revolutionary coup in 1952, was led by the charismatic Colonel Gamel Abdel Nasser, a Soviet ally. Nasser adopted a hard-line attitude toward Israel, threatening its extinction. By the end of March 1956, Egypt had massed troops and equipment along its border with Israel and closed the Gulf of Aqaba and the port of Eilat to Israeli shipping. In a demonstration of nationalistic independence, Nasser also seized the Suez Canal and closed it to Israeli traffic, thereby aligning Britain and France with Israel in a secret plan to retake the canal and reopen it to Israeli shipping. On October 29, Israel surprised the world by invading Egyptian-held Sinai and Gaza. In 100 hours, Israel totally defeated the Egyptian army in Sinai and reached the banks of the Suez Canal.

In Washington, President Eisenhower was livid and issued a tough warning to Israel to withdraw immediately. He threatened not only to suspend government economic aid to Israel, but also to restrict all private funds raised through the sale of Israel Bonds and contributions to the United Jewish Appeal. Israel was reluctant to withdraw without assurances for its safety from threats and attacks. Supporters of Israel in the United States responded with rallies and telegrams to Congress. The American Jewish community was united as never before in a no-holds-barred push for Israel's support. American sympathy, which had originally supported the president, shifted within a few days in favor of Israel, as did the attitude toward Israel in Congress and the press. Throughout the crisis, the "shared attitudes of Jewish identification and support for Israel bound together virtually all American Jewish organizations into a potentially strong pressure group."[5]

Israel ultimately withdrew from the Sinai under an agreement whereby the United States formally issued a commitment to Israel that United Nations peacekeeping troops would be stationed in Gaza and the Sharm-al-Sheikh area to guarantee Israel's security. The war united the American Jewish community in political action. Perhaps remembering the Holocaust years, American Jews had become more assertive. With the White House largely insensitive to their cause, American Jews found members of Congress more receptive. National Jewish organizations took activist positions on U.S. policy toward the Middle East and encouraged their members to contact their elected representatives with their views. When Congress approved the Eisenhower Doctrine in March 1957 to strengthen friendly governments in the Middle East, intense Jewish lobbying resulted in an amendment that guaranteed that the United States would come to Israel's aid if the Jewish state were attacked.

The 1956 war did raise the consciousness of the U.S. government regarding Israel's security. But it was not until John F. Kennedy became president in 1961 that relations between the two countries materially improved. Kennedy had received support during his political career from Jews who were heavily committed to Israel. Several months after the election, Kennedy pulled Israeli prime minister David Ben Gurion aside at the United Nations for a quiet talk. "You know," Kennedy said, "I was elected by the Jews of New York. I will do something for you."[6]

President Dwight Eisenhower Greets Prime Minister Ben Gurion
The warmth portrayed in this photograph, taken at the White House in March 1960, does not accurately reflect relations between Eisenhower's administration and that of Israel. On the eve of the 1956 Suez War, President Dwight Eisenhower had sent a letter to Israeli Prime Minister concerning the mobilization of Israeli troops in response to Egyptian forces massed on Israel's border:

Dear Mr. Ben Gurion:

Yesterday I forwarded to you a personal message expressing my grave concern regarding reports of mobilization in Israel and renewing my previous plea, which had been transmitted by the Secretary of State, that no forcible initiative be taken by Israel which would endanger peace in the Middle East.

This morning I have received additional reports which indicate that mobilization of Israel's armed forces is continuing and has become almost complete ...

Again, Mr. Prime Minister, I feel compelled to emphasize the dangers inherent in the present situation and urge your government to do nothing which would endanger the peace. (Eisenhower, October 28, 1956)

Even though U.S.-Israeli relations had improved following the Suez War, tension remained high between the two leaders in 1960 as Ben Gurion requested new Hawk missiles to defend against increasing Arab threats. Eisenhower did not want to escalate tensions by providing advanced technology to Israel. Eisenhower Presidential Library

Kennedy acted on Israel's requests for modern arms with which to counteract the growing Arab arsenal, becoming the first American president to treat Israel as an ally. When the United States agreed to provide Israel with Hawk missiles, it was with the provision that Israel pay in advance. "We can't," an Israeli official said. "We don't pay cash for anything. We buy everything on credit." Further investigation revealed that the United States had previously arranged to sell arms to Australia on good credit terms. Kennedy told the secretary of defense, "Let's lend them [Israel] the money on the same terms as the Australians." Myer Feldman, the president's advisor on Jewish affairs, recounted that this action "broke the dam," and all future sales of arms to Israel were on equally generous terms.[7]

Ben Gurion with John F. Kennedy
On a 1951 trip to Israel, Congressman John F. Kennedy met with Prime Minister David Ben Gurion. This was the beginning of a meaningful relationship between Kennedy and the State of Israel. He is shown here with another congressman, Franklin Roosevelt Jr. John F. Kennedy Presidential Library

The Cold War

With the end of World War II, America found itself in a "Cold War" with a former ally, the Soviet Union. Hostility between the two nations dated back to the 1917 Communist Revolution and the long-standing threats of world revolution. Americans watched warily as in the late 1940s and early 1950s China fell to the Communists and the Soviet Union announced its development of an atomic bomb. Paranoia over the Soviets and Communist infiltration gripped the nation as Americans questioned how the Soviets had gained the knowledge to become a nuclear power. Congressional hearings and the institution of "loyalty oaths" challenged traditional American values. Jewish commitments to equal rights, social action, and liberal agendas often made them suspects, as politicians sought to root out "Reds, pinkos, and Commies." It was the era of professional blacklists, where noted writers, actors, and filmmakers were arbitrarily fired because of their political views or simply because they had been anonymously accused. In 1953, Ethel and Julius Rosenberg were executed after being found guilty of handing atomic secrets to the Soviets. Their accused conspirators were also Jewish. For American Jews, the news could not have been any worse, fueling the deep-rooted belief held by many that Jews were Communist sympathizers and disloyal citizens.

The Rosenbergs
Julius and Ethel Rosenberg are led from the courthouse in 1953. Library of Congress

The Watershed Year

Prior to the mid-1960s, American Jews focused their energies primarily on their own Jewish communities. Thoughts of Israel and the Holocaust took second place until the 1967 Six-Day War, when both issues overtook other concerns as the prime ways in which Jews identified themselves. The year 1967 was a critical turning point not only for Israel, but for the American Jewish community as well.

J. Robert Oppenheimer

Often referred to as the "father of the atomic age," J. Robert Oppenheimer, born in 1904, headed the Manhattan Project during World War II, which created the first atomic bomb. He was the creative head of the Los Alamos nuclear laboratory. After the first successful test of the atomic bomb, Oppenheimer worried about the consequences unleashed by the new weapon. When, a decade later, he spoke out against creating an even more powerful hydrogen bomb, he found himself enmeshed in the McCarthy-era witch hunts, accused of being "anti-American." He turned back to academic life. In 1963 the Atomic Energy Commission, which had earlier revoked his security clearance, honored him with its highest honor, the Enrico Fermi Award. He died in 1967.

Although American Jews more actively supported Israel after the 1956 war both politically and financially, events in early 1967 increased concern. Aiming for a political foothold in the Arab world, the Soviet Union had provided economic and military aid to Egypt and its leader, Nasser. In 1963 Nasser federated his country with Syria to form the United Arab Republic, creating a two-front threat to liberate "the Arab Nation from the peril of Zionism." Tensions along Israel's borders increased, and on May 16, 1967, Egypt requested the United Nations to withdraw the Emergency Force troops (UNEF) from the northern Sinai and Sharm-al-Sheikh, thereby negating the assurances that had allowed Israel to withdraw from those areas after the

1956 war. Since the UNEF troops had been stationed on Egyptian soil, the withdrawal request was honored by the United Nations. This time Israel would face larger, better-prepared, and more-unified Arab armies, provisioned generously by the Soviet Union. As war clouds gathered over the area, there was much sympathy and moral support among other nations for Israel, but little tangible aid.

Israel felt isolated, its very existence threatened. Abba Eban later recalled, "Nobody who lived those days in Israel will ever forget the air of heavy foreboding that hovered over our land ... for Israel there would be only one defeat."[8] American Jews were frightened and gloomy, sharing the same sense of doom felt by Jews around the world. Images of the Holocaust prevailed. Rabbi Heschel wrote, "Terror and dread fell upon Jews everywhere. Will God permit our people to perish? Will there be another Auschwitz, another Dachau, another Treblinka?"[9] Arthur Hertzberg observed, in the August 1967 issue of *Commentary*, that "many Jews would never have believed that grave danger to Israel could dominate their thoughts and emotions to the exclusion of all else."

But events in the Middle East instantly traumatized most American Jews and transformed them into active Zionists. Jewish groups such as the American Jewish Committee, which had never been a strong supporter of the Jewish state, joined with other religious and communal organizations to raise money and exert political pressure on Israel's behalf. The American Israel Public Affairs Committee (AIPAC) and the Conference of Presidents of Major American Jewish

164

Israel, indicating land under Israeli control after the Six-Day War. www.maps.com

Organizations, both founded in the 1950s, coordinated lobbying and political activities. By the end of the Six-Day War, with Israel prevailing dramatically—some would say, miraculously—over its Arab foes, American Jews had raised $240 million in aid and purchased $190 million worth of Israel Bonds. Ten thousand Americans rushed to Israel to work in agricultural and other noncombat positions as substitutes for hastily mobilized reserve soldiers. The anti-Zionist American Council for Judaism, practically speaking, ceased to exist.

New Victories, New Problems

Israel had recaptured the Sinai Peninsula and gained control of the West Bank from Jordan and the Golan Heights in the north from Syria. Most meaningful of all was reclaiming the Western Wall, which had been under Jordanian control since 1948. "We have unified Jerusalem, the divided capital of Israel," Defense Minister Moshe Dayan stated. "We have returned to the holiest of our holy places never to depart from it again." The 1967 war was a supremely paradoxical turning point in the history of modern Israel, bringing the new nation grave long-term consequences along with a clear military victory. Prior to 1967, the image of a beleaguered nation maintaining itself against all odds had captured the sympathy of many around the world. With the decisive end of the Six-Day War in Israel's favor, the position of underdog shifted to the Arabs and altered the balance of power between Israel and its neighbors.[10]

The United Nations Declares that Zionism Is Racism

These excerpts from UN General Assembly Resolution 3379 show how the United Nations arrived at its conclusion that Zionism was a form of racism:

Recalling its resolution 1904 (XVII) of 20 November 1963, ... in particular its affirmation that "any doctrine of racial differentiation or superiority is scientifically false, morally condemnable, socially unjust and dangerous" and its expression of alarm at "the manifestations of racial discrimination still in evidence in some areas in the world, some of which are imposed by certain Governments by means of legislative, administrative or other measures,"

Recalling also that, in its resolution 3151 G (XXVIII) of 14 December 1953, the General Assembly condemned, inter alia, the unholy alliance between South Africa and Zionism ...Taking note also of resolution 77 (XII) adopted ... at Kampala from 28 July to 1 Augusut 1975, which considered "that the racist regime in occupied Palestine and the racist regime in Zimbabwe and South Africa have a common imperialist origin, forming a whole and having the same racist structure and being organically linked in their policy aimed at repression of the dignity and integrity of the human being,"

... [the United Nations] determines that Zionism is a form of racism and racial discrimination.

165

Henry Kissinger

The first Jew to be appointed secretary of state, Henry Kissinger was born in Germany in 1923 and fled with his family in 1938. A brilliant student, he earned a Ph.D from Harvard University after serving in the U.S. Army during World War II. As a professor at Harvard, he gained attention through his writings on national security. Kissinger advised President Richard Nixon, who appointed him secretary of state in 1973.

Sadat, Carter, and Begin at White House, 1979 Peace Treaty
While President Jimmy Carter was lauded for his part in the talks that resulted in the historic peace treaty between Israel and Egypt in 1979, he was humble about his accomplishments, calling the treaty "a first step on a long and difficult road." Here (from left to right) President Anwar Sadat of Egypt, President Carter, and Israeli Prime Minister Menachem Begin appear in the White House Rose Garden during the treaty-signing ceremony. Carter Presidential Library

Suddenly, Israel found itself targeted internationally as a vicious aggressor of "people of color" by left-wingers in Western countries, at the United Nations, and by Third World countries. The Israeli government policy encouraging Jews to settle in the occupied areas of the West Bank and Gaza increased diplomatic tensions with the United States. Many American Jews, while publicly supporting the positions of the Israeli government and the militarily strategic importance of the new settlements, privately questioned the political wisdom of settling Jews amid a sea of Arabs. An era of renewed anti-Semitism began, cloaked in not-so-subtle international loathing of Zionism. In 1975, due in large part to support from Arab and Soviet bloc countries, a United Nations resolution equating Zionism with racism passed on a vote of 72 to 35 with 32 abstentions, mainly from Western countries. The U.S. ambassador, Daniel Patrick Moynihan, declared to the other members, "The United States rises to declare before the General Assembly of the United Nations and before the world that it does not acknowledge, it will not abide by, it will never acquiesce in this infamous act." The resolution was ultimately repealed in 1991.

The 1973 Yom Kippur War began badly for Israel. The surprise Egyptian attack on Judaism's holiest day had caught the country unprepared. In spite of Israel's plea for military aid, the United States was slow in responding. Some blamed Secretary of State Henry Kissinger, himself Jewish. Kissinger later said, "The strategy was to prevent Israel from humiliating Egypt again. From the beginning, I was determined to use the war to start a peace process."[11] The calculated U.S. policy sought to prevent Israel from achieving a total victory and to keep the Soviet Union from intervening on the Arab side. The war fundamentally changed once again the balance of power in the Middle East and allowed for discussions to begin that ultimately resulted in the 1979 peace treaty between Israel and Egypt, facilitated by President Carter.

A New Self-Image Emerges

American Jews felt a renewed pride in their religion and their connections to Israel. They told stories of non-Jewish friends saying to them, "You really showed them." Jewish pride swelled as Jews internalized the Israeli victory and, in so doing, strengthened their own self-image. Israel's triumph "seemed to have unleashed among American Jewry a new kind of assertiveness …"[12] According to the 1998 *American Jewish Year Book*, of the more than 400 national Jewish organizations in the United States, close to 100 were Israel related. Israel became the central tenet that unified all segments of the American Jewish community. David Clayman of the American Jewish Committee noted that "fund-raising was the key. You worshiped at the altar of Israel by contributing. Jewish observance was raising money, not going to the synagogue."[13]

One goal of Zionism was to facilitate the mass emigration of worldwide Jewry to the Jewish State, but despite generous financial support of Israel, most American Jews were not pulling up stakes and moving there. While earlier Israeli leaders had admonished American Jews for not leaving Los Angeles, Detroit, and New York to make aliyah, later leaders accepted reality. Speaking to American Jewish leaders visiting Israel in 2004, Prime Minister Ariel Sharon said, "The future of Israel depends, first of all on Aliyah to Israel … Not all of you will be coming, but, in any case, you have to help, you have to support, you have to send your children to study here, to learn here, to spend a year here."[14] The end of the 20th century marked a change in the American Jewish relationship with Israel. Rather than viewing Israel as merely a recipient of American Jewish funding, some began to perceive Israel as an important vehicle for strengthening Jewish identity within their families. American Jewish parents stayed home, by and large, but did send their children to study and tour. In spite of these actions, however, the 2000 National Jewish Population Survey revealed that only 35 percent of all American Jews had ever visited the Jewish State. By 2004, pollsters discovered a significant decline in the outright support of Israel by American Jews, even as many look to Israel to strengthen Jewish identity for the young. Israel's thriving economy has also made it less dependent on American Jewish dollars.[15]

Liz Claiborne

Born in Belgium in 1929, Claiborne became a noted women's clothes designer in the United States. In 1976, she founded her own company, which became one of the world's largest designers and manufacturers of clothing and accessories for women, men, and children. In a 1986 interview in *Vogue* magazine, she stated that her goal was "to dress the women who didn't have to wear suits—the teachers, the doctors, the women working in Southern California and Florida, the women in the fashion industry itself."

Judith Resnik

Judith Resnik was the second American woman to travel in space, as a mission specialist on the first voyage of the space shuttle *Discovery* in 1984. She was born in 1949 in Akron, Ohio, and developed a passion for mathematics. More interested in numbers than concepts, she obtained her doctorate in electrical engineering from the University of Maryland. She was accepted into NASA's astronaut program in 1978 and used her engineering background to train as a mission specialist. Her second mission ended in tragedy on January 28, 1986, when the space shuttle *Challenger* exploded seconds after take-off, killing her and the other six astronauts aboard. NASA

Barriers Fall

Since 1967, due in part to their own self-confidence and the passage of civil rights legislation, Jews have found previously unattainable opportunities opened to them. By the end of the 20th century, Jews had become the best-educated American ethnic or religious group. In the business and academic world, qualified Jews broke through the invisible "glass ceiling" to reach the highest offices. In contrast to 1945, when Jews considered it a great feat when Bess Myerson was chosen Miss America, in 1973 Irving Shapiro was elected chief executive officer of DuPont, one of America's industrial giants. Since then, from sports to politics and from the medical and legal professions to every other aspect of American life, Jews have experienced open access to positions formerly closed to them. Ivy League universities, which instituted quotas on Jewish students in the 1920s and '30s, were headed by Jewish presidents. "White shoe" law firms had Jewish partners. "The more prestigious the law firm, the more Jewish attorneys it had on its staff."[16] In the 1950s there were no Jewish members of the U.S. Senate. By the 1970s there were two. During the 1990s, the Senate always included at least 10 Jewish members—a minyan for a traditional Jewish religious service.

Arnold Auerbach

It may be difficult to comprehend today, but at one time basketball was considered a "Jewish" sport. Arnold "Red" Auerbach grew up in that environment to become the most respected coach in that sport's history. Born in New York in 1917 to immigrant parents, he played basketball in high school and college before becoming a professional coach. With the Boston Celtics, he created what have become classic innovations to the game, leading the team to unprecedented championships. He was elected to the Basketball Hall of Fame in 1968.

Race Relations Deteriorate

Unfortunately, the close ties that had existed between African Americans and Jews began to fray during the 1960s. Decades of built-up frustration within the African American community resulted in riots in the ghettos of major cities. Ironically, just a generation earlier these ghettos had been home to vibrant Jewish communities. While many Jews had left for the suburbs, Jewish businesses that remained—often the only white contacts in the community—were burned and looted. As the decade proceeded, African Americans took charge of their own civil rights institutions, and American Jews increasingly focused on their own issues.

Jews had played a prominent role in the Civil Rights movement right from the beginning. Yet, following the legal successes of the 1960s, a new group of young African American activists embarked on removing all white people from leadership positions within the movement. James Baldwin, the noted African American writer, explained, "One does not wish, in short, to be told by an American Jew that his suffering was as great as the American Negro's suffering. It isn't and one knows that it isn't from the very tone in which he assures you that it is."[17] The spirit of cooperation that had marked the Civil Rights movement to that time weakened considerably, as conflicting agendas created serious tensions and blacks and Jews became absorbed in their own concerns. For African Americans, issues such as Black Power and frustrations with economic and educational advancement widened the rift, at the same time that Jews were becoming increasingly concerned with issues of Israel and affirmative action.

Ruth Bader Ginsburg

Ruth Bader Ginsburg's encounters with discrimination—not as a Jew but as a woman—shaped her determination to succeed as a lawyer. Born in Brooklyn in 1933, she graduated first in her class at Columbia Law School after transferring from Harvard Law School. At Harvard, she and other women students were chided for pursuing legal careers and "taking the places of more-deserving men."

Unable to obtain a position in a New York City law firm because of her gender, she taught at Rutgers University School of Law and worked for the American Civil Liberties Union. In 1972, Columbia University Law School made her the first woman at the school to be awarded tenure. In 1980 President Jimmy Carter appointed her to the U.S. Court of Appeals for the District of Columbia. In 1993, President Bill Clinton nominated her to fill a vacancy on the U.S. Supreme Court. The Senate overwhelmingly confirmed her by a vote of 97 to 3.

169

What began as a labor dispute in New York City in 1968 marked a turning point in black–Jewish relations. In an effort to improve education in the predominantly black

Ocean Hill–Brownsville section of Brooklyn, the school board created a new school district under community control, with power to hire and fire teachers without regard to established regulations. The teachers' union objected. Ninety percent of New York City's public school teachers were white, and two-thirds of them were Jewish. The preponderance of Jews reflected their high concentration in the population and years of previous discrimination, which had locked them out of professional careers in the private sector.

In May of that year, the local Ocean Hill–Brownsville board fired 19 teachers, 18 of whom were white and Jewish. The United Federation of Teachers, led by Albert Shanker, protested the violation of established procedures under the existing union contract. What ensued was the longest public school teachers' strike in American history, pitting Jewish teachers against African American community activists. During the two-month strike, inflammatory anti-Semitic literature and taunts spread throughout the community.

Julius Lester, then the host of a WBAI radio talk show, encouraged an activist black teacher to read a particularly strident poem written by a student. The first few lines of "Anti-Semitism" set the tone.

Rosalyn Yalow
Rosalyn Yalow, born in 1921, attended public school in New York City. She received her doctorate in physics from the University of Illinois. Later, working closely with Dr. Solomon Berson, she joined her expertise in physics with his in medicine to create a method for measuring circulating insulin. Yalow was instrumental in creating the radioimmunoassay procedures now commonly used in laboratories around the world. She was awarded the Nobel Prize in Medicine in 1977, only the second woman to receive this honor. Library of Congress

Hey, Jew boy, with that yarmulke on your head
You pale-faced Jew boy—I wish you were dead.
I can see you Jew boy—no you can't hide
I got a scoop on you—yeh, you gonna die ...[18]

Lester had hoped that the words would disturb listeners enough to encourage the black community to cease the anti-Jewish nature of the controversy. Instead, the ferocity and hatred of the poem against Jews worsened the already tender situation. The Anti-Defamation League reported that "raw undisguised anti-Semitism had reached a crisis level in New York City ..." Shortly thereafter, a special exhibit called Harlem on My Mind opened at New York's Metropolitan Museum of Art. The exhibit catalogue contained an inflammatory introduction written by a black high school student:

Behind every hurdle that the Afro-American has yet to jump stands the Jew who has already cleared it. Jewish shopkeepers are the only remaining "survivors" in the expanding black ghettos …. The lack of competition in this area allows the already exploited black to be further exploited by the Jews. Another major area of contact involves the Jewish landlord and the black tenant. Our contempt for the Jews makes us feel more completely American in sharing a national prejudice.[19]

Her words created yet another national furor as the tension between both minority groups grew. Underlying the situation was the fight for affirmative action in America, and its related issue of quotas. Jews viewed affirmative action with apprehension. Numerical quotas for admission to American institutions of higher learning would restrict Jewish applicants to available spaces equal to their small percentage in the population. Jews had fought hard to gain admission to prestigious universities by merit alone and constituted larger percentages in such professions as law, education, and medicine. Quotas would prevent the brightest and best of young Jews from professions they had worked so hard to enter. Jews vividly remembered the discrimination they had to overcome over the years to earn places in the educational and work world.[20]

In 1978, Jewish organizations submitted legal briefs to the U.S. Supreme Court in a case brought by a non-Jew, Allen Bakke, who had been denied admission to the University of California Medical School at Davis. Bakke argued that had it not been for affirmative action policies at the school, he would have been admitted based on merit. The Supreme Court, in a 5 to 4 landmark decision, ruled in Bakke's favor by banning the use of quotas while upholding the use of race in university admissions.

Toward New Forms of Observance

In the 1960s and '70s, a series of seemingly unconnected situations converged to directly challenge traditional Jewish religious practices. It was the time of anti-Vietnam War demonstrations, the

Philip Roth

In his highly acclaimed novels and short stories, Pulitzer Prize–winning author Philip Roth focuses on his Jewish and neighborhood roots to create characters and situations that mirror his view of Jewish life in America. He was born in 1933 and grew up in a heavily Jewish neighborhood of Newark, New Jersey. Much of his work is satiric in nature, poking holes in the lower-middle-class mores that surrounded him in his youth, and often revolves around the themes of Jewish identity, sex, and the role of the individual in American society. His breakthrough novel was *Goodbye, Columbus* (1959), followed by other works including *Portnoy's Complaint* (1969), which incorporated a controversial—at the time—sexual theme, and a trilogy including *American Pastoral* (1997), *I Married a Communist* (1998), and *The Human Stain* (2000). In addition to the Pulitzer Prize, Roth has won numerous prestigious awards, including the National Book Award (1959).

Library of Congress

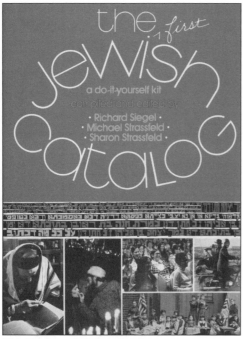

The First Jewish Catalog
Published by The Jewish Publication Society in 1973.

Civil Rights movement, hippies, feminism, individuality, and personal choice. Jews, particularly the young, were not immune to the social and political upheaval around them (in which they were also active participants).

In 1968, a group of young activist Jews in Somerville, Massachusetts, disaffected with established religious communities, created Havurat Shalom, a congregation in which they could "redeem the current bleakness of American Jewish religious life" and whose "aim was to re-create Judaism in their own generation's image."[21] The *havurah* (fellowship group) experience was replicated in other college communities, where participants created personalized rituals, prayers, and music and experimented with different art forms through which to express their Judaism. What began as a hippie/commune experience quickly entered the mainstream, as established congregations absorbed the spirit and practices of the *havurah* movement. The popular *Jewish Catalog*, a "do-it-yourself kit" for Jewish observance, grew out of Havurat Shalom's activities and was published by the mainstream Jewish Publication Society.

It was a measure of America's increasing tolerance for religious and ethnic differences that by the end of the 20th century, Orthodox Jews had begun to go public in their dress and ritual. Where fathers once discreetly covered their heads with hats and caps, sons now nonchalantly wore *kippot* and displayed tzitzit (prayer shawl fringes). Orthodox Jewish parents, whose own parents had given them "American" names, now proudly gave their children obviously Jewish names. By the 1990s the erection of *eruvim*—delineated, artificial boundaries within which observant people could obey Biblical injunctions and carry items (or wheel baby carriages) on Shabbat and holidays—became a topic of heated discussion in towns with large Orthodox populations. Lubavitch Hasidism proudly displayed Hanukkah menorahs in public places, infuriating liberal Jews who for years had fought against the public display of Christian symbols. In America, Orthodox Jews have become revitalized and more comfortable than their parents in publicly asserting themselves. Earlier Jewish immigrants subscribed to the "melting pot" theory, which required them to downplay their differences while assimilating into the majority culture. Later arrivals took advantage of American diversity and multiculturalism to visibly maintain their own identities.

Chabad Rabbi Making a Shofar with Neighborhood Children
Chabad Rabbi Gedaliah Lowenstein, Philadelphia, Pennsylvania, teaches two young boys how to make a shofar. Photo: Beth Rosenwasser

The Russians Arrive

Far-off influences continued to play a role in the evolution of American Jewish identity. Just as the Six-Day War had heightened Jewish self-awareness in the United States, so also did it trigger among Soviet Jewry a heightened sense of the injustices they were suffering at the hands of their own government. Anti-Semitism had become an unofficial doctrine of state, and discrimination against Jews and Judaism were facts of life. Many Jews in the Soviet Union reacted to their harsh lives by publicly demonstrating a strong stand with Israel and demanding free emigration. As Russian Jews secretly began to organize toward that end, American Jews gradually became aware of the deteriorating condition of their fellow Jews in the Soviet Union. In April 1966, 69 U.S. senators issued a statement asking that "the three million Jews of the Soviet Union be allowed to live creatively and in dignity as Jews."[22] "Let my people go" became the clarion call for a mass movement dedicated to convincing the Soviet government to allow their Jewish citizens to freely emigrate.

The arrest and mistreatment of Jewish activists strengthened the Soviet Jewry advocacy movement in America. Using strategies involving public relations, political action, and education, American Jews had by early 1972 strengthened their

174

This Year in Russia

Poster issued by the National Conference on Soviet Jewry. During the 1960s and '70s, the Jews of the Soviet Union experienced increased discrimination. In response, activism by American groups ultimately encouraged the Soviet Union to allow Jews to emigrate in large numbers. Aside from lobbying Congress, these activist groups sponsored marches and public protests.
Library of Congress

varied efforts to free Soviet Jewry into a crusade. Organizations such as the Student Struggle for Soviet Jewry (founded in 1964) and the National Conference on Soviet Jewry (1971) rallied support for the beleaguered Jews of the Soviet Union. In 1974, political action led Congress to adopt the Jackson–Vanik Amendment, which directly linked Soviet–U.S. economic cooperation to the treatment of Soviet Jews. American Jews traveled to the Soviet Union to surreptitiously bring support to Jewish "refuseniks." While some Soviet Jews were able to leave during the 1970s, arrests and show trials of dissident Jews continued, as did levels of persecution. The heroism of Natan Sharansky, Yosef Begun, and Ida Nudel was heralded in the United States.

In 1987, on the eve of a summit meeting between President Ronald Reagan and Soviet Premier Mikhail Gorbachev, the American Jewish community arranged a highly publicized demonstration on the Washington Mall that was attended by 200,000 people from around the country—the largest rally ever staged by the American Jewish community. Noted Holocaust chronicler Elie Wiesel said in his benediction, "Had there been such a demonstration in 1942, then in 1943 and in 1944 millions of Jews would have been saved … Too many of us were silent then. We are not silent now."[23]

Meeting with a Soviet "Boiler Watcher"

During the 1970s and '80s, international activism on behalf of Jews in the Soviet Union escalated. One way to connect with refuseniks* in Russia was through clandestine visits by Jewish travelers. Late in 1987, Dr. Solomon Schimmel visited Moscow and met the Rabinovich family. Misha, the father, was in the 31st day of a hunger strike. The following is excerpted from a reminiscence of Dr. Schimmel's:

Misha told us of how he had been a very professionally successful applied mathematician working at a meteorological institute in Moscow, directing many graduate students. In response to his request for an exit visa he was stripped of his professional degrees, dismissed from his position and for seven years has worked as a "boiler watcher,"** currently earning seventy rubles a month. … We asked Misha why he was on this hunger strike, what does he hope to accomplish with it. He answered that it is an act of despair—he cannot bear any longer the life situation which has been coerced upon him because of his desire to leave Russia and live as a Jew in Israel. He felt a need to do something more active than protest or demonstrate in some public setting. He cannot tolerate being ignored any longer and hopes that his hunger strike will bring him to the attention of the authorities and perhaps induce them to give him permission to go. He also hopes that his strike will benefit other refuseniks as well, by calling attention to their plight. (Schimmel 1987)

* Russian Jews who were denied permission to emigrate

** a term used for any menial occupation below one's educational and professional background

As the political underpinnings of the Soviet Union began to crumble, Jewish emigration increased markedly. Between 1989 and 1992, "more than three-quarters of a million people fled what they saw as a collapsing economy, state and social order."[24] In the entire period 1968–1994, a total of 1,214,448 Jews left, with nearly a third of them going to Israel. Half of them resettled in the United States, many given refugee status. The American Jewish community, largely through its network of local federations, raised millions of dollars to provide extensive support to

Elie Wiesel

Elie Wiesel is known as the conscience of our generation. Beginning with the publication of *Night* (1960), Wiesel's semi-autobiographical writings have given the world deeper insight into the personal tragedies of the Holocaust. Wiesel, born in 1928, was awarded the Nobel Peace Prize in 1986 for his continual efforts to confront inhumanity around the globe. "The only role I sought," he wrote, "was that of witness. I believed that, having survived by chance, I was duty-bound to give meaning to my survival, to justify each moment of my life."

Art Spiegelman

From his early days as a successful creator of bubble gum cards, stickers, and underground comic books, Spiegelman, born in 1948, helped create a publishing niche for adult-oriented graphic novels. His cutting-edge *Maus: A Survivor's Tale I: My Father Bleeds History* (1986), catapulted him into the world of mainstream publishing. *Maus,* an allegorical tale of the Holocaust featuring mice and cats, has resonated with readers around the world.

the refugees. Unlike the earlier wave of Russian Jewish immigration, which began in the 1880s, these newcomers did not bring with them a strong religious identity. But unlike earlier immigrants, these later arrivals were largely highly educated and maintained strong cultural associations to Russian culture and life. The established American Jewish community provided housing and cultural assistance to the new arrivals, but many Russian Jews preferred to set up their own social and political activities.

Remembering the Holocaust

Until the 1960s, little public mention was made of the Nazi killings of 6 million Jews during World War II. Perhaps feeling guilty for previous political impotence or embarrassed by the symbolism of victimhood, American Jews kept their feelings about the Holocaust to themselves. When an attempt was made to construct a Holocaust memorial in New York in the late 1940s, leaders of major Jewish organizations reacted negatively. They viewed a public display as "a perpetual memorial to the weakness and defenselessness of the Jewish people." The head of the American Jewish Committee stated at

United States Holocaust Memorial Museum

Chartered by a unanimous Act of Congress in 1980, the United States Holocaust Memorial Museum is adjacent to the National Mall in Washington, D.C. Through exhibitions and educational programs, the museum enhances understanding of the Holocaust.
United States Holocaust Memorial Museum

the time, "We must normalize the image of the Jew ... the Jew should be represented as like others rather than unlike others."[25] But as Israel faced the threat to its existence just before the Six-Day War and the plight of Soviet Jews surfaced, Jews realized that more had to be done to keep the memory of the Holocaust alive. The results were books for adults and children, museums, public school curricula, and popular movies. Even as memorials were being established in cities around America, dissenting opinions surfaced. Some were concerned that activism related to the memory of the Holocaust would diminish interest in other Jewish areas of concern. The highly public establishment of the United States Holocaust Memorial Museum just off the Mall in Washington, D.C., evoked this reaction from Steven Bayme of the American Jewish Committee:

The vision of the Holocaust as centerpiece of Jewish identity suggests that our connection with our past is a connection of sadness, that being a Jew is a matter of commemorating terrible events. This is a very distorted focus on the Jewish historical experience and the meaning of being a Jew.[26]

The impact of the Holocaust resonated through the American Jewish community. As a group, American Jews, remembering their ineffective impact on governmental policy to save the Jews of Europe, became more vocal and politically attuned. President Ronald Reagan's 1985 announcement that he would visit a German war cemetery during an upcoming state visit touched a raw nerve among Holocaust survivors and the American Jewish community. Many denounced the planned visit when it was discovered that the Bitburg cemetery contained the remains of Nazi Waffen SS troops. The *Washington Post* declared: "President Reagan cannot go to Bitburg. It is out of the question for the leader of the Western world to lay a wreath in a war cemetery where Nazi storm troopers are buried ..."[27]

Steven Spielberg

Spielberg was born on December 18, 1947, in Cincinnati, Ohio. Interested in film at an early age, he is credited with directing and producing some of the most important films of the latter 20th century. Beginning with *Close Encounters of the Third Kind* and *E.T. The Extra-Terrestrial*, he moved on to such classics as *Saving Private Ryan* and *Amistad*. His 1993 Oscar-winning film, *Schindler's List*, moved interest in the Holocaust to a new level. A year after its release, he founded the Steven Spielberg Shoah Foundation, which has collected over 50,000 videotaped testimonies of Holocaust survivors to keep the memory of the Holocaust alive for future generations

Ironically, just prior to his German trip, President Reagan was scheduled to present Elie Wiesel with the Congressional Gold Medal at the White House. At the ceremony, Wiesel publicly lectured the president on the upcoming Bitburg visit. "That place, Mr. President," Wiesel said, "is not your place. Your place is with the victims of the SS." The trip did go on but with a hurried change in plans. Before going to Bitburg, Reagan and his host, German chancellor Helmut Kohl, first visited the Bergen-Belsen concentration camp, where Reagan said, "Out of this tragic and nightmarish time, beyond the anguish, the pain and suffering, and for all time, we can and must pledge: Never Again!"

Caspar Weinberger's Declaration on the Pollard Case

On March 3, 1987, the day before Jonathan Pollard's sentencing, Secretary of Defense Caspar Weinberger submitted the following Supplemental Declaration:

It is difficult for me, even in the so-called "year of the spy," to conceive of a greater harm to national security than that caused by the defendant in the view of the breadth, the critical importance to the U.S., and the high sensitivity of the information he sold to Israel ... I respectfully submit that any U.S. citizen, and in particular a trusted government official, who sells U.S. secrets to any foreign nation should not be punished merely as a common criminal. Rather the punishment imposed should reflect the perfidy of the individual's action, the magnitude of the treason committed, and needs of national security. (Weinberger Supplemental Declaration, *United States v. Pollard*, 959 F.2d at 1017, 1025)

An Old Fear Surfaces

On November 21, 1985, an American Jewish naval intelligence analyst and his wife were arrested by the FBI at the gates of the Israeli embassy in Washington, D.C., where they had gone to seek asylum. Jonathan Pollard, convicted two years later of spying for Israel, readily admitted to providing thousands of classified documents to agents of the Jewish state and was sentenced to life imprisonment with no chance of parole. A major factor in his harsh sentence was due to the still-classified, 46-page report submitted to the court by Secretary of Defense Caspar Weinberger in January 1987. While most American Jews shared his idealistic concern for Israel's survival, they were aghast that he had gone so far as to commit espionage against the United States. As comfortable as the American Jewish community had become by the mid-1980s, fears that Pollard's actions could lead to charges of dual loyalty hovered just below the surface. Some Jews at the time criticized what they viewed as an overreaction by the Conference of Presidents of Major American Jewish Organizations, which issued a statement endorsing Pollard's life sentence.[28] Others felt that the punishment did not fit the crime and, indeed, was overly harsh given the situation. Nonetheless, the Pollard Affair provoked a feeling of insecurity among American Jews, who had by then become desensitized to the age-old view of Jews as outsiders.

While institutional anti-Semitism in America largely disappeared from the scene during the later decades of the 20th century, Jewish insecurity did not. Jews in America were never numerically significant, but their high profile made them highly visible. Through Bitburg, the Pollard Affair, and the rise of Christian fundamentalism, American Jews kept their collective antennae on constant alert, but with the disappearance of external threats to their well-being, they began to focus on themselves. The National Jewish Population Survey in 1990 shocked the community with the revelation that the intermarriage rate of Jews had climbed to 52 percent. Continuity became the watchword for the next decade, as initiatives were developed and implemented to stem the outflow of Jews—which turned out to be less drastic than originally reported, although still high enough to cause concern, and still rising between 1990 and 2000. But even beyond the intermarriage statistics, the survey indicated a large percentage of people who self-identified themselves as "just Jewish" rather than belonging to an organized religious denomination. The self-definition of "just Jewish" rose in 2000 to 31 percent of Jewishly connected respondents.

Who Is a Jew?

As Orthodoxy turned to the right, the complicated question of "Who is a Jew" surfaced in Israel and directly affected the majority of American Jews, who followed the more liberal branches of organized Judaism. Because of a "status quo" arrangement made when Israel was established as a state in 1948, the Orthodox rabbinate retained decision-making power over religious aspects of Jewish life in Israel. When questions related to the recognition in Israel of marriages performed by Reform and Conservative rabbis arose, the legitimacy of non-Orthodox rabbis was questioned. Unable to resolve the issue, the "Who is a Jew?" question has become a political hot potato in Israel and has divided American Jews as well. Ismar Schorsh, chancellor of the Jewish Theological Seminary of America, explained, "Jews in Israel and in the Diaspora can no longer avoid confronting the question of how a Jewish state dominated by the Orthodox can serve as the center of the Jewish world, where the Orthodox are only a small part of the population."[29]

Dividing Lines Among Jewish Sects

"It is in regard to the principles of the divinity and immutability of halakah [sic] that Orthodoxy opposes Conservative and Reform Judaism. Conservative Judaism affirms the divinity of halakah, but questions its immutability. Reform Judaism denies the authority of both principles. Because of these views and their control over the religious establishment, Orthodox Jews have been able to keep rabbis of either persuasion from establishing full legitimacy in Israel. But because the majority of Jews in the Western democracies, if they are affiliated at all, are affiliated with Reform or Conservative congregations, and because of the high intermarriage rates, as of 1988 Orthodox Jews have been unable publicly to invalidate Reform or Conservative conversions to Judaism under the Law of Return by amending the law again to stipulate specific conformance with halakah as the sole mode of conversion. Yet many new immigrants (and some long-time residents) whose status is in doubt have undergone Orthodox conversions—often added onto their previous Reform or Conservative ones—once resident in Israel."

(Metz 1990, 178)

179

A negative result of Orthodoxy's turn to the right in America was a greater reluctance to work cooperatively with the more liberal Jewish denominations. Growing rifts in Judaism began to polarize American Jews. As early as 1954, Orthodox rabbi Joseph D. Soloveichik issued a ruling that prohibited Orthodox Jews from even entering Reform or Conservative synagogues. Later, the movements divided on public policy when the Orthodox, with their well-established network of day schools, joined with Christian groups to support state and federal aid to parochial schools. Liberal Jews continued their traditional support of public schools even as their own movements were opening more day schools. By the mid-1990s, ideological shifts caused the veneer of joint cooperation among the branches of Judaism to disappear. The Synagogue Council of America, which had existed for 68 years,

Self-Identification of Jews by Denomination

Orthodox	8%
Conservative	25%
Reconstructionist	2%
Reform	34%
Just Jewish	31%

Report Series on the National Jewish Population Survey 2000/01, October 2004, 7.

served as the central religious umbrella organization for all Jews until Orthodox groups withdrew their funding and participation. With its demise in 1994, official dialogue came to an end.

The Demands of Ezrat Nashim

In March 1972, members of the feminist group Ezrat Nashim (the name given to the segregated women's section of traditional synagogues) presented a flyer titled "Jewish Women Call for Change" and excerpted below, to the rabbis attending the annual convention of the Conservative movement's Rabbinical Assembly.

It is not enough to say that Judaism views women as separate but equal, nor to point to Judaism's past superiority over other cultures in its treatment of women. We've had enough of apologetics: enough of Bruria, Dvorah, and Esther; enough of eshet chayil*!

It is time that:

    women be granted membership in synagogues

    women be counted in the minyan

    women be allowed full participation in religious observances

    women be recognized as witnesses before Jewish law

    women be allowed to initiate divorce

    women be permitted and encouraged to attend Rabbinical and Cantorial schools, and to perform Rabbinical and Cantorial functions in synagogues

    women be encouraged to join decision-making bodies, and to assume professional leadership roles, in synagogues and in the general Jewish community

    women be considered as bound to fulfill all mitzvot equally with men ...
(Hyman 1972)

* Written in Hebrew on the flyer, *eshet chayil* (woman of valor) is a reference to Proverbs 31:10–31, traditionally recited by husbands on Friday night, praising the perfect wife who is the mainstay of her home.

Women Move Forward

Another divisive action was the ordination of women. During the late 1960s and early 1970s, women began to challenge their second-class status in American society. In spite of incremental advances in the workplace and their educational attainments, women encountered institutional roadblocks that confined their talents to the home or to traditional careers such as teaching and social work. Jewish women, many of whom were in the forefront of the feminist movement, broke down the religious barriers to ordination. Beginning with ordination of Sally Priesand by the Reform movement's Hebrew Union College in 1972, the liberal branches of Judaism have seen sharp rises in the numbers of women clergy. Also in 1972, a feminist group called Ezrat Nashim presented specific demands for religious equality within the Conservative movement that foreshadowed the rights now enjoyed by non-Orthodox Jewish women.

Intermarriage

In 1983, the Reform movement, which was particularly sensitive to the high rates of intermarriage, made a decisive but divisive decision to recognize as Jewish a child born to either a Jewish mother or father. The patrilineal decision created a rift with Orthodox and Conservative Jews, who continue to recognize the traditional halakhic practice of accepting as a Jew only a person born of a Jewish mother. The issue of intermarriage provided a "cup half-full or half-empty" problem for

American Jewry. On the one hand, the escalating number of Jews marrying out of their faith carried the threat of a benign end to a vibrant Jewish world in America. A highly controversial 1964 issue of *Look* magazine focused on "The Vanishing Jew," foretelling the end of the Jewish people. On the other hand, intermarriage was seen by some as a positive indication of just how accepted Jews had become as individuals in multiethnic America. Historian Jonathan Sarna observed, "To oppose marriages between men and women of different ethnicities, faiths and races seems to many people to be un-American and racist."[30] By the final third of the 20th century, even though Jewishness had little influence on how most Jews lived their lives, Hanukkah candle lighting and Passover seders had been elevated to nearly obligatory observances and Jews were increasingly obsessed about Jewish continuity in America.[31] Some Jewish leaders saw the need to become more proactive. Efforts to make the Jewishness of American Jews more central to their lives began slowly in the 1960s and reached a critical mass in the 1990s.

Rising Intermarriage Rates

The *National Jewish Population Survey 2000/01* reported the following rates of inter-marriage. This table shows the corrected figure for the period from 1985 to 1990, which was originally quoted in 1990 as 52 percent due to a flawed statistical method.

Time Period	Percentage of Jews Marrying Non-Jews
Before 1970	13
1970–1979	28
1980–1984	38
1985–1990	43
1991–1995	43
1996–2001	47

National Jewish Population Survey 2000/01, January 2004, 16.

Education

One crucial, yet manageable way for Jews to affect the thinking of their children and grandchildren about being Jewish was through education. By the 1960s, the Jewish education of most children ended at bar and bat mitzvah, and the learning they did receive often focused on the rote skills needed to perform at their coming-of-age ceremonies and were soon forgotten. In effect, the Jewish education for most children, much like that received by their parents, ended when they were in

Birthright Israel Group Arrives in Israel

Over 100,000 Jewish young adults ranging in age from 18 to 26 have visited Israel on one of the first-time, educational trips sponsored by Taglit-birthright israel. These 10-day trips, supported by private philanthropists, the State of Israel, and United Jewish Communities, are designed to diminish the growing division between Israel and the Diaspora and to strengthen personal Jewish identity and connection to the Jewish people.
birthright israel: Sivan Farag

the eighth grade, just at the age when intellectual curiosity begins. Steps were begun within the organized community to enhance the religious educational status of American Jews. Day schools, once the exclusive province of the Orthodox world, spread into the more liberal streams of Judaism. Beginning with Conservative-affiliated Solomon Schechter schools, the Reform movement followed in the 1970s with schools of their own. In larger cities, all-day Jewish high schools were founded. In Boston, where Rabbi Soloveichik's well-established Orthodox Maimonides School continued to grow and flourish, Conservative and Reform day schools appeared. A new transdenominational Jewish high school opened and within a few years built a state-of-the-art campus to serve a growing student body. Meanwhile, enrollment in Boston's supplementary Prozdor high school division of Hebrew College, founded in 1926, grew from a static under-200 enrollment in the 1970s and 1980s to nearly 1,000 by 2005. Between 1960 and 2000, the number of day schools tripled and by 2000 provided education to 200,000 students, with the largest growth occurring in schools affiliated with the Conservative and Reform movements. Outreach initiatives such as Birthright Israel brought young Jews to Israel, while Aish HaTorah and Jewish Family and Life encouraged Jews of all ages to connect with Jewish learning and culture. Other experiential programs which fostered continuity included Jewish summer camping and retooled educational experiences. Jewish studies departments at leading American universities began to offer advanced courses in Jewish subjects. Hebrew College's successful Me'ah program opened the study of Jewish texts to adults eager to reclaim a formal connection to Jewish education.

Political Power and Leanings

In an October 1967 article in *Commentary*, Milton Himmelfarb had stated that because of the Six-Day War, Jews "relearned the old hard truth that only you can feel your own pain." Immediately after the conclusion of World War II, Jews had strengthened their existing defense organizations by passing leadership roles on from the older generation of philanthropists to a younger group of professionally trained social workers and attorneys. The new activism they created included highly structured public campaigns against prejudice and discrimination. They had broadened the fight against intolerance to include all minority groups, thereby avoiding an image of Jewish singularity. This public activism gave rise to the myth of Jewish political power. As with all myths, this one contained a kernel of truth. The Jewish lobby succeeded because their causes were also supported by the larger American community. In a 1981 London *Times* article, Henry Fairlie remarked, "The Jewish lobby in America is an American lobby. That is the dark secret of its influence."[32]

Because of their geographic concentrations and higher than average participation in the election process as voters and financial contributors, Jews often did make a significant difference, particularly in close elections, despite being less than 3 percent of the American population. A key factor was the unique connection of Jewish voters to the Democratic Party. Unlike other immigrant groups, which over time veered politically toward the Republican Party as they became more assimilated and successful, Jews maintained strong loyalty to the

Democrats. By the end of the 20th century, Hispanic voters, including Puerto Ricans, were voting in larger numbers for Republicans while their Jewish counterparts largely continued their support for Democrats.

But that support is softening. Concern for Israel and increased worldwide terrorism led to a larger Jewish vote for George W. Bush in the 2004 election than that received by earlier Republican candidates. That year, the Republicans made significant inroads among several Jewish voting subgroups, including the Orthodox and also the newly franchised Russian immigrants,[33] many of whom departed from the liberal politics of other Jews and voted Republican.

"Who Is a Jew?" Revisited

The question of "Who is a Jew?" has expanded beyond the original debate involving Orthodox relations with liberal Judaism. Can a person be Jewish without attending religious services? Is an individual Jewish simply through involvement with Jewish charitable and social organizations? Is Judaism a religion or an ethnicity? Here in the early 21st century, the complexion of the

Jewish Percentage of U.S. Population, 1877–2001

Year	Number	Percentage
1877	250,000	0.52
1897	937,800	1.31
1907	1,776,885	2.0
1917	3,388,951	3.27
1927	4,228,029	3.58
1937	4,770,647	3.69
1949	5,000,000	3.5
1959	5,367,200	3.02
1969	5,869,000	2.9
1982	5,725,000	2.5
1992	5,828,000	2.3
2001	6,155,000	2.2

Data from the American Jewish Year Book. Estimated information for early years was provided by local communities.

American Jewish population has broadened beyond the stereotypical White-European model. African American Jews, Latino Jews, Asian Jews, intermarried Jews, and mixed-race Jews have taken their places in the Jewish community. A corollary question to "Who is a Jew?" has become "How can a diverse Jewish population transmit Jewish values and learning to a new generation?" Rabbi Ephraim Buchwald, director of the National Jewish Outreach Program, said in 2003, "It's not lighting Shabbat candles, it's not sending a Rosh Hashanah card or ethnic pride, it's not belonging to a JCC or love of Israel or Jewish philanthropy or memorializing the Holocaust. We know from 3,000 years of empirical evidence that the key to Jewish survival is Jewish practice."[34] Although efforts to increase religious awareness have grown, statistics tell us that Jewish practice continues to wane among American Jews as a whole.

A Growing Apathy

"In the 1980s, three-quarters of American Jews did not observe kashrut within the home, two-fifths did not fast on Yom Kippur, and 90 percent did not attend a religious service once a month or more."[35] As the 20th century ended, despite efforts to raise the importance of Jewish faith and practice among American Jews,

A Baseball First

On August 8, 2005, an event occurred that, while not historically world altering, nonetheless served as a marker of just how "normal" Jewish participation had become in American life. For the first time in a major league baseball game, one team (the Boston Red Sox) had three Jewish players on the field during a single inning (the ninth): Kevin Youkilis, Gabe Kapler, and Adam Stern.

"Is This a Great Country or What?"

To Eastern European Jewish immigrants, anything was possible in America—even seeing a Jew in the White House some day. With the selection of Senator Joseph Lieberman of Connecticut as the 2000 Democratic Party nominee for vice president of the United States, that dream came close to realization. After losing a close election that year, Lieberman spoke of his selection:

I began by asking: Is America a great country or what? Last night, we ended that remarkable journey in a disappointing way. But nevertheless, I want to answer my question this morning by declaring: Yes, America is a great country.... In selecting me, a Jewish American, to be his running mate, Vice President Gore did what no presidential candidate before him had done ...The absence of bigotry in this campaign... should, I think, encourage every parent in this country to dream the biggest dreams for each and every one of their children. Anything is possible in America. (Finkelstein 2002, 165)

most Jews had little connection to the organized Jewish world and lacked any kind of meaningful knowledge of Jewish history, culture, and religion. In part, this was due to the pressures placed upon suburban residents and the drive to succeed in the secular world. It was a legacy of earlier generations of American Jews, who too quickly gave up elements of Judaism to hasten their assimilation. By 2000, 60 percent of American Jews held bachelor's degrees and 28 percent had earned master's degrees. But this high rate of secular educational achievement did not carry over into the world of Jewish learning.

The causes that particularly united Jews during the latter part of the 20th century—Israel, Soviet Jews, and the memory of the Holocaust—did not bring about an revived interest in traditional Jewish learning and religious practice. And although initiatives taken to bolster traditional learning and foster the continuity of the Jewish community were hailed as positive indicators, the corresponding decrease in the Jewish population revealed a paradox. As the religious and cultural cohesiveness of American Jews has weakened, the social, political, and economic situations of "just Jews" have never been better. When the 20th century ended, Jews had achieved secular success in America unparalleled in Jewish history. From "minyan" status in the U.S. Senate to their appearance on best-seller lists, from the presidential offices of Ivy League universities to the boardrooms of America's leading corporations, Jews have become accepted, full-fledged members of the American elite.[36]

Hope for the Future

Yet, in spite of these advances, after 350 years in America, Jews still face the same question today that confronted the original 23 arrivals in 1654: how to ensure the continuation of Jewish life. In a 1948 essay, historian Simon Rawidowicz spoke of Jews as "the ever-dying people." "The world has many images of Israel," he wrote, "but Israel has only one image of itself: that of an expiring people, forever on the verge of ceasing to be … He who studies Jewish history will readily discover that there was hardly a generation in the Diaspora period which did not consider itself the final link in Israel's chain. Each always saw before it the abyss ready to swallow it up … Often it seems as if the overwhelming majority of our people go about driven by the panic of being the last."[37] Notwithstanding this wryly pessimistic view, the legacy of the past may very well be, as Jonathan Sarna wrote, "that today, as so often before, American Jews will find creative ways to maintain and revitalize American Judaism."[38]

1948–present
A TIMELINE

1948
Israel's War of Independence

1953
Ethel and Julius Rosenberg executed for treason

1954
Brown v. Board of Education

1956
Suez War between Israel and Egypt

1960
Sit-ins begin in South to protest discrimination against African Americans

1963
Civil Rights March on Washington; Egypt and Syria form United Arab Republic

1964
Murders of three civil rights workers: Goodman, Schwerner, and Cheney

1965
Vatican II positively alters Catholic relations with Jews

1967
Six-Day War

1971
National Conference on Soviet Jewry founded

1972
Ordination of Sally Priesand by Hebrew Union College

1973
Yom Kippur War

1974
Henry Kissinger is first Jew appointed secretary of state

1975
"Zionism is racism" resolution adopted by United Nations

1977
Rosalyn Yalow wins Nobel Prize for Medicine

1978
Isaac Bashevis Singer receives Nobel Prize for Literature

1979
Peace Treaty signed between Israel and Egypt

1983
Reform movement accepts patrilineal descent

1985
Conservative movement recognizes women rabbis

1986
Elie Wiesel awarded Nobel Peace Prize

1987
Rally on Mall for Soviet Jewry attended by 200,000

1993
Opening of the United States Holocaust Memorial Museum in Washington

1994
Rabbi Schneerson, head of Chabad Lubavitch movement, dies with no successor

2000
Senator Joseph Lieberman nominated as Democratic Party candidate for vice president of the United States

Notes

Chapter 1
Mid-1300s–1654: Before the Beginning

1   Cecil Roth, *A History of the Marranos* (New York: Schocken Books, 1974), 17.

2   Norman H. Finkelstein, *The Other 1492: Jewish Settlement in the New World* (New York: Charles Scribners Sons, 1989), 22–23.

3   B. Netanyahu, *Don Isaac Abravanel* (Philadelphia: The Jewish Publication Society, 1953), 43.

4   Roth, *A History of the Marranos*, 20.

5   Netanyahu, *Don Isaac Abravanel*, 44.

6   Ibid., 175.

7   Seymour B. Liebman, *The Jews in New Spain* (Coral Gable, Fla.: University of Miami Press, 1970), 69–72.

8   Anne J. Cruz and Mary Elizabeth Perry, *Cultural Encounters* (Berkeley: University of California Press, 1991), 178.

9   Arnold Wiznitzer, "Crypto Jews in Mexico during the Sixteenth Century," *American Jewish Historical Quarterly*, no. 3 (March 1962): 186–87.

10 Quoted in Liebman, 290.

11 Roth, *A History of the Marranos*, 283.

12 Quoted in Paul Masserman and Max Baker, *The Jews Come to America* (New York: Bloch Publishing Company, 1932), 14.

Chapter 2
1654–1820: The Earliest Settlers

1   Norman H. Finkelstein, *The Other 1492: Jewish Settlement in the New World* (New York: Scribners, 1989), 60–63.

2   Finkelstein, *The Other 1492*, 65.

3   Samuel Oppenheim, "The Early History of the Jews in New York, 1651–1664," *Publications of the American Jewish Historical Society* 18 (1909), 4–5.

4   Oppenheim, "Early History," 9–11.

5   Ibid., 8.

6   Leon Hühner, "Asser Levy," *Publications of the American Jewish Historical Society* 8 (1900), 13.

7   Hühner, "Asser Levy," 13.

8   Oppenheim, "Early History," 20.

9   Ibid., 21.

10 Ibid., 19.

11 From the diary of Levi Sheftall, quoted in Mordecai Sheftall, "The Jews in Savannah," *The Occident and American Jewish Advocate*, 1:8 (November 1843), 2.

12 American Jewish Desk Reference (New York: Random House, 1999), 4, 35.

13 *Gomez Mill House* (Marlboro, N.Y.: The Gomez Foundation for Mill House, 1998), 11.

14 Hasia R. Diner and Beryl Lieff Benderly, *Her Works Praise Her: A History of Jewish Women From Colonial Time to the Present* (New York: Basic Books, 2002), 20.

15 Morris A. Gutstein, Aaron Lopez and Judah Touro: A Refugee and a Son of a Refugee (New York: Behrman, 1939), 14.

16 Abram Vossen Goodman, *American Overture: Jewish Rights in Colonial Times* (Philadelphia: The Jewish Publication Society, 1947), 63.

17 Abraham Karp, ed., *The Jews in America: A Treasury of Art and Literature* (Southport, Conn.: Hugh Lauter Levin Associates, 1994), 48–50.

18 Malcolm H. Stern, "Two Jewish Functionaries in Colonial Pennsylvania," *American Jewish Historical Quarterly* 57, 45.

19 Joan Nathan, *Jewish Cooking in America* (New York: Knopf, 2001), 11.

20 Doris Groshen Daniels, "Colonial Jewry: Religion, Domestic and Social Relations," *American Jewish History Quarterly* 66 (1976–77), 391.

21 Max Kohler, "Phases of Jewish Life in New York Before 1800," *Publications of the American Jewish Historical Society* 21 (1894), 89.

22 Samuel Openheim, "The Jews and Masonry in the United States Before 1800," *Publications of the American Jewish Historical Society* 19 (1910), 2.

23 Letter dated 1819 in the Collections of the American Jewish Historical Society (Collection I–4, Box 8).

24 Paul Masserman and Max Baker, *The Jews Come to America* (New York: Bloch, 1932), 134.

25 Daniels, "Colonial Jewry," *American Jewish Historical Quarterly* 66 (1976–77), 381.

26 Quoted in B. H. Levy et al., "History of Mickve Israel," www.mickveisrael.org/history, 2.

27 Eli Faber, *A Time For Planting* (Baltimore: Johns Hopkins University Press, 1992), 64.

28 Faber, *A Time For Planting*, 81.

29 Jonathan Sarna, *American Judaism* (New Haven: Yale University Press, 2004), 45.

30 Kohler, "Phases of Jewish Life in New York," 90.

31 Faber, *A Time For Planting*, 92.

32 Solomon Solis-Cohen, "Note Concerning David Hays and Esther Etting His Wife and Michael Hays and Reuben Etting, Their Brothers, Patriots of the Revolution," *Publications of the American Jewish Historical Society* 2 (1894), 66.

33 Leon Hühner, "The Jews of New England," *Publications of the American Jewish Historical Society* 11 (1903), 84.

34 Quoted in Faber, *A Time for Planting*, 105.

35 Kohler, "Phases of Jewish Life in New York," 91.

189

Chapter 3
1813–1880: Settling In

1   Norman H. Finkelstein, *Friends Indeed* (Brookfield, Conn.: Millbrook Press, 1998), 14.

2   Jacob R. Marcus, *Memoirs of American Jews 1775–1865* (Philadelphia: The Jewish Publication Society, 1955), 1:247.

3   Dana Even Kaplan, "A Historical Perspective," *Judaism* 48 (Summer 1999): 259.

4   *Jewish Encyclopedia*, s.v. "America, Judaism in."

5   David Philipson, "The Progress of the Jewish Reform Movement in the US," *Jewish Quarterly Review* (1898): 60.

6   Israel Goldstein, *A Century of Judaism in New York* (New York: Congregation Bnai Jeshurun, 1930), 52.

7   Leon Jick, *The Americanization of the Synagogue 1820–1890* (Hanover, N.H.: Brandeis University Press, 1976), 61.

8   Jacob Rader Marcus, *United States Jewry 1776–1985* (Detroit: Wayne State University Press, 1989), 1:293.

9   American Jewish Historical Society, *American Jewish Desk Reference* (New York: Random House, 1999), 35.

10 Jick, *Americanization*, 134.

11 Ibid., 25.

12 Hasia Diner, *A Time for Gathering* (Baltimore: Johns Hopkins University Press, 1992), 146.

13 *Jewish Encyclopedia*, s.v. "The American Israelite."

14 Diner, *Time for Gathering*, 162.

15 Jick, *Americanization*, 80.

16 Pamela S. Nadell, "The Americanization of the Synagogue, 1820–1870: An Historiographical Appreciation," *American Jewish History* 90 (2002): 56

17 Ibid., 99.

18 Harriet and Fred Rochlin, *Pioneer Jews* (Boston: Houghton Mifflin, 1984), 206.

19 Quoted in Nadell, "The Americanization of the Synagogue," 51.

20 Karla Goldman, "The Path to Reform Judaism: An Examination of Religious Leadership in Cincinnati 1841–1855," *American Jewish History* 90 (March 2002): 36.

21 Jick, *Americanization*, 157.

22 Goldman, "The Path to Reform Judaism," 35.

23 Jonathan Sarna, *American Judaism* (New Haven: Yale University, 2004), 150.

24 Philipson, "Progress of the Jewish Reform Movement," 98.

25 Peter Wiernick, *History of the Jews in America* (New York: Jewish Press Publishing Co., 1932), 194.

26 Norman H. Finkelstein, *Heeding the Call* (Philadelphia: The Jewish Publication Society, 1997), 27.

27 Ibid., 39.

28 Gloria R. Mosesson, *The Jewish War Veterans Story* (Washington: The Jewish War Veterans of the United States, 1971), 16.

29 Quoted in Isaac Markens, "Lincoln and the Jews," *Publications of the American Jewish Historical Society* 17 (1909): 135.

30 Abraham Karp, *Haven and Home* (New York: Schocken, 1985), 374-75.

31 Finkelstein, *Heeding the Call*, 53.

Chapter 4
1881–1913: The Great Wave

1 Quoted in Judah Gribetz et al., *The Timetables of Jewish History* (New York: Simon & Schuster, 1993), 301.

2 Salo Baron, *The Russian Jew Under the Tsars and Soviets* (New York: Macmillan, 1964), 95.

3 Library of Congress, Printed Ephemera Collection, Portfolio 131, Folder 30.

4 Errera, "Les juifs russes," *Journal du Nord* (1892), 120–21: Quoted in *Jewish Encyclopedia*, s.v. "Russia."

5 Paul Masserman and Max Baker, *The Jews Come to America* (New York: Bloch, 1932), 228.

6 Irving Howe, *World of Our Fathers* (New York: Schocken, 1976), 33.

7 Ibid., 36.

8 Copy of letter in "The Attitude of American Jews to East European Jewish Immigration (1881–1893)," *Publications of the American Jewish Historical Society* 40 (March 1951): 265.

9 Quoted in the *Jewish Messenger*, September 8, 1882.

10 George M. Price, "The Russian Jews in America," *Publications of the American Jewish Historical Society* 48, no. 2 (December 1958): 119.

11 Rufus Learsi, *The Jews in America* (New York: Ktav, 1972), 128.

12 Gerald Sorin, *A Time for Building: The Third Migration 1881–1920* (Baltimore: Johns Hopkins University Press, 1992), 12.

13 Hyman B. Grinstein, "The Efforts of East European Jewry to Organize Its Own Community in the United States," *Publications of the American Jewish Historical Society* 49 (December 1959): 73–74.

14 Moses Rischin, *The Promised City* (Cambridge: Harvard University Press, 1977), 263.

15 Ibid., 97.

16 Ibid., 103.

17 Ibid., 98.

18 Sorin, *A Time for Building*, 11.

19 Peter Romanofsky, "To Rid Ourselves of the Burden . . . New York Jewish Charities and the Origins of the Industrial Removal Office. 1890–1901," *American Jewish Historical Society Quarterly* 64 (1975): 42.

20 Jacob Riis, "Jews of New York," *Review of Reviews* 13 (1896): 59.

21 Stephen F. Brumberg, "Going to America: Going to School: The Immigrant–Public School Encounter in the Twentieth Century," *American Jewish Archives* 36, no. 2 (November 1984): 88.

22 Max Dimont, *The Jews in America* (New York: Simon & Schuster, 1978), 165.

23 Hutchins Hapgood, *The Spirit of the Ghetto*, ed. Moses Rischin (Cambridge, Mass.: Belknap Press, 1967), 24.

24 Abraham J. Karp, "New York Chooses a Chief Rabbi," *Publications of the American Jewish Historical Society* 44, no. 3 (1955): 29ff.

25 Quoted in Jacob Neusner, "The Impact of Immigration and Philanthropy upon the Boston Jewish Community (1880–1914)," *Publications of the American Jewish Historical Society* 46 (1957): 77.

26 Peter Beinart, "Education and Rise of Jewish Schools," *Atlantic Monthly* (October 1999), 21.

27 Arthur A. Goren, ed., *Dissenter in Zion* (Cambridge: Harvard University Press, 1982), 101.

28 Masserman and Baker, *The Jews Come to America*, 296.

29 Dimont, *The Jews in America*, 168.

30 Lance J. Sussman, "New York Jewish History," New York State Archives, http://www.archives.nysed.gov/a/researchroom/rr_pgc_jewish_essay.shtml.

Chapter 5

1914–1948: From Home to Homeland

1 Mel Scult, ed., *Communings of the Spirit: The Journals of Mordecai M. Kaplan—Volume I: 1913–1934* (Detroit: Wayne State University Press and Reconstructionist Press, 2001), 118–19.

2 Quoted in *The Maccabean* 23 (July 1915): 9.

3 Paul Masserman and Max Baker, *The Jews Come to America*, (New York: Bloch, 1932), 336.

4 Alphos T. M. Mason. *Brandeis, A Free Man's Life* (New York: Viking Press, 1956), 455.

5 Selig Adler, "The Palestine Question in the Wilson Era," *Jewish Social Studies* 10 (October 1948): 318.

6 Quoted in Melvin Urofsky, "Zionism: An American Experience," *American Jewish Historical Quarterly* 63:1–4 (September 1973): 215.

7 Melvin Urofsky, *A Voice That Spoke for Justice* (Albany: State University of New York, 1982), 240.

8 www.spartacus.schoolnet.co.uk/usaceller.htm

9 Masserman and Baker, *The Jews Come to America*, 366.

10 Gerald Sorin, *A Time For Building* (Baltimore: Johns Hopkins University Press, 1992), 76.

11 *New York Times*, March 21, 1933.

12 Ibid., March 28, 1933.

13 Ibid., July 21, 1935.

14 David Brody, "American Jewry, the Refugees and Immigration Restriction, 1932–1942," *Publications of the American Jewish Historical Societ* 45 (September 1955): 219.

15 Leonard Dinnerstein, *Anti-Semitism* (New York: Oxford University Press, 1994), 147.

16 Stephen S. Wise, *As I See It* (New York: Jewish Opinion Publishing, 1994), 67.

17 *The Times,* London, issue 46967 (January 21, 1935): 11.

18 Quoted in Jack R. Fischel, "Rabbis and Leaders—Silver and Wise," *American Zionist* 72 (April-May 1983): 6.

19 Norman H. Finkelstein, *Forged in Freedom* (Philadelphia: The Jewish Publication Society, 2002), 129.

20 Norman H. Finkelstein, *Heeding the Call* (Philadelphia: The Jewish Publication Society, 1997), 114.

21 Brody, "American Jewry, the Refugees and Immigration Restriction," 219.

22 Quoted in Walter Laquer, *A History of Zionism* (New York: Holt, Rinehart and Winston, 1972), 566.

23 *American Jewish Year Book* (New York: American Jewish Committee; Philadelphia: The Jewish Publication Society, 1950), 51:248.

24 Eddie Jacobson to Harry Truman, 3 October 1947, Harry S. Truman Library.

25 President Truman to Dean Alfange, 18 May 1948, President's Secretary Files, Harry S. Truman Library.

26 Quoted in Michael J. Cohen, *Truman and Israel* (Berkeley: University of California Press, 1990), 186.

27 Norman Finkelstein, *Friends Indeed, The Special Relationship of Israel and The United States* (Brookfield, Conn.: The Millbrook Press, 1998), 42.

Chapter 6

1948–present: Into the Mainstream

1 Edward Shapiro, *A Time for Healing* (Baltimore: Johns Hopkins University Press, 1992), 147.

2 Norman H. Finkelstein, *Heeding the Call* (Philadelphia: The Jewish Publication Society, 1997), 128–29.

3 Ibid., 132–33, 159.

4 Norman H. Finkelstein, *Forged in Freedom* (Philadelphia: The Jewish Publication Society, 2002), 145.

5 Isaac Alteras, "Eisenhower, American Jewry, and Israel," *American Jewish Archives* 37 (November 1985): 272.

6 David Ben Gurion Oral History, July 16, 1965, from the John F. Kennedy Presidential Library.

7 Myer Feldman Oral History, August 26, 1967, from the John F. Kennedy Presidential Library.

8 Quoted in Yaacov Bar Siman-Tov, *Israel, the Superpower, and War in the Middle East* (New York: Praeger, 1987), 123.

9 Arthur Hertzberg, "Israel and American Jewry," *Commentary* 44:2 (August 1967): 70.

10 Norman H. Finkelstein, *Friends Indeed* (Brookfield, Conn.: Millbrook Press, 1998), 84.

11 Henry Kissinger, *Years of Upheaval* (Boston: Little, Brown, 1982), 542–43.

12 Hasia Diner, *The Jews of the United States* (Berkeley: University of California Press, 2004), 324.

13 Allan C. Brownfeld, "Consensus Grows That Israel as Surrogate Religion for American Jews a Failed Strategy," *Washington Report on Middle East Affairs* 22 (November 2003): 66.

14 Ariel Sharon speech to United Jewish Communities leaders, Jerusalem, July 18, 2004.

15 David Borowich, "US Jews Disengaging from Israel," *Ynet news.com*, January 26, 2005.

16 Samuel Z. Klausner, "Anti-Semitism in the Executive Suite: Yesterday, Today, and Tomorrow," *Moment* 13 (September 1988): 33–39.

17 Finkelstein, *Heeding the Call*, 169.

18 Quoted in *American Jewish Year Book, 1969* (New York: American Jewish Committee; Philadelphia: The Jewish Publication Society, 1969), 84.

19 Ibid., 78.

20 Finkelstein, *Heeding the Call*, 10-11.

21 Jonathan Sarna, *American Judaism* (New Haven: Yale University Press, 2004), 320.

22 Irving Spiegel, "Senators Appeal to Soviet on Jews," *New York Times*, April 17, 1966.

23 Charles A. Radin, "With Cries of 'Let My People Go,' 200,000 Rally for Soviet Jewry," *Boston Globe*, December 7, 1987.

24 Murray Friedman and Albert D. Chemin, eds., *A Second Exodus: The American Movement to Free Soviet Jews* (Hanover, N.H.: University Press of New England, 1999), 86.

25 Arnold Jacob Wolf, "The Shoah in America," *Judaism: A Quarterly of Jewish Life and Thought* 48 (Fall 1999), 490.

26 Marilyn Henry, "AJC Survey," *Jerusalem Post*, March 3, 1998 .

27 *Washington Post*, April 23, 1985.

28 Yosef Goell, "The Lessons of the Pollard Affair," *Congress Monthly* (May/June 1987): 4.

29 *International Herald Tribune*, April 29, 1998.

30 Sarna, *American Judaism*, 361.

31 Diner, *The Jews of the United States*, 314.

32 Henry Fairlie, "Jews Yes, But America Comes First," The London *Times,* July 29, 1981.

33 Jay Lefkowitz, "The Election and the Jewish Vote," *Commentary* 119:2 (February 2005): 63.

34 Joe Berkofsky, "Study Finds Positive Trends Along with Rising Intermarriage," *Jewish Telegraphic Agency*, September 10, 2003.

35 Shapiro, *A Time for Healing*, 163.

36 Henry L. Feingold, "The American Jewish Condition After 350 Years," *Midstream* 50 (September/October 2004): 4.

37 Quoted in Leon Wieseltier, "Hitler Is Dead," *The New Republic* (May 27, 2002).

38 Sarna, *American Judaism*, 374.

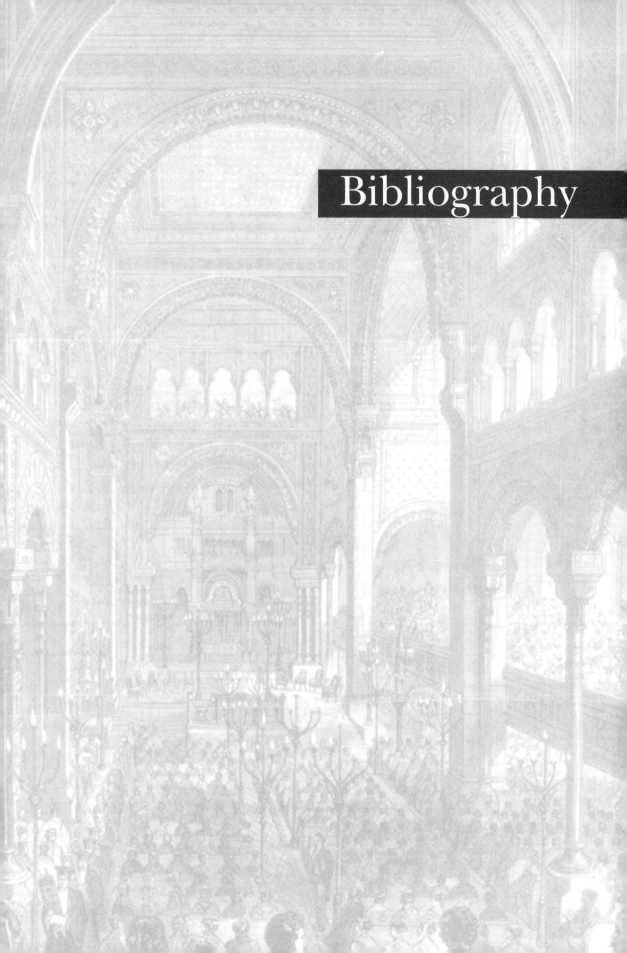

Bibliography

Adler, Selig. "The Palestine Question in the Wilson Era." *Jewish Social Studies* 10 (October 1948): 304—344.

Alteres, Isaac. "Eisenhower, American Jewry and Israel." *American Jewish Archives* 37 (1985): 272.

American Jewish Committee. *American Jewish Year Book.* New York: American Jewish Committee, 1969, 2000, 2002.

American Jewish Historical Society. *American Jewish Desk Reference.* New York: Random House, 1999.

Antin, Mary. *The Promised Land.* Boston: Houghton Mifflin, 1912.

Baron, Salo. *The Russian Jew Under the Tsars and Soviets.* New York: Macmillan, 1964.

Bar Siman-Tov, Yaacov. *Israel, the Superpower and War in the Middle East.* New York: Praeger, 1987.

Beinart, Peter. "Education and Rise of Jewish Schools." *Atlantic Monthly* 284:4 (October, 1999): 21–22.

Berkofsky, Joe. "Study Finds Positive Trends Along with Rising Intermarriage." *Jewish Telegraphic Agency* (September 10, 2003).

Bingham, Theodore. "Foreign Criminals in New York." *North American Review* 188, no. 3 (September 1908): 383–94.

Brownfeld, Allan C. "Consensus Grows that Israel as Surrogate Religion for American Jews a Failed Strategy." *Washington Report on Middle East Affairs* 22 (2003): 66.

Brumberg, Stephen F. "Going to America: Going to School: The Immigrant-Public School Encounter in the Twentieth Century." *American Jewish Archives* 36 (1984): 88.

Cohen, Michael J. *Truman and Israel.* Berkeley: University of California Press, 1990.

Cruz, Anne J., and Mary Elizabeth Perry. *Cultural Encounters.* Berkeley: University of California Press, 1991.

Dabru Emet: A Jewish Statement on Christians and Christianity. Originally published as a full-page statement in the *New York Times,* September 10, 2000, New England edition, 23. Available online at http://www.bc.edu/research/cjl/meta-elements/texts/cjrelations/resources/documents/jewish/dabru_emet.htm.

Daniels, Doris Groshen. "Colonial Jewry: Religion, Domestic and Social Relations." *American Jewish Historical Quarterly* 66 (1976–77): 391.

Dimont, Max. *The Jews in America.* New York: Simon and Schuster, 1978.

Diner, Hasia. *The Jews of the United States.* Berkeley: University of California Press, 2004.

_____. *A Time for Gathering.* Baltimore: Johns Hopkins University Press, 1992.

Diner, Hasia, and Beryl Lieff Benderly. *Her Works Praise Her.* New York: Basic Books, 2002.

Dinnerstein, Leonard. *Anti-Semitism.* New York: Oxford University Press, 1994.

Eisenhower, Dwight David. Papers. Vol. XVII, part XI, chap. 22, doc. 2048. Available online at www.eisenhower memorial.org/presidential-papers/first-term/documents/2048.cfm.

Faber, Eli. *A Time for Planting.* Baltimore: Johns Hopkins University Press, 1992.

Feingold, Henry L. "The American Jewish Condition After 350 Years." *Midstream* 50 (2004): 4.

_____. *A Time for Searching.* Baltimore: Johns Hopkins University Press, 1992.

Finkelstein, Norman H. *The Other 1492: Jewish Settlement in the New World.* New York: Charles Scribner's Sons, 1989.

_____. *Friends Indeed: The Special Relationship Of Israel and the United States.* Brookfield, Conn.: The Millbrook Press, 1998.

_____. *Heeding the Call: Jewish Voices in America's Civil Rights Struggle.* Philadelphia: The Jewish Publication Society, 1997.

_____. *Forged in Freedom: Shaping the Jewish American Experience.* Philadelphia: The Jewish Publication Society, 2002.

Fischel, Jack R. "Rabbis and Leaders—Silver and Wise." *American Zionist* 72 (1983): 6.

Freedman, Murray, and Albert D. Chenin, eds. *A Second Exodus: The American Movement to Free Soviet Jews.* Hanover, N.H.: University Press of New England, 1999.

Goldman, Karla. "The Path to Reform Judaism: An Examination of Religious Leadership in Cincinnati 1841–1855." *American Jewish History* 90 (2002): 35–36.

Goldstein, Israel. *A Century of Judaism in New York.* New York: Congregation B'nai Jeshurun, 1930.

Gomez Mill House. Marlboro, N.Y.: The Gomez Foundation for Mill House, 1998.

Goodman, Abram Vossen. *American Overture: Jewish Rights in Colonial Times.* Philadelphia: The Jewish Publication Society, 1947.

Goren, Arthur A., ed. *Dissenter in Zion.* Cambridge: Harvard University Press, 1982.

Gribetz, Judah, et al. *The Timetables of Jewish History.* New York: Simon and Schuster, 1993.

Grinstein, Hyman B. "The Efforts of East European Jewry to Organize Its Own Community in the United States." *Publications of the American Jewish Historical Society* 49 (1959): 73–74.

Gutstein, Morris A. *Aaron Lopez and Judah Touro: A Refugee and a Son of a Refugee.* New York: Behrman, 1939.

Halevy, Schulamith C. "Anusim in North America: The Ingathering." *Tradition* (1995). Also available online at http://www.cs.tau.ac.il/~nachumd/sch/sch/anusim.html.

Howe, Irving. *World of Our Fathers.* New York: Schocken, 1976.

Hühner, Leon. "Asser Levy." *Publications of the American Jewish Historical Society* 8 (1900): 13.

_____. "Francis Salvador, A Prominent Patriot of the Revolutionary War." *Publications of the American Jewish Historical Society* 9 (1901): 109–13.

_____. "Jews in the Legal and Medical Professions in America Prior to 1800." *Publications of the American Jewish Historical Society* 22 (1914): 163.

_____. "The Jews of New England." *Publications of the American Jewish Historical Quarterly* 11 (1903): 84.

Hutchins, Hapgood. *The Spirit of the Ghetto.* Cambridge, Mass.: Belknap Press, 1967.

Hyman, Paula. Personal archive. *Ezrat Nashim* flyer, "Jewish Women Call for Change," March 14, 1972. Available online at http://www.jwa.org/feminism/_html/_pdf/JWA039a.pdf.

Jastrow, Morris, Jr. "Documents Relating to the Career of Colonel Isaac Franks." *Publications of the American Jewish Historical Society* 5 (1897): 9.

Jewish Encyclopedia. 12 vols. New York: Funk and Wagnalls, 1901–1906.

Jewish Reconstructionist Federation Growth Fact Sheet. Found at www.jrf.org/jrf-growth.html.

Jick, Leon. *The Americanization of the Synagogue 1820–1890.* Hanover, N.H.: Brandeis University Press, 1976.

Kaplan, Dana Evan. "A Historical Perspective." *Judaism* 48 (Summer 1999): 259.

197

Kaplan, Mordecai. Diary entry of 15 January 1931. Found at www.jrf.org/rt/diaries.html.

Jewish Reconstructionist Federation. *Reconstructionism Today* (Spring 2000). (JRF). All rights reserved.

Karp, Abraham. *Haven and Home.* New York: Schocken, 1985.

_____. "New York Chooses a Chief Rabbi." *Publications of the American Jewish Historical Society* 44, issue 1–4 (June 1955): 128–201.

Karp, Abraham, ed. *The Jews in America: A Treasury of Art and Literature.* Southport, Conn.: High Lauter Levin Associates, 1994.

Kaufman, David. *Shul With a Pool.* Hanover, N.H.: Brandeis University Press, 1999.

Klausner, Samuel Z. "Anti-Semitism in the Executive Suite: Yesterday, Today and Tomorrow." *Moment* 13 (1988): 33–39.

Kohler, Max. "Phases of Jewish Life in New York before 1800." *Publications of the American Jewish Historical Society* 21 (1894): 89.

Kohut, George Alexander. *Ezra Stiles and the Jews.* New York: Philip Cowen, 1902.

Laquer, Walter. *A History of Zionism.* New York: Holt, Rinehart and Winston, 1972.

Learsi, Rufus. *The Jews in America.* New York: Ktav, 1972.

Lebeson, Anita Libman. *Pilgrim People.* New York: Harper & Brothers, 1950.

Liebman, Seymour B. *The Jews in New Spain.* Coral Gables, Fla.: University of Miami Press, 1970.

Lindbergh, Charles A. Speech given 11 September 1941, Des Moines, Iowa. Found at http://www.charleslindbergh.com/americanfirst/speech.asp.

Long, Breckinridge. Assistant Secretary of State Breckinridge Long to State Department officials, 26 June 1940. Found at www.pbs.org/wgbh/amex/holocaust/filmmore/reference/primary/barmemo.html.

Marcus, Jacob R. *The American Jewish Woman: A Documentary History.* Cincinnati: American Jewish Archives, 1981.

Markens, Isaac. "Lincoln and the Jews." *Publications of the American Jewish Historical Society* 17 (1909): 135.

Martin, Bernard. "The Americanization of American Judaism." *Journal of Reform Judaism* (Winter 1980): 43–93.

Mason, Adphos T. M. *Brandeis: A Free Man's Life.* New York: Viking Press, 1956.

Masserman, Paul, and Max Baker. *The Jews Come to America.* New York: Bloch, 1932.

Metz, Helen, ed. *Israel: A Country Study.* Washington, D.C.: U.S. Government Printing Office, 1990.

Metzker, Isaac. *A Bintel Brief: Sixty Years of Letters from the Lower East Side to the Jewish Daily Forward.* New York: Schocken Books, 1990.

Mosesson, Gloria R. *The Jewish War Veterans Story.* Washington, D.C.: The Jewish War Veterans of the United States, 1971.

Nadell, Pamela S. "The Americanization of the Synagogue, 1820–1870: An Historiographical Appreciation." *American Jewish History* 90 (2002): 51.

Nathan, Joan. *Jewish Cooking in America.* New York: Knopf, 2001.

Netanyahu, B. *Don Isaac Abravanel.* Philadelphia: The Jewish Publication Society, 1953.

Neusner, Jacob. "The Impact of Immigration and Philanthropy upon the Boston Jewish Community (1880–1914)." *Publications of the American Jewish Historical Society* 46 (1957): 77.

198

Oppenheim, Samuel. "The Early History of the Jews in New York, 1651–1664." *Publications of the American Jewish Historical Society* 18 (1909): 4–11.

_____. "The Jews and Masonry in the United States Before 1800." *Publications of the American Jewish Historical Society* 19 (1910): 2.

Panitz, Esther. "In Defense of the Jewish Immigrant." *American Jewish Historical Quarterly* 55 (September 1965): 57–97.

_____. "The Polarity of American Jewish Attitudes Towards Immigration (1870–1891)." *Publications of the American Jewish Historical Society* 53 (1963): 99–130.

Penkower, Monty Noam. *The Jews Were Expendable: Diplomacy and the Holocaust.* Detroit: Wayne State University Press, 1998.

Perry, Mary Elizabeth, and Anne J. Cruz, eds. *Cultural Encounters: The Impact of the Inquisition in Spain and the New World.* Berkeley: University of California Press, 1991.

Philipson, David. "The Progress of the Jewish Reform Movement in the US." *Jewish Quarterly Review* (1898): 60.

Phillips, N. Taylor. "The Levy and Seixas Families of Newport and New York." *Publications of the American Jewish Historical Society* 50 (1950–51): 198–99.

Pool, D. DeSola. "Descriptions of the Synagogues in New York in 1776 and 1828." *Publications of the American Jewish Historical Society* 40 (1950–51): 187.

Price, George M. "The Russian Jews in America." *Publications of the American Jewish Historical Society* 59 (1958): 115.

Riis, Jacob. *The Children of the Poor.* New York: Scribners, 1892.

_____. *How the Other Half Lives.* New York: Scribners, 1890.

Rochlin, Harriet, and Fred Rochlin. *Pioneer Jews.* Boston: Houghton Mifflin, 1984.

Romanofsky, Peter. "To Rid Ourselves of the Burden . . . New York Charities and the Origins of the Industrial Removal Office, 1890–1901." *American Jewish Historical Society Quarterly* 64 (1975): 42.

Salaman, Nina, trans. *Selected Poems of Jehudah Halevi.* Philadelphia: The Jewish Publication Society, 1924.

Sarna, Jonathan. *American Judaism.* New Haven: Yale University Press, 2004.

_____. *JPS: The Americanization of Jewish Culture 1888–1988.* Philadelphia: The Jewish Publication Society, 1989.

Scult, Mel, ed. *Communings of the Spirit: The Journals of Mordecai M. Kaplan.* Detroit: Wayne State University Press, 2001.

Senior, Max. Speech to National Conference of Jewish Charities, Chicago, November 2000. Quoted in Harold Rosen, "A Century of Caring," *Jewish United Fund News,* Jewish United Fund/Jewish Federation of Metropolitan. Available online at www.juf.org/news_public_affairs/article.asp?key=6208.

Shapiro, Edward. *A Time for Healing.* Baltimore: Johns Hopkins University Press, 1992.

Sheftall, Mordecai. "The Jews in Savannah." *The Occident and American Jewish Advocate* 1:8 (November 1843): 2.

Sheskin, Ira. M. "Geographic Differences Among American Jews, Report 8." *Report Series on the National Jewish Population Survey, 2000–2001.* New York: United Jewish Communities, 2004.

Schimmel, Solomon. "Report on Trip to the Soviet Union in January 1987 to Visit Jewish Refuseniks." Found at http://www.angelfire.com/sc3/soviet_jews_exodus/English/WhoHelped_s/WhoHelpedSchimmel_1.shtml.

Solis-Cohen, Solomon. "Note Concerning David Hays and Esther Etting His Wife and Michael Hays and Reuben Etting, Their Brothers, Patriots of the Revolution." *Publications of the American Jewish Historical Society* 2 (1894): 66.

Sorin, Gerald. *A Time for Building.* Baltimore: Johns Hopkins University Press, 1992.

Stern, Malcolm S. "Two Jewish Functionaries in Colonial Pennsylvania." *American Jewish Historical Quarterly* 57 (1949): 45.

Stiles, Ezra. *The Literary Diary.* Edited by F. B. Dexter. New York: Scribners, 1901.

Truman, Harry. Truman speaking to Rabbi Abba Hillel Silver, January 1948. Quote found at http://www.mideastweb.org/us_supportforstate.htm.

United Jewish Communities. *The National Jewish Population Survey 2000–01.* New York: United Jewish Communities, 2004.

_____. Report Series on the National Jewish Population Survey, 2000-2001. New York: United Jewish Communities, 2004.

Urofsky, Melvin. *A Voice that Spoke for Justice.* Albany: State University of New York, 1982.

_____. "Zionism: An American Experience." *American Jewish Historical Quarterly* 63 (1973): 215.

Wiernick, Peter. *History of the Jews in America.* New York: Jewish Press Publishing Company, 1932.

Wieseltier, Leon. "Against the Panic of American Jews: Hitler Is Dead." *The New Republic* (May 27, 2002): 73–78.

Wise, Isaac Mayer. *Reminiscences.* Cincinnati: Leo Wise Company, 1901.

Wise, Stephen S. *As I See It.* New York: Jewish Opinion Publishing, 1994.

Wiznitzer, Arnold. "Crypto Jews in Mexico During the Sixteenth Century." *American Jewish Historical Quarterly* 51 (1962): 191.

_____. "Crypto Jews in Mexico During the Seventeenth Century." *American Jewish Historical Quarterly* 51 (1962): 237.

Wolf, Arnold Jacob. "The Shoah in America." *Judaism: A Quarterly of Jewish Life and Thought* 48 (1999): 490.

Yezierska, Anna. *Salome of the Tenements.* Chicago: University of Chicago Press, 1996.

Index

217

Wise, Rabbi Isaac Mayer
    background of, 67, 67*f*
    on Benjamin, 77*f*
    Board of Delegates of American
          Israelites opposed by, 72
    Central Conference of American
          Rabbis established by, 115
    on fraternal orders, 63
    Minhag America of, 67, 70
    on peddlers/storekeepers, 59
    political activism of, 71
    publications by, 69, 73
    Reform movement role of, 66–67,
          67*f*, 68, 69, 70, 104–5
Wise, Rabbi Stephen S.
    on Americanism of Jews, 134
    American Jewish Congress founded
          by, 124, 133
    as American Zionist Emergency
          Committee cochair, 139
    background of, 94
    on the Holocaust, 137–39
    on the Nazi threat, 132
    quiet diplomacy of, 135, 140, 142
    on rescuing endangered Jews, 135
    and Franklin D. Roosevelt, 135, 137,
          140, 142
    as spokesman for American Jewish
          community, 123
    on the Wagner-Rogers bill, 136–37
    as World Jewish Congress president,
          137
    Zionist Organization of America
          formed by, 93–94
Wolf, Simon, 74, 79
women
    colonial, 38
    counted in *minyan,* 67
    emerging role of (1800s), 70–71
    equality under Reform Judaism/Jews,
          70
    Jewish identity of family maintained
          by, 19
    ordination of, 180, 186
    religious rights for, 180
    rights for, 73–74
    separate seating abolished, 67
    in volunteer organizations, 149–50
Women's American ORT, 149–50
working conditions in sweatshops, 12, 12*f*,
    98–99
Workmen's Circle (formerly *Arbeiter Ring*),
    104, 115
World Jewish Congress, 137–38
World War I, 120–21, 123, 124, 125, 146
World War II, 139*f*

    anti-Semitism prior to, 134
    outbreak of, 146
    U.S. entry into, 137, 146
    See also Holocaust/Nazis
World Zionist Organization, 124

Y

Yale University, 42
Yalow, Rosalyn, 170*f,* 186
Yeshuat Israel (Salvation of Israel;
    Newport), 36, 39, 43
Yezierska, Anna
    "Fat of the Land," 103
    Salome of the Tenements, 119
Yiddishkeit, growth of, 131
Yiddish language/culture
    decline of, 130, 148
    vs. English, 102–3
    Jewish immigrants united by, 93
    literature, 148–49*f*
    music, 102
    newspapers, 95, 102, 115, 119, 125
    theater, 102, 104*f,* 115, 118–19
    in wartime America, 118–19
YMCA (Young Men's Christian
    Association), 78, 80*f*
YMHA (Young Men's Hebrew Association),
    78
Yom Kippur, 19, 20
Yom Kippur War (1973), 166–67, 186
Youkilis, Kevin, 184
Young Israel, 110
Young Men's Christian Association
    (YMCA), 78, 80*f*
Young Men's Hebrew Association (YMHA),
    78
Young Women's Hebrew Association
    (YWHA), 78
Yulee, David Levy, 62, 81
YWHA (Young Women's Hebrew
    Association), 78

Z

Ziegfield Follies, 130*f*
Zion College, 67*f*
Zionism
    after the Holocaust, 141–42
    American, rise of, 121–22
    vs. American Council for Judaism,
          141, 146, 159, 165
    American Zionist Emergency
          Committee, 139–41
    and anti-Semitism, 166
    and the Balfour Declaration, 122–24,